The Cunning Craft

A Tortuous Path of the Wise Art

ABOUT THE AUTHOR

Nicholaj de Mattos Frisvold graduated in psychology, anthropology/science of religion and cinema studies at the University of Oslo and NTNU, Trondheim, Norway. He is the owner of Sacred Alchemy Store and the retreat center The Monastery of St. Uriel, Archangel. He has been living in Brazil since 2003 where he has dedicated much of his time studying, both as a practitioner and as an ethnographer, the varieties of Brazilian spirituality and sorcery.

The Cunning Craft

A Tortuous Path of the Wise Art

Nicholaj de Mattos Frisvold

Chicago, Illinois

Paperback ISBN: 978-1-959883-93-7
Hardcover ISBN: 978-1-964537-33-7
Library of Congress Control Number on file.

Published by:
Crossed Crow Books, LLC
6934 N Glenwood Ave, Suite C
Chicago, IL 60626
www.crossedcrowbooks.com

Printed in the United States of America.
IBI

OTHER BOOKS BY THE AUTHOR

Invisible Fire: Traditional Themes in Western Mysticism and Sethian Gnosticism (Crossed Crow Books, 2024)

Seven Crossroads of Night: Quimbanda in Theory and Practice (Hadean Press Limited, 2023)

The Canticles Of Lilith (Troy Books, 2022)

Trollrún: A Discourse on Trolldom and Runes in the Northern Tradition (Hadean Press Limited, 2021)

Ifá: A Forest of Mystery (Scarlet Imprint, 2016)

Obeah: A Sorcerous Ossuary (Hadean Press, 2013)

Exu: Exu and the Quimbanda of Night and Fire (Scarlet Imprint, 2012)

Craft of the Untamed: An Inspired Vision of Traditional Witchcraft (Mandrake of Oxford, 2011)

Pomba Gira: Pomba Gira and the Quimbanda of Mbumba Nzila (Scarlet Imprint, 2011)

Palo Mayombe: The Garden of Blood and Bones (Scarlet Imprint, 2010)

Arts of The Night (Chadezoad Publications, 2009)

Kiumbanda—A Complete Grammar of the Art of Exu (Chadezoad Publications, 2006)

ACKNOWLEDGEMENTS

Most of those who deserve to be acknowledged are those who are kings and queens in the kingdom of Silence and Shadows—you know who you are—but I want to give thanks to Tzillah and the brethren of the Conclave of the True Cross, Alogos, Radomir Ristic, Peter Hamilton-Giles, Arkaitz Oroitz Urbeltz, and Etxe Dragokoia (hurrah ya!), as well as the wayfarers on the Via Nocturna and the Lonely Road. Thanks to Jim Yahazim for all his help in the process and to Crossed Crow Books for manifesting this work in the world!

CONTENTS

FOREWORD

The origin of the word *cunning* derives from the fourteenth century *conning,* meaning "learned, skilful, possessing knowledge," via the Old English *cunnan,* ultimately from the Proto-Indo-European **gno,* "to know." It also possesses the sense of "skilfully deceitful" and is "characterised by crafty ingenuity." By the actual period of the fourteenth century, *cunning* had also acquired the meaning of the "ability to understand, intelligence; wisdom, prudence," a sense of "cleverness, shrewdness, practical skill in a secret or crafty manner." These are all concepts that are normally associated with the witch, both historically and in today's culture and, as is shown within this text, all are valid associations. However, it is the root term "to know" that is the most salient here, and one that is examined in great depth by the author. A closer look at the root of this word sees that it gives rise to the term "gnosis," which is categorised as knowledge, particularly "special knowledge of spiritual mysteries" and also "higher knowledge of spiritual things."[1] It is these very "spiritual things" that are examined in this book. For the Cunning person or witch, it is not enough to simply have knowledge of an art, craft, or form of magic. The knowledge of the spiritual reality behind this knowledge is equally important. Ultimately, it is the knowledge of Self that is sought, in all its myriad and devious forms and ways, with the aim of returning to—or gaining knowledge of—the ultimate Source of that knowledge, however it is conceived. Hence, this Craft of Cunning is often called by its adherents the "Nameless Arte," rejecting the constriction of strict definition of its ways and practices.

1 Etymological definitions from Online Etymology Dictionary, www.etymonline.com.

Far from the image of many forms of modern witchcraft, Nicholaj de Mattos Frisvold states right from the beginning that this text deals with the historical forms of Craft, known as Traditional or Old Craft, practised prior to the "revised" forms promoted by Gerald Gardner in the 1950s and 60s. These forms of Craft, now known as Wicca, and their myriads of offshoots are now generally seen as the "norms" of witchcraft. But there are other, less well-known forms that generally do not seek such publicity and continue perhaps more secretly. It is now fairly well-established by researchers such as Philip Heselton that Gardner was indeed inducted into an established lineage of Craft, possibly more than one, which were obviously pre- "Gardnerian" in type. Among some that are now publicly known and claim an older lineage are the Clan of Tubal Cain (as propounded by the late Robert Cochrane), the Cultus Sabbati, and Y Plant Bran. Others prefer not to have a public face and are descended from individual family or clan groupings; others yet derive from or are practised by solo adherents. However, Gardner heavily adapted what he received from his traditional sources to his own way of thinking and patterns of knowledge and practice. These included such sources as Freemasonry, ceremonial magic—particularly after the manner of the Hermetic Order of the Golden Dawn—and various paths of modern Druidry, as conceived with and by his close friend and associate Ross Nichols, founder of the modern Order of Bards, Ovates, and Druids. Gardner's avowed aims were to restore the worship of the pagan gods of old and to craft a nature-based, fertility religion of natural worship and seasonal veneration, mainly in a closed, initiatory form. He hoped this would eventually gain popularity and expand to become one of the world's major faiths. That he indeed included elements of older forms of magic and historical witchcraft is undeniable, but that he also changed many of the forms that he received into his personal vision is also no longer without a doubt. One of the main influences that he almost completely abolished was that of the Christian religion and those earlier faiths and beliefs that fed into it. As will be amply shown within this book, earlier historical forms of witchcraft were intricately and intimately involved with and bound up within these other strands and derived much of their practice and background thinking from them. Indeed, if asked, most historical witches within Europe would have declared themselves to be Christian, their magical work notwithstanding, and would have considered themselves to be practising within that milieu. Whilst certainly not denying or ignoring the pagan origins of much of old-style witchcraft, herein some of those informing strands of origin that led to the cultural amalgamation that is the Cunning Craft are examined in detail. In the words of the author: "For an art to be considered traditional, it needs some level of consistency in being passed down, typically over an extended period. A tradition does not emerge instantaneously; it gradually becomes a vehicle for maintaining connectedness with the sacred centre through its capacity to preserve wisdom and adapt to changes."

In particular, one of the strands involved in traditional transmissions deals with the dual nature, or dual faith practice, of the more old-style forms of Cunning Craft. An aspect of this involves looking at the lineage of what has come to be known as "Devil worship." The author looks in depth at the origins of both the term itself and the forms of thinking that lead to this concept. Deeply involved within Devil worship is the concept of working "with both hands": the Left Hand Path and the Right Hand Path, both Maleficia and Beneficia. Working with the Christian-based ideas found in the Bible and its antecedent literature, the Cunning person also had no problem working with the avowedly pagan in origin spirits or deities disguised therein. This involved working with the being painted as the source of all ill, frequently known as simply "the Devil," who was still a powerful entity in its own right, able to give the witch the knowledge and power that they desired and needed to accomplish their magical tasks and ideals. This being, whatever its origins (and they are many and complex), was seen as the initiator of the Cunning person: the source of their power and the bestower of the ability to work in two worlds. I have talked about this aspect in my own recent work, *Blackthorn Whitethorn: Ways of Witchery* (published by Troy Books), and have described Him thus:

> *He is the firstborn from the Darkness of Night, but contains within Himself Night's opposite — the bright and blinding Light. He is therefore a complete duality in Himself, both Dark and Bright, which exemplifies the liminal nature so prominent in the Witch themselves. He is ancient, terrible, awesome, wise and learned. He contains elements of many of the Horned Gods of prehistory, (or should I say that they contain elements of Him?), but is not simply one or a combination of any of them. He is very much the Trickster, the Guiser, lurking in shadow, teasing and misleading to bring about a greater learning in His followers. He is the Opposer, going against the general norms of society and standard religion*

> *or belief patterns, forcing His People to look beyond the surface of things and look deeper, to challenge, to consider different realities. He is also very much Lucifer, the Light Bearer, as it is through Him that knowledge and enlightenment are gained and He carries the torch of Illumination between His horns. Again, the horns can be seen as exemplifying both the Light and the Dark, Blackthorn and Whitethorn if you will, both within one individuality. He can be a hard Master, pushing and challenging the Witch to achieve things that they didn't think possible or attainable. He can be kind and supportive, but is never soft or gentle, although He can be forgiving and patient. His face changes with the natural tides and seasons, but he is not a "fertility god", however lusty He can be at times; He far transcends this and His origin is far beyond just this planet, in the realms of the stars and beyond. Ultimately, He is the great Mystery, to be worked with and called upon to open oneself up to greater things than can be readily achieved otherwise.*

This liminal nature of witch practises gave them the ability not only to work their magic, but also to have the vision of two worlds and to perceive and affect the Fate, or *Wyrd,* of their clients and, ultimately, themselves. To quote Frisvold in this context:

> *It is also crucial to learn and master an oracle as an aspect of the sorcerer's trade, as it is through the manipulation of oracles that Fate shows herself and reveals what lies ahead. In this is found friction between established religious orders and the cunning ones, similar to how it was in Antiquity when someone who threw lots and could see Fate and thus the future would be a threat to the existing priesthood. In both cases, they made themselves independent of the politico-religious structures, convening with Spirit and Fate in a way that generated uneasiness amongst the ruling priesthood, which for the sorcerer, became redundant.*

This independence from "normal" society gave a freedom of expression and existence that further empowered the Cunning One and enhanced both their image and abilities. That this involved working with both hands was not seen as a problem; it merely gave a greater picture of the whole of reality, more holistic than simply following a single idea of spirituality, based on wider perception from a completely different viewpoint.

Continuing with the concept of liminality and viewing the world from a different perspective, Frisvold introduces the theme of the crossroads, standing with a foot in more than one world and the transformational abilities and opportunities this provides the Cunning One with. Standing at the crossroads, the witch partakes both metaphorically and literally of the energies of more than one realm; they are able to both communicate with and travel to different realms, gaining both experience and knowledge of these states "in-between." Techniques for manifesting these skills are variously known as shape-changing, skin-turning, soul-flight, and sending forth the fetch, which enable the Cunning One to converse with the denizens of these Other realms, among whom are found the counterpart(s) to the Devil initiator figure. Here are Dame Venus, Hekate, and Lilith, all initiators in their own rights and ways, with whom the witch may compact, train, and join in spirit, attending the Otherworldly Sabbat of ecstasy and knowledge.

Involved within the Cunning stream of knowledge was the possession of the Faerie blood and its manner of transmission. The author describes in great detail the origins and importance of the idea of transmission, and whether it was necessary indeed to possess this attribute for the practice of the Cunning Craft. Examined here is the example of the Reverend Robert Kirk, Minister of Aberfoyle in Scotland, who allegedly consorted with the Faire Folk, gaining much insight into their nature, ways, and practices. This he recorded in his small volume *The Secret Commonwealth of Elves, Fauns, and Fairies,* which was not published until years after his strange "death" or disappearance bodily into the realm of Faerie. Allied with the concept of the transmission of the Faerie blood is the concept of the origin of the Witch blood itself and its ultimate beginnings in the conjoining of the Watchers, or Nephilim, with early women of the human race. The idea of the Nephilim is common to several cultures in the ancient Middle East, these angelic "Sons of God" who fell from grace or heaven and walked the Earth, teaching early humanity the secret arts and crafts that were originally forbidden by autocratic divinities. Engendering offspring with human women brought about the race of Elven folk, who carried the inheritance of these Sons of God that became the Witchblood, necessary for the practice of the Craft. This again led to a different perception on the part of the Cunning One: an enchanted worldview that gave access not only to otherworldly abilities, but also knowledge of handling those abilities and the effect that it would have on the client and the witch themselves. This worldview conveyed the ability to see the inter-connectivity of all of creation, of Humanity as a part of Nature, not apart from it, hence the correspondences of and between all things in Creation. That all is connected was readily apparent for those with the eyes to see, standing between two worlds.

Whilst it is acknowledged that the heart and origin of the Cunning Craft is within the wild places of the natural world—within the woods with the woodland deities—and it is, essentially, pagan at its core, there is also a cultured and learned or literate aspect to many strands found within it. Discussed herein is the concept of the Book, both material and non, which can be a fountain of learning for the Cunning One to further their Craft. Such examples as the Armadel, Lemegaton, Greater Key of Solomon, and the works of such notaries as Giordano Bruno, Cornelius Agrippa, and the Greek Iamblichus, as well as other kinds and types of grimoiric literature, all lent rich pickings for the enquiring witch. Many types of ritual drawn from these volumes have found their way into the historical and modern Cunning Craft and have inspired adaptations and offshoots of their own.

To finish this foreword, I would like to give one further quote from this book:

> *"Humanity's modern psyche is a product of their belief in their own greatness and loss of spiritual connection."*

As amply exemplified in these pages by the exceedingly erudite Nicholaj de Mattos Frisvold, the Cunning Craft is, and always has been, a supreme antidote to loss of spiritual connection and a belief in one's own greatness. Herein are found not only previously unreleased rites from a working conclave of Cunning Folk that may be employed to deeply benefit personal illumination, but also a sincere and profoundly considered exposition of the Cunning Craft and its origins, history, and contents from a myriad of viewpoints.

Nigel G. Pearson

PREFACE

The practice of witchcraft has suffered a myriad of interpretations over time. In the British Isles, "witchcraft" was considered a crime until 1735 and was punishable by death. However, the eighteenth century marked a cultural shift known as the Age of Reason, where science and engineering became the focus of humanity's material condition. The world gradually turned towards science to explain phenomena and magic, and the concept of "unbelief" became an accepted theological and religious stance as the Western world underwent a process of disenchantment.[2] As a result, the image of the witch transformed from the diabolical witch or volatile and dangerous village witch to the fantastical witch of folklore and fairytales.[3]

The folkloric witch maintained ambiguous and dangerous qualities, as seen in the stories collected by the Brothers Grimm in Germania and Asbjørnsen and Moe in Norway in the nineteenth century. However, the witch became a mythical being, a Lacanian nightmare as we advanced into the modern age where a renewed interest in faith, witchcraft, and spirituality swept across the post-war world from the 1950s onward.[4]

Due to the many names given to the Nameless Art today, Pennick comments on the difficulty of defining "witchcraft."[5] Given this ambiguity and the resulting quandary, to avoid confusion I was tempted for some time to cease using the term "witchcraft"; however I discarded this idea since historically, "the craft of witches also fell under the domain

---

2 Charles Taylor, *A Secular Age* (Belknap Harvard Press, 2007).

3 Julian Goodare, *The European Witch-Hunt* (Routledge, 2016) p.12.

4 The Witchcraft Act was repealed in 1951 in Great Britain.

5 Nigel Pennick, *Witchcraft & Secret Societies of Rural England* (Destiny Books, 2019).

of conjurers, sorcerers, wizards, and cunning folk."[6] Consequently, I have discarded forms of witchcraft that are religious and dogmatic in nature and distinctively modern and New Age in their outlook on the world.

The term "cunning one" has been in popular use since the fifteenth century and, like the elusive word "witch," refers to anyone who knows the art of enchantment, healing, herbalism, divination, and any form of magic. A cunning one is generally considered a "white witch," someone helpful in their village, in contrast to the wicked witch filled with envy and lust. However, the wicked witch also possessed cunning, which was considered antisocial and negative, a *maleficum* that brought disorder and chaos.[7] Therefore, if the idea of *maleficum* takes a backseat in the discourse, we can investigate the realm and landscape of the cunning ones from their specific perspective. *The Cunning Craft* will address themes and motifs of the Craft that have a global reach, such as the importance of the crossroad, the diabolic, the stars, and snakes. These elements carry power and meaning in Africa, Asia, and Europe in general. For instance, when we speak of the Devil, what does this mean in the context of West African faiths that do not have a concept of the Devil as an enemy of humanity like in Christendom? African entities and spirits like the Èsú and Legba were identified as "The Devil" with ease by Christian explorers and friars when they encountered these ithyphallic and horned deities. In dark woods, cemeteries, and crossroads, we find hungry vampiric and ghostly *vetalas* in Hindu myths, and these same places are also where many cunning encounters are explored in American, Brazilian, and European mythologies.

After addressing the previous matters, I will turn towards the mysteries of the two keys: the silver key of Night and Earth and the golden key of Heaven and Sun. These keys exemplify the importance of working with both hands for the cunning one, as well as the idea of wisdom and what the craft of the wise might look like in its structures. This will lead to a simple cosmic panorama focusing on the two luminaries of heaven, the Sun and the Moon, which, together with Saturn, might be said to generate a cunning triad, similar to how the Sun, Moon, and Venus generate their own triad.

Lastly, I would like to note that this book is a heavily revised, expanded, and rewritten version of my previous work, *The Craft of*

6 Owen Davies, *Cunning-Folk* (Hambledon & London, 2003) p.ix.

7 Stuart Clark, *Thinking with Demons* (Oxford University Press, 1997) p.88.

the Untamed, which was originally published in 2011 by Mandrake of Oxford. Additionally, several rituals from the traditional conclave Via Vera Cruz, which have never been published before, are included in this publication offered to the world for the very first time. As I was once told, "hele, heal, and never reveal," and I will forever stand true to this, as the secrets embedded in the Nameless Art can never truly be revealed, as the Greek poet Kostes Palamas once wrote:

We are neither Christians nor Pagans
With Crosses and Pagan symbols
We are trying to build the new life
Whose name is not yet known

Nicholaj de Mattos Frisvold
Holy Friday 2023
In the Valley of Vera Cruz

CHAPTER ONE

STRIGAE, SORCERERS AND CUNNING ONES

Regardless of whether the craft is used for nefarious or constructive purposes, the practitioner has often been both feared and respected, up until the early Modern Age, due to the knowledge they possessed. The cunning one, witch, wizard, conjurer, or any other name given to this practitioner of magic understood something about the world and creation that was withheld from people in general. In Scandinavia, these individuals were consistently referred to as "wise folk" and were largely considered benign; however, it was unwise to provoke them, lest they resorted to diabolism and the Black Book.[8] A cunning or wise one displaying their dark side would frequently be labelled a witch, which in many ways perpetuated the association witches had with accusations of *maleficium.*

Nevertheless, times have changed, and with the advent of Wicca in the 1950s, the term "witch" took on a quite different connotation than it once had, derived from the Old English *wicce,* which gave us the word "wicked." Anglo-Saxon glossaries from the twelfth century associate *wicce* with divination and the art of the pythoness in the temple of Delphi. In contrast, the male form of the witch or sorcerer, the wizard, is derived from the Middle English *wys*, meaning "wise." In Scandinavia, the wise one was contrasted with the hex or *hekse*, borrowed from Old High German, which took on many connotations given to the *lamia,* a spirit that haunted the night, as popularised in the folk tales collected

[8] Ørnulf Hodne, *Trolldom i Norge* (Cappelen Damm, 2008).

by the Grimm brothers in Germany and the Norwegians Asbjørnsen and Moe in the nineteenth century. Gerald Gardner's 1954 publication, *Witchcraft Today,* marked a radical change in the perception of the witch from an ambivalent diabolic figure to a benign, earth-venerating practitioner of natural magic and paganism, ultimately becoming a fertility-based earth religion.

Wicca, as a product of the spirit of modernity, naturally discarded the pre-modern enchanted worldview in favour of a person-centred eclecticism that led to an epistemology based solely on the mind as the source for generating meaning.[9] Personal agency became vital, as in the pre-modern enchanted world, the line between the practitioner and the many forces in and within nature was not easily separated. Additionally, meaning and interpretation were often surrounded by a certain mystique in a world populated with spirits, both good and bad, that were as real as anything else. This created a unique connection with nature, and in this enchanted reality, wisdom was found in ways of understanding and manipulating nature. The wisdom transmitted within such a worldview will naturally deviate from the teachings handed down in a disengaged world that posits meaning as constructed by an individual's mind and perception alone. As such, it may not qualify as traditional when the traditional enchanted worldview is absent from the transmission.

Examining the word "tradition," derived from the Latin *traditio,* it refers to something that has been passed down, usually in the sense of teachings handed down over time and through generation after generation. It was only in the 1590s that "tradition" acquired the usage we often see today, denoting a custom handed down in more material and less doctrinal ways. The Latin word *traditio* implies both surrender and something handed down and can signify handing down a craft, such as a handicraft or a particular *officio* or trade, as exemplified by the craft guilds. This means that for something to be traditional in a spiritual sense, it must have some connection to a mystery or legacy passed down over time through generations. Moreover, it is essential to consider the substance being passed down; it should have the merit of the keeper of the tradition being regarded as wise. Consequently, we increasingly encounter misuse or misunderstanding of the word "tradition" as it relates to the Cunning Craft, and from this, we lose our sense of what a cunning one is and what a witch used to be.

---

9 Charles Taylor, *A Secular Age* (Belknap Harvard Press, 2007) p.33.

If we continue to explore the word "tradition," we find that the Kabbalists of medieval Safed understood their mystical interpretation of the Torah and Talmud to be tradition in the sense of reception, receiving prophetic inspiration through the light kernels of gnosis. This was only possible through ardent study and surrender to the Law. We should understand the esoteric meaning of "law" as more akin to the idea of "dharma," as in those laws of nature that generate stability and harmony and the sense of profound duty that arises in support of that stability and harmony.

When people or esoteric groups claim to be traditional without their work, belief, or aspiration being informed by what has been handed down, to what is connected to the profound stillness of the Hyperborean centre, then the word "tradition" is misused. Since the advent of Theosophy, tradition has been more frequently employed as a label to inform the "out-group" about something exclusive concerning the "in-group," as so the term "tradition" has lost its meaning. In fact, when one seeks to give form to truth, as is the tendency among many modern occult practitioners, the effect is often that the group, as a collective unit, conforms to some form of illusory traditionalism, a form that reinforces false hierarchies of power and group politics instead of supporting empowerment of the true self, which in turn positively effects community. The idea of creating one's own system is perhaps the most blatant and banal way pseudo-tradition is presented by these actors. Such considerations are often put forth by people who utilise modern tools of distorted formats of magic and sorcery to re-evaluate the past. It is not uncommon for pop psychology to come into play, using psychoanalytic language to colour the pseudo-tradition with a false sense of academic substance, as well as the use of baseless and meaningless parallelisms, often in terms of pantheons and philosophy. Furthermore, there is a hunger and thirst among these individuals, often displayed in deliberate obscurantism and inventive new perspectives on the grammars and handbooks of past sages, as if they see themselves fit to make some sort of upgrade without bothering to understand the foundation of the birth of these manuals and grammars.

The term "witchcraft" is used to refer to various pagan practices and an array of practices of a darker strain. With its many variations, the concept of witchcraft becomes diluted, enriched, and truncated by the diversity of practices and inclinations that seek to appropriate this label. It might be that the witches' art can be acquired by anyone, just as anyone can teach themselves a trade or handicraft from a few books. However, a person who ventures into the terrain of the wild ones, either purposely or accidentally, is recognised as "the other" by one of their own.

Judging all of this is difficult, but one can share their perspective on its nature. For me, my understanding of Traditional Craft has evolved over nearly two decades, during which I have been fortunate to encounter pilgrims and masters of various persuasions that I would classify as the Craft of the Wise with a traditional pedigree. Like many, I first became aware of the term "Traditional Witchcraft" through the letters and writings of Robert Cochrane, and my search was rewarded by meeting numerous exceptional practitioners of the art, with whom kinship was mutually recognised. Some have contributed to this compilation, while others have opted to remain in the shadows and maintain the secrecy befitting them.

The art and craft of the witch often involves transgression, but it is the type of transgression and practices that honour nature and defy profane social order in favour of truth. Truth—what a troublesome word! Truth is not about facts and evidence, but about the immanence of the Source. Thus, we might say that the "sorcerer" meddles with the Source, while the witch has crafted their work upon the Source. Truth is an active state of being. In a world that favours deception over truth, it is natural for those who advocate it to risk being vilified and becoming the subjects of hatred and suspicion.

Perhaps it is accurate to assume that the craft of the witch can be defined as possessing natural and occult knowledge, enabling one to manipulate or appease the spirits of nature and the soul of the world to be favourable. If so, many can be said to be practitioners of witchcraft through sorcerous virtue or intimate knowledge of spellcraft and sympathetic means to achieve their goals. Naturally, when hidden knowledge is revealed in divination and through classical astrology, it can arouse suspicion—as can the utterance of spells and enchantments that transform an unfavourable current into a benevolent and rewarding one.

The cunning one who charms away a wart, the astrologer who casts an election and creates a talisman for a given purpose, or the solitary walker who blesses a barren womb to produce a child all practice aspects of the craft. Nigromancy, *venefica* (originally "venerated" and "venereal" works, later associated with poisoning due to the popularity of magical potions in sex work and erotic issues in general), and *maleficia* (negative workings) also form part of the cunning arsenal. The craft itself might be viewed as the wisdom contained in both "the cursing hand" and "the giving hand." It is the same power and secrets that are manipulated, but by one to the benefit of the community and by the other to the detriment of common welfare. Thus, the witch's role as a potential embodiment of wickedness and a constant threat to social order is a reality that the witch accepts willingly or reluctantly.

Witchcraft accusations were levelled on people accused of *maleficia* and those acting in ways that did not conform to "lawful" magic. Lawful magic largely consisted of wortcunning and sympathetic workings performed by a cleric. Therefore, those who dabbled in such practices outside official ecclesiastical or royal boundaries risked being condemned for *maleficia*, even if their work was intended for good purposes. From the Middle Ages to the maturity of the Modern Age, witchcraft has undergone many phases of understanding, but it has always retained an air of something wicked and uncanny about it. The word "witch" has become so problematic that practitioners of Traditional Craft often accept the label only to escape it, as in the case of Robert Cochrane, who accepted the label as having some sort of meaning but would not define himself as a witch. For Cochrane, this discomfort with the term "witch" was partly due to a group of Wiccans he called "Gardnerians," who also considered themselves witches. I will leave this issue aside and simply state that Gerald Gardner, as demonstrated in recent research by Philip Heselton, most likely received a traditional induction into a lineage of traditional witches.[10] However, he also wanted to modernise the transmission he received and add his personal touch. For Gardner, this involved transforming witchcraft into a ritualistic system influenced by fringe Masonry with a sprinkling of some Crowleyan and Rosicrucian elements. In creating the icon of the modern witch found in Wicca today, the witch became quite distant from the figure targeted by ecclesiastical courts, the anti-social evildoer in league with demons, an image that lasted up to the nineteenth century.

Given this transformation of the word "witch" and how those pertaining to the true persuasion—or perhaps better, the Nameless

---

10 Philip Heselton, *Gerald Gardner and the Cauldron of Inspiration* (Capall Bann, 2003).

Art—resonate less and less with its modern conceptual form, it is crucial to remind that the "traditional witch" is someone considered "other." As Henningsen commented in his discourse in the *Sicilian Donas de Fuera*, "the Ladies from the Outside," he described them as "something of a fairy and something of a witch, although one cannot distinguish which is which."[11]

The "witch" is that constant and still element at the outskirts of the world, true to itself because it possesses a different essence from the many, and with this, becomes "the other" —an embodied reminder that the world has a living, vibrant soul anchored deep within its origin. The presence of this unique essence manifests in a natural and arcane perception of the world that comes easily to "the other," who sees the world as enchanted, filled with possibilities and secrets. This goes far beyond the mere worship of nature and its spirits, seeking to rediscover true connection with the Source.

The ideas of witchblood and elven blood surface repeatedly in any discourse concerning the cunning arts, especially when discussing nocturnal mysteries and the concept of otherness. It is a constant theme, and indeed the question of blood is precisely what sets the witch apart from a cunning one or a sorcerer—a secret pedigree that lives on from forgotten times when all was mystery, and the visible and invisible worlds were free from the need to be veiled. Possessing the blood or not is an issue sometimes seen as provocative and caused by elitism, but this is not the case. It is about pedigree and belonging, related to family and kin. Over time, many of these families dissolved and were broken, leading those of the blood to find themselves again through calling upon the blood of the land and finding their rekindling of the fiery essence. For others, the cunning meeting and unbroken family ties have made the recognition and acceptance of elven blood less enigmatic, and its mystery clearer than it is for many, a solitary pilgrim who walks woodlands and mountains, who follows the whispers of a silent, throbbing call within the soul of the world.

The Craft of the Wise is diverse, but diverse across the poles of blood and land. This means that one specific practice can manifest through a myriad of variations all mediated by land, blood, and person—and for those with keen eyes, these bonds become salient and evident wherever

---

[11] Gustav Henningsen, "The Ladies from Outside," in *Early Modern Witchcraft* (Oxford University Press, 1990).

they are found. It is also my conviction that, even if the blood is forgotten, it does not mean that it is not there.

The icon of the witch we have today owes much to Fernando de Rojas' *La Celestina* (1499) and Jules Michelet's *The Sorceress* (1862). In *La Celestina,* we find the lovesick Calisto seeking the help of brothel madam Celestina to subdue the object of his desire with potions and spells, painting a seductive and dangerous image of the witch as a siren of debauchery who possesses forbidden cunning, a mirror of Circe. Michelet follows up this imagery in many ways, but within the historical annotations and explanations, he allows the witch to emerge as a poetic reality—a fairy tale made flesh—and it is perhaps this poetic icon that has coloured our perception of the witch more than any other account. Julio Caro Baroja and Carlo Ginzburg refined this icon. I would also place Emma Wilby and Gustav Henningsen in this succession of investigation, as they widened the scope of their study and brought more nuances into the study of witchcraft.

As mentioned, Michelet argued that witchcraft occurred as a rebellion against the feudal system and clerical abuse in the Middle Ages, suggesting that witchcraft originated during this period as a countermovement to clerical and political abuse. However, as research by Keith Thomas and Eva Pocs has demonstrated, this claim is erroneous. It appears that the sorcery he focused on for his presentation actually developed within the ecclesiastical walls of churches and monasteries. It is possible to suggest that clerics and friars entered the holy office with this wisdom or simply made use of the tricks and spells they learned from the countryside dwellers. This is also supported by the fact that Michelet and many others saw the Black Mass and the Witches' Sabbath as one and the same thing. The Witches' Sabbath is largely a motif found among the Basque people and is thus recognized by witches from other places in the world accustomed to spirit congress. It might be that the Black Mass is a corruption of this Sabbath or Aquelarre of the Witches, given an unholy form and meaning. At least the occurrences of the Black Mass and the investigations of the Witches' Sabbath coincide along the same timeline and geography. The historical precedence of the Black Mass is largely rooted in the scandals surrounding the Ursuline convents in Loudon and Aix-en-Provence, where diabolic possessions and marriages with demons were performed in an orgiastic style befitting the popular imagination of the Black Mass and continued by Abbé Etienne Guibourg (1610–1686). Guibourg died in prison, but the celebration of the Black Mass, whether in truth or by rumour, persisted among French and Germanic clergy, leading up to the orgiastic worship of the Carmelite Msgr. Eugene Vintras and his successor, Abbé Boullan. Boullan incorporated the Black Mass into workings of a sexual and magical nature more akin to sorcery than celebrations to appease Nature and Night. We can genuinely ask if these clerics were of the blood or not—an answer that will not be possible to provide, only assumed or denied. The terrain of Traditional Witchcraft is, and perhaps should remain, a mystery.

The mark of the witch is that they seek "the other" in places of power, which are found everywhere. Like the kith and kin of the witch who has been dispersed like seeds all around the world, these crossroads are found everywhere. It is here that the idea of Traditional Witchcraft enters; it is about a connection with Origin by virtue of shared blood and ancestry. It is about family in the most radical sense of the word, as *famulus*—denizens of a household, be they disembodied or alive, echoing the idea of the totem pole among Indigenous peoples of northwestern North America. The witch who is traditional will have such kinship, and while most of these families maintain a seal of secrecy, seeking to uphold their stillness and silence, there are some who have, and still do, demonstrate the play of famulus in the way they present themselves to the world, knowingly or not—it is about the otherness that speaks from the silence, where truth lingers and slithers.

Most dictionaries, such as Merriam-Webster, define witchcraft as "a power more than natural," "the power of influence," or "to charm people"—hence *enchantment,* the power to bind someone or something through use of natural bonds or spirit agency. *Sorcery* and *witchcraft* are often synonymous and defined as "the witches' art"—as well as the congress in dream, the "orgy" with spirits (in its real Elysian meaning, a magical communion of the senses), often deemed evil, while they are, in truth, the denizens of the Night.

The crossover between sorcery, witchcraft, tradition, and cult is a complex one, and it becomes even more perplexing when we consider, for example, India, where witchcraft today is synonymous with wickedness and is viewed as a threat to social order. Despite this, witchcraft might be seen as something passed down among Kapalikas and tantric sects of various orientations, focusing on *yathuvidah*— "the sorcerous knowledge." It might be more accurate to consider these practitioners as similar in type to the North European concept of the traditional witch, as they possess a *darshana* or *samaya,* a traditional doctrine, upon which they enact their spellcraft in company with spirits. Likewise, the obscure Jewish *keshupherim*—those who know *keshup* (the secret workings of the Moon)—are individuals brought into these mysteries by the intercession of past Rabbis and Rebbas who continue to work from the other side and open the world of night for the practitioner. Can these people be considered "traditional witches," or are they more akin to sorcerers who work with the mighty Djinn, as described in this text? If so, where is the dividing line between the art of the witch and the witch itself? To some extent, it involves induction into a group that possesses lineal succession based on traditional knowledge, which varies in focus and scope.

If we turn to West Africa, from the perspective of the Yoruba people, witchcraft is considered an innate power some people are born with, a chaotic and eruptive fire that must be tempered, not battled. This witch power, *ajé,* is found among women called to undergo initiation into the Lady of the Birds of Night, *Iyami Osoronga.* These women are part of the Ogboni council—the society of wise ones—and they alone possess the power to crown or dethrone a king. It is only when malefica is enacted with boiling passion and in the spirit of wrath and vengeance that these women are understood to be witches in a negative and wicked sense. From the perspective of a traditional witch, this might be seen as a recognition of "otherness" that leads to initiation and induction into the mysteries. Additionally, there is also the *Imole Oso,* given the form of a wizard and serving as the spirit protector of a secret cult loosely connected to the Ogboni. Access to the cult is granted by divination, and only a few are called to enter. They are then subject to initiation into these mysteries and must merge with the spirit of Oso, becoming Oso themselves. Are any of these—or perhaps all—applicable to the label of Traditional Witchcraft when their cultural trappings are removed?

The issue is that when you call upon the spirit and they answer, who can deny this connection? If you deem this connection to be one of blood, rest only in your own irrevocable conviction of having found your Self, and this will automatically cause a humble remembrance of the forgotten. In finding yourself, you might discover kith and kin—or not. In stating this, I am also aware that I open doors—but I also know that Truth speaks in silence, and thus any need for profane verification of one's discovery of Self will turn itself into dust and broken illusions. Blood recognises blood because the initiation, as such, was a pact from before...one which can be found and lost and then found again and again.

We might understand Traditional Witchcraft as a poetic reality of night and nature that, whilst taking various shapes, gives form to the possibility of the "other." Traditional Witchcraft is a set of practices born from need, land, and blood. It is the art of working one's Fate and the art of working hedge, hill, and mound for one's benefit. This benefit can be limited to one's immediate needs or a group or conclave of people and their needs. The witch, in the traditional sense, is someone who is aware of their pedigree—the particular blood that sets the witch apart as other.

Robert Cochrane stated that a witch is never a pagan, but a pagan might be a witch, pointing at the error in conflating paganism and pagan reconstructions with Traditional Witchcraft proper. The distinction lies in the difference between reverence and worship, and what is known as dual observance, which is quite characteristic of several strands of Traditional Witchcraft. A dual observance indicates that one is able to see the same mystery playing itself out in various cultural manifestations and is capable of embracing both—the most salient one being witches who use saints as well as their own famulus and spirit guides to accomplish their ends.

Due to its diverse possibilities, Traditional Witchcraft is often misunderstood, and some even view it as an empty term that can be filled with any meaning one chooses. However, that is not quite accurate. Even though traditional witchcraft varies—sometimes dramatically—in its diverse expressions, there are a few pillars that consistently appear in its kaleidoscopic dance. First and foremost, we have the idea of "tradition." Tradition is not only a lineal succession of initiation. It can be passed on through fiery blood horizontally, blood to blood, flesh to flesh, or it can also be awakened by the celestial flame striking down. No matter how the induction or initiation is conferred, it will always lead to the same results and realisations—that one is of "the other"—which comes with a natural understanding of the enchanted worldview. The secrets of the world are found unbridled within the witch's own soul where God and Satan, angel and demon toast cheerfully at the same table, or, as Najm Razi said:

> *Know that the soul, the devil, the angel are not realities outside of you; you are them. Likewise, Heaven, Earth, and the Throne are not outside of you, nor paradise nor hell, nor death, nor life. They exist in you; when you have accomplished the mystical journey and have become pure you will become conscious of that.*[12]

A History of Cunning Craft

Up to the late fifteenth century, the *Cunning Craft* referred to the secret wisdom passed on through various craft guilds like shoemakers, gardeners, masons, millers, Bonesmen,[13] Horsemen, and others.[14] At some point, the words "cunning craft" became tied to *cunning folk* and were used in England to describe practitioners of magic or sorcery in general. Different from the malefic *witch*, the *cunning one* was generally perceived as a benevolent force who possessed occult knowledge, could perform acts and deeds judged supernatural, and often specialized in divination, healing, and finding lost objects.[15] The cunning arts could be thought of and mastered by whomever had access to the teachings or teachers with the greater goal to, in the words of Nigel Pennick, "open up the way."[16] Pennick sees little difference between the Cunning

---

12 Henry Corbin. *The Man of Light in Iranian Sufism* (Omega Publications, 1971) p.60.

13 Bonesmen were, like the Society of Horsemen's word and Toadsmen, a secret sorcerous society in Rural Britain from the late eighteenth century organized upon fringe masonic ritual and symbolism

14 Nigel Pennick, *Witchcraft & Secret Societies of Rural England* (Destiny Books, 2019) p.124–130.

15 Up to the sixteenth century in England cunning folk was largely untouched by the law, this changed with the Witchcraft Act of 1542, that gave the potential death penalty for conjurations, sorcery, divination and using supernatural means for finding hidden objects and treasures. The Witchcraft Act of 1542 saw the cunning folk as similar to witches, that were perceived as practitioners solely involved in harmful and anti-social practice.

16 *Ibid.*

Craft and the Nameless Art, as he sees both terms as ways of speaking about East Anglian magic and witchcraft. Yet, in his book *Secrets of East Anglian Magic* (1995), he makes a few distinctions between Toadsmen, Bonesmen, and cunning men related to the presence of the diabolic amongst the former two.

The Bonesmen underwent a Masonic type of initiation at the cemetery where both the Devil and the Dead were crucial elements in the initiation. This initiation would then bestow upon the Bonesmen a power to influence men and horses gained from the Devil and were often also part of the Society of Horsemen. The Toadsman, however, was expressively made into "a witch" whose powers involved influence and control over people, spirits, and the weather. This power was ultimately gained from the Devil, and the Toadsman had to go through a series of supernatural tests to secure the power they had taken, or in other words, they had to gain sufficient respect from the Devil so that he would allow them to keep the power they had stolen. We might conclude from this that the Nameless Art can be acquired through Promethean courage in the way of the Toadsmen, through teachings and teachers like the cunning ones, or through the passing on of power as in the case of the Bonesmen and Horsemen.

Owen Davies points out that from the fourteenth century and onward the cunning one was associated with the arts of necromancy, divination, enchantments, and sorcery. Embedded in the word *wizard,* which was used as a synonym for a cunning one, was the sense of a wise or sagacious person. He also points out that the cunning ones were not pagans and that the Cunning Craft was considered more an art than a movement or religion as such. Further, he states that the line drawn between a cunning one and a witch or warlock was the extent of diablerie involved in their work. A cunning one conceived to be in league with the Devil or his demons was classified as a witch with more ease than a cunning or wise one who was not. Naturally, these ideas were, like the label "witch," shaped by the people around the practitioners who were trying to define what these unusual people were doing while attempting to decide if they were working harm or healing. Hence, someone morally ambiguous associated with evil would be judged a "witch."[17]

---

17 Owen Davies, *Cunning Folk: Popular Magic in English History* (Hambledon & London, 2003) p.12– 13.

The Cunning Craft is sorcerous knowledge and technique that are taught or passed on, hence the passing on of knowledge and magically endowed objects becomes the means for transmitting the cunning forge. Even if, in terms of magical capacity, there is not much that differs between the cunning one and "those of the blood," there still remains the idea that the other blood constitutes something different at its core. This something different, when it was given names in Europe, could be as *sorginak,* wise one, *vampir, volva,* witch, and other terms that possess ideas of malefica and forbidden or occult knowledge. Perhaps the Basque *sorginak* is the word that describes the witch best, as it roughly translated means "fatemaker." This is in harmony with the Nordic Tradition where the witch properly is someone of a distinct blood that is in allegiance with the Norns, the spirits that weave Fate. This other blood can also be found in encounters where otherworldly beings seek to interact with particular humans. Although there are layers and depth also in this mystery insofar as purpose, it is vital to give space for the fetch, *fylgja,* the familiar, and the cunning congress of various forms with the other side, be they in night-flights, sabbath-flights, or other forms.

In this book, we shall concern ourselves with the emergence of witchcraft beliefs in the wake of reformation and use the witches' Sabbath, ecclesiastical witchcraft, and the cunning arts as our nucleus. It appears that witchcraft largely received a form and function in relation to the Church, and as the dissent within the Church became more and more deep and eruptive, so became the need for chiselling out the enemies of the Church. Clearly, the practices of witches were defined in relation to ecclesiastical protocol and the sacraments of the Church. We might go as far as to say that the Church was dependent on the existence of witches and devils to sustain their hold on people and to validate their theology. The following account can testify to how deeply related the origins of today's Traditional Witchcraft and heretic ecclesiastical activity were:

> *This is the kind of order (ordo) by which I have been seduced, he said. It is necessary initially for the future disciple and his teachers (magistri) to go into a church early on Sunday morning, before the holy water has been consecrated. There, in front of them he has to deny Christ, his faith, his baptism, and everything about the church. Then he must do homage to the Magisterulus, that is, the Little Master, for thus, and*

> *in no other way, do they name the demon. Finally, he drinks from the above-mentioned wineskin. As soon as he has done this, immediately, in the deepest part of himself, he feels himself conceived and retaining the images (ymagines) of our art and the principal rites of this sect.*[18]

This description is related to a larger context where the mystery of the Eucharist is used to invoke a quite different kind of power. It is interesting in this confession to see that the reception of the witch-power is conducted within the Church by using wine and bread, but instead of worshiping the powers residing in the Church, they go to their temple to renounce them. It is a radical act described and the effects noted are just as radical as, upon reception of the powers, an instant transformation occurs within the candidate where the images, or symbols of the witchblood return to the candidate's consciousness. There might be importance in that the presiding devil is referred to as a Magister, denoting a linguistic similarity with the Roman *collegias,* which fits very well in the assumption presented in this book and also indicates that the name "The Roman Catholic Church" was indeed properly chosen.

Let us focus on Elias Ashmole (1617–1692), the founder of the Royal Society, a diligent astrologer, a Rosicrucian, and the first man to present an account of initiation into Accepted Freemasonry. He grew up with a deep resonance with the marshlands of Lichfield, reputed to host the bones of St. Chad, the patron of madmen. In the thirteenth century, the moors themselves were frequently referred to as the fields of the dead with a powerful relationship to Saxon deaths by Roman hands. Ashmole was marked by the spirit presences he witnessed here, such as the piper that had eyes "out of the ordinary" that imparted hidden knowledge in the young Elias, as he encountered beings from the fairy realm in the moors and the fairies dancing on the moorlands and around springs. Churton writes in this regard:

> *Ashmole's mature philosophy certainly held room for the secret life of these supposed strange, intermediate beings. It was customary to give fayrie-like characteristics to the spirits of the elements: of earth, gnomes; of water, undines; of air, sylphs; and of fire, salamanders. A Midsummer Night's Dream and The Tempest were modern plays*

---

[18] This account was noted in 1430 by Nidinger and Beierman and further discussed in Walter Stephen's *Demon Lovers* in 2002 (p.202).

> *when Ashmole was a boy. But whereas the four traditional elements were everywhere and constituted everything, the "fayries" were quite particular about their chosen place. Not every house was suitable for fairies. It was a question of location, of locus, of genius loci, and of locus genii. Ashmole could hardly have been a stranger to the concept of magic of place, whether that magic induced ecstasy or panic.*[19]

What is imperative with this observation is that Ashmole represented the typical cunning one in their time, a learned person, who knew that the "other side" was a reality, and who, we might say, maintained a heathen philosophy in spite of his veneration for the Church and the Christian Mysteries. You might object to this by referring to the absence of fairy-faith in Ashmole's thinking; however, congress with fairies at this time was veiled by taboo, and a common belief was that unnecessary talk about one's dealings with the fairy folk would ensure that one lost whatever grace they had bestowed on you. Cunning folk who were reputed to gain their gifts from fairies would accordingly demonstrate great diligence in not divulging anything regarding "the other side." Likewise, both Katharine Briggs and Emma Wilby point out the ease with which Irish peasants engaged in dual-faith observance, meaning the observance of two distinct different faiths that co-exist in a paradox without doing anything to reconcile them.[20] As seen in a number of observations from this time, it was quite common to view the Christian Devil as the god of earth and the Christian God as the god of heaven, and it was perceived that a relationship between them was dynamic and workable. For the cunning one, the coexistence of mutable opposing principles would be accepted as a cosmic fact, what we understand as "working both hands." It would appear that a man like Elias Ashmole was influenced by this worldview, what we may call the Elizabethan worldview, and it was in this climate that we see the work of Dr. John Dee come into fruition.[21] It was a fruitful time of exchange and renewed appetite for the mysterious and magical. It was also a time of contrast and significant religious shifts, particularly when it came to

---

19 Tobias Churton, *The Magus of Freemasonry* (Inner Traditions, 2007) p.47.

20 Katherine Briggs, *The Vanishing People: A Study of Traditional Fairy Belief* (Batsford Ltd, 1978); Emma Wilby, *Cunning Folk and Familiar Spirits* (Sussex Academic Press, 2005).

21 E.M.W. Tillyard, *The Elizabethean World Picture* (Vintage Books, 1942).

Catholicism, Lutheranism, and, in the case of England, Anglicanism. In this regard, it is of interest and importance to remember where the term "old faith" actually came from.

A more rational attitude that discarded the cunning arts as nonsense, delusion, and superstition entered the continent with the Protestant Reformation. In England, Catholicism was abolished in 1530, and as Emma Wilby comments, the Protestants saw the "popish addiction" as a problem. She writes:

> *Devotion to the saints continued, pilgrimages to wells, springs and holy places continued, as well as the use of rosaries, primers, vestments, altars and images, liturgy, prayers and the belief in miracles persisted in spite of Catholicism being outlawed. A British vicar lamented in 1584 of the people that were 'still hanging on to the old superstitions in their popish addiction.' Parts of the liturgy seeped out in use amongst the peasants, as in nominee patris filii et spiritus sancti of the healing charm from the cunning man William Kerrow in 1623:*
>
> *The quaqu and fever and the trembling fever*
> *And the sea fever and the land fever*
> *Bot and the head fever and the hart fever*
> *And all the fevers that God creatit*
> *In Sanct Johnes name, Sanct Peteris name*
> *And all the sancts of heavin's name*
> *Our Lord Jesus Chrystis name.* [22]

It is also worthy to remember that the Mass was held in Latin, a language few of those attending understood, which led to an impression of Latin as a magical language. Hence, it made sense to use parts of the liturgy for the purpose of spellcraft. After all, the whole Mass claimed a miraculous transformation of simple bread and wine into blood and flesh, and since the Mass emphasized the use of words, it was not difficult to see this is a form of institutionalized charm work.

[22] Emma Wilby, *Cunning Folk and Familiar Spirits* (Sussex Academic Press, 2005) p.11.

In particular, it was prayer that was problematic for many Protestant reformers such as William Tyndale (1494–1536), who compared the cunning conjuration with prayer.

We shall, however, be careful with exaggerating how important the Church, as a vehicle for Christian dogma, was in the life of people. Folk Catholicism demonstrates a practical and pragmatic use of sacraments and saints as intermediaries between mankind and the heavens. The role of saints would be similar to the function of fairies, denizens in a parallel invisible realm that interacted with the human world, and what we would term "fairy faith" with its belief in fairy familiars, ghosts, and powerful presences in nature. Wilby suggests that these heathen remains constituted continuous accounts of familiars and ecstatic journeys into the night as integral and natural ways of interacting with the other world and the cunning ones that were able to traffic between the visible and invisible dimensions were considered as out of this world or different, and they gained epithets like witches, wizards, sorcerers, charmers, conjurers, magicians, nigromancers, and necromancers. The people themselves were not that occupied with exactly what they were—they were more occupied with effectiveness. It is this wide array of practitioners, both learned and unlearned, that were referred to as "cunning folk." What they had in common was the rather pragmatic way of their dual practice. The use of the host and wine smuggled out of the Church, scrapings from the images of saints, holy water, and other Catholic artifacts were used in dolls, cords, and the effectuation of spells and curses. Often Latin liturgical elements were used, and quite often they were mixed up with local "fairy faith." The use of keys and the Bible for divination or the laying of stolen hosts on wounds to stop bleeding while reciting psalms were not uncommon elements in the arsenal of the cunning folk.

As people did not bother to segment the different classes of practitioners but rather jumbled things around using whatever term seemed proper, so too did they do to the fairy familiar or witch familiar. It helped little if the cunning one described their familiar as an angel or saint, while the ecclesiastical agitator saw only a pagan remnant or the Devil. A problematic issue here is that many cunning folk used their fairy familiars to converse with the Dead. This was natural for these people as the relationship between fairies and the realm of the Dead was an intimate one where, in many cases, fairies were seen as inhabitants of the realm of death or even as the elevated dead themselves. Whether the familiar was seen as a fairy, angel, or demon was quite often due to the local reputation of the witch. Bad witches had demon familiars, while good cunning folk had fairy familiars. The demon would promise earthly wealth, while the fairy was helpful with common tasks and inspired good deeds. Generally, bad magic was seen as demonic, and good magic was from kind fairies.

There has also been some dissent regarding the term "cunning folk" as if this was a phenomenon confined to the British Isles, but if we agree with Davies, these kinds of people were found everywhere in Europe working a variety of practices related to love magic (bindings and dissolving bindings), finding lost objects and thieves, divination, herbalism, un-bewitching, and blessing.[23] In Denmark they were called *kloge folk* (wise people), in Norway *blessers* or *readers,* in Germany *Hexenmeister, Curanderos* in Spain, *Saludadores* in Portugal, and likewise *benezedieras* or *curandeiros* in Brazil. These people represent a particular form of dual observation, as they were commonly Christian, but also lived in the reality of the fairy faith—they were cunning ones who were also charmers of spirits and animals.

Davies comments that there was a difference between a charmer and a cunning one, but it seems that these segmentations were not a concern, lest it brought some profit. Hence, we see in the late sixteenth and early seventeenth centuries cunning folks of a great variety advertising their services, and it is from this popularization of the cunning ones that we also see the emergence of the quack. From this more commercial interest in the wise arts, a number of charlatans set up their practices and started to propagandize their abilities or services. As a response, from 1660 until 1850, British law had to take repeated severe measures regarding quackery, the promise of medicinal healing under false pretences, and what today we would call "charlatanism." Gradually, the law started to cover more and more areas under the broad category of "medicine." Interestingly enough, side by side with the genuine practitioners, a

[23] Emma Wilby, *Cunning Folk and Familiar Spirits* (Sussex Academic Press, 2005) p.11.

subgroup of merchants and commercial charlatans surfaced who are still amongst us—more well-versed in the art of deception than ever. Taking Scandinavia as an example, they had similar problems as England with what they called *kvaksalvere.* These were merchants who profited off their miraculous medicine, yet the results of their medicine often remained in their promises only. As early as 1794, a "kvaksalver law" was approved in Denmark, which was particularly directed against those that "...took upon themselves to cure illness among the peasantry in spite of being completely unknowing in the art of medicine."[24]

When we look at the practice of the cunning folk, it is reasonable to suggest that the basis of modern-day Traditional Witchcraft is rooted in some sodalities of the cunning folk of this period. But this is merely a suggestion, as it is quite difficult to produce evidence to support or deny such a claim. We have only the history and nature of certain craft guilds to refer to and it is difficult, if at all useful, to make any conclusive judgement about this. As the eighteenth century is taking shape, we see a revival of folk magic in the practice of the *Curandeiros* and *Hexenmeisters,* partly due to a renewed interest in heathenism and witchcraft amongst intellectuals, artists, and occultists that can be said to find a reference point in the work and occult influence upon the world instigated by Alphonse Louise Constant (Eliphas Levi), who spawned the French occult revival. Amongst the many notable thinkers in this period, we find Stanislas de Guita (1861–1897), who, in his well-received and equally well-read 1891 publication *Le Temple de Satan,* gave erudite descriptions of the diabolic arts of witches and cunning ones. We also have the birth of Helena Blavatsky in 1831 and Aleister Crowley in 1875. The founding of the Theosophical Society and the Golden Dawn brought the East into the Western Mysteries and presented a fusion of Eastern elements, such as meditation and yoga, Kabbalah (mainly Lurianic), and more classical magic mixed with Masonic and quasi-Masonic myth. It is not strange to think that this revival, this coming together of various elements of magic also happened in terms of witchcraft in the eighteenth century. The beginning of modernity

[24] Emma Wilby, *Cunning Folk and Familiar Spirits* (Sussex Academic Press, 2005) p.165.

was a time of "coming together," and consequently, fragmentation and the beginning of eclecticism and uninformed opinions started. The multi-faceted curriculums of the occult orders founded during this time testify to this with modern magical orders embodying their eclectic continuation.

The Good Folk

There is a curious text we shall bring forth at this point: Robert Kirk and his little monologue *The Secret Commonwealth*, originally written in 1691 but not published until 1893. Kirk was said to be a minister and the seventh son of a minister, and he advocated for the supernatural belief that the seventh child would benefit from something extraordinary in terms of faerie gifts—Kirk himself was said to be able to heal severe afflictions with just a touch. So, again we see how a man of faith was engaged in dual observation, recognizing the reality of both the commonwealth of fairies and that of God. Quite commonly, the existence of a hidden realm of spirits that was not associated with God's kingdom would run the risk of being considered part of the empire of Satan. While this was common in the 1600s and 1700s, this is not the case with Kirk's explanations, and his experience and opinion are similar to those of Elias Ashmole. Andrew Lang, who commented extensively on Kirk's little booklet, actually vaguely suggests that the land of Fairies merged with the idea of Purgatory and, in the centuries after the Reformation, the Church contributed to making the land of Fairies even more inaccessible to people. This understanding fits in with the nature of the fairy realm as we see in the myths of Anwynn, for instance. Likewise, the sub-terrestrial and hill-sealed kingdom evokes the memories of the realm of Hades, Hel, and the importance of the castle that is only accessible after crossing the river in Robert Cochrane's vision of the "other side." Kirk's work presents a wealth of immensely valuable information that can help us understand the nature of fairy lore and its transition both prior to and after the 1700s.

We see from Kirk's accounts that storytelling, or rather fairytales, were a vehicle for the preservation of these mysteries, and those who were engaged in telling fairytales and stories concerning the state of the Dead were indicated as witches. Kirk writes about the Scottish Archbishop Sharp, who was accused of "entertaining 'the muckle black Devil' in his study at midnight, and of being 'levitated' and dancing in the air."[25] Even if Kirk tried to present a distinction between the Fairy Domain and witchcraft as such, it was fused anyway into an amalgamation of practices rightly belonging to the synagogue of the Satanic Sabbath. Kirk resided in the Scottish Highlands at Aberfoyle, an area with rich roots in Celtic settlements such as the Picts. Here in Aberfoyle, there is a hill close to the Church where the fairies were said to dwell. In many parts of Scotland, it was considered crucial to build churches close to fairy hills in order to ease the transition to the other side for those that were about to enter the Kingdom of the Dead. Early folklorists have commented that sub-terrestrial people were reputed to live either underground or in caves in these areas and were referred to as "Feens." We might have a common reference to "fiend" and "fairy" from this term. These people have been understood to be the original Picts by the rather outdated folklorist MacRitchie, described as a weird dwarfish race, and he suggests that these people originated fairy beliefs.[26]

I think it is more plausible to assume that fairy beliefs are rather universal and legends about beings and settlements hidden from the gaze of ordinary sight are found in the mythical heritage of most cultures. But, in order to keep within the historical thread in this book, let us call forth the observation of Chaucer who refers to Proserpina as the Fairy Queen. The word *prosperpina,* the Roman equivalent of the Greek word *persephone,* means "to emerge," and the myth of Proserpina informs about how she was playing with the nymphs picking flowers when Pluto came out of the volcano Etna in Sicily with four black horses to seduce her, and if that failed, to abduct her. The myth tells that this scenario was caused by Venus who sent her son Cupid to Pluto in order to bring some love to his heart and kingdom. As a result, he kidnapped Proserpina and made her his queen in Hades. To retrieve her, her mother Ceres annihilated the fertility of the Earth, and through Hermes' intervention, an agreement was accomplished, and fertility was reinstated. Proserpina's position is one of ambivalence, and by being the Queen of the Underworld, she possesses all power as she keeps total destruction in her hand, her tool for control.

---

25 Robert Kirk, *The Secret Commonwealth* (1893).

26 David MacRitchie, *The Testimony of Tradition* (Kegan Paul, Trench, Trübner & Co. Ltd, 1890).

Kirk comments at the beginning of his book that the Fairies, or *Siths*, also known as *Sleagh Maith* or the "Good People," appear as apparitions that are of a cloudy texture and that they are benevolent when they are given due respect and attention. He further states that they are a particular blend between human and angel and that the ancients called them *daemons*, intelligent fluid spirits with changeable bodies. They are reputed to be more prone to visibility in twilight and one needs to possess the second sight to see them. It is interesting to note their connection with funerals where they are frequently seen partaking of the banquette and feeding on the essence of the food.[27]

The spirits of witches, commonly understood as familiars, were seen as hostile spirits, feeding upon fear, melancholy, and pain. They are associated with foul or strong smells and the North which indicates an antipathy between the powers of the North and those of the fair folk. He sees the iron and loadstone as items naturally drawn to the North as a means of manifesting these ambiguous powers. Hence, we find the belief that iron nails nailed to the ground will drive away the Good People. We also find a subtle reference to the Cainite mythos and the stories of the first blacksmith who is the carrier of the seed of witchblood, the seed that counters natural flow and order. Kirk refers to these ambiguous spirits as "Divels conjured up in the country" as they are intimately linked to geographical location and said to be of a less talkative nature than the Good People.[28]

The account of the witch Isobel Gowdie is interesting in this regard, as she says in her confession that it is the Devil that sharpens the Elf arrows and prepares their powers. This she had seen herself in her visits to Elfland. She also said that witches make these Elf arrows by forging coffin nails that they have taken from tombs. The confessions of Isobel Gowdie are found in the third volume of Pitcairn's *Scottish Criminal Trial.* To this, Kirk comments: "They contain little or nothing of the 'psychical;' all is mere folklore, fairy tales, and charms derived from the old Catholic liturgy. The poor woman, having begun to with the manifest enjoyment of considerable power. It seems from her account that each 'Covin,' or assembly of witches, had a maiden in it, and 'without our maiden we could do no great thing.'" This might suggest that the reference to the old religion indeed concerned the Catholic faith and

[27] Robert Kirk, *The Secret Commonwealth of Elves, Fauns, and Fairies* (1893).

[28] *Ibid.*

the use of the word "coven" among present day witchcraft revivalists is truly derived from Roman Catholic convents. It is evident from seeing the "old Catholic liturgy" and "fairy tales" being ascribed to the same practitioners.

The kind of Seers especially gifted to communicate with these familiars and devils are called *tabhaisver* whom Kirk identifies with the famous Witch of Endor in the Bible, which suggests that necromancy and pyromancy were a vital aspect of their practice. Further, they are reputed to "have nothing of the Bible," possess a vast number of charms and counter-charms, and be deeply related to the werewolf mysteries and shapeshifting. It seems that the heart of the problem lies in the deliberate use of inhabitants from the kingdom of the Dead. Kirk mentions that witches use the souls of condemned ones to do their work and bidding, and it also looks like he suggests that there is a difference between the spirits of the Dead that come voluntarily and those who are summoned in the form that they take, like the *taibhshe*, meaning "death's messenger," that is said to come in the shape of a dog. The crossroad signifies a crossing, a place of choice, a place where the mysteries take shape, where the other side bleeds into this realm we often call reality. Like the cross, the crossroad is the creation of a timeless centre where the vertical or spiritual axis and the horizontal or temporal axis of being meets, and thus a rift occurs where the two roads meet. The crossroad doesn't necessarily have to be in the shape of a cross. It is a place of convergence, where the meeting and parting takes place, where the door opens and where the well whispers its enchantments and invites us to dive in to the unknown.

CHAPTER TWO

THE ROWDY CROSSROAD

If we look at the cross itself, it is made from two bridges that cross one another, making four paths, but this bridge can also part into two or three avenues and still be a crossroad. Hence the *triskelion,* the witches' foot, the Sun cross, the Basque *lauburu,* and the Slavic *kolovrat*—whether they be three-arm, four-arm, or eight-arm crosses, they represent the powers of the Sun shining in the Land of the Dead as well as the movement through the four stations of the day reflected in the four stations of life: birth through life to death and then rebirth. This is also true for the Kongo *Yowa* cosmogram, which marks the stations of life from within the abysmal waters throughout the cycle of life and death before finally returning to the abysmal waters.

The cross with its lower end planted into the earth, the grave of Adam, thus resurrects the Sun and becomes a code for the most infamous of the patrons of the witches' craft, *Sol Invictus*—Lucifer. The cross itself marks the four quarters, the four elements, and the path of the Sun, Moon, and stars rooted in the terrestrial centre, mirroring itself in the polestar. The Romans had several words to refer to types of crossroads, such as *Bifrons, Trifrons,* and *Quadrofrons,* which would be a road in the shape of a stang, a trident, or in the shape of a cross respectively. Janus, god of passages and transitions, was subject to variants of all these forms of intersection—a legacy Hecate inherited.

Also, the cross was at times fused or confused with the Greek *staurus,* meaning "rod" or "pole," evident from the Latin word *crux.* The crossing rods generate four roads and a point of exact cosmic meeting, a point of possibility and becoming, where this world and the other side meet, and all possibility becomes reality for a while. This simple fact can at times be lost as one chases the Sabbath or occupies oneself with formalities that bring the seeker away from its centerpoint. The crossroad is a place where choice happens, the spirit-denizens of the crossroad are said to be tricky and unreliable, and it is, of course, where we find the Devil himself, like in the cinematic masterpiece from 1926, F.W. Murnau's *Faust—A German Folktale,* with its photographic excellence of depicting Dr. Faust summoning Mephistopheles at a fog-ridden crossroad. Communion with the Devil at the crossroads goes back at least as far as the late thirteenth century, when the process of the Germanic city of Simmental in the years 1398–1406 revealed something that looked like a sect of practitioners of witchcraft. Accused of Sabbath flight and *malefica,* the cunning man Stedelen was inducted into the "black arts" by the aristocrat Scavius in 1375.[29] Of interest in the accusations was the sacrifice of a black rooster at a crossroad prior to Sabbath flight.

[29] Johannes Nider, *Formicarius* (1437); Edward Peters and Alan Charles Kors, *Witchcraft in Europe, 400-1700: A Documentary History* (University of Pennsylvania Press, 2001).

Meeting diabolic powers at the crossroad is rich in the Gullah Conjure and Hoodoo traditions, where communion through gifts and calling to spirits are done at the crossroad in a myriad of forms. What took place at the crossroad in terms of gaining a "Faustian" talent is probably most famously embedded in the myths surrounding the famous blues legend Robert Johnson (1911–1938). The myth tells us that one night, just before midnight, he had gone to the crossroad. He had taken out his guitar and played some notes whereupon a large dark shape appeared to him. This figure took his guitar, tuned it, played a song backward, and then handed it back to him. This incident was said to alter Johnson's way of playing, and his finest and most everlasting compositions were the fruit of these few years of life left after the pact was done. What the legend does not tell is how he needed to have made a burial of himself at the crossroad, and as such, offered himself in allegiance with the powers dwelling at the crossroad. All business done with the Devil is said to give him the upper hand. All ill omens and all malefica associated with making deals with the Devil are present in Johnson's story. So, he got fame and women, but he died before he reached thirty and his truly inspired period spanned less than three years. His body was found at a crossroad in the countryside. Evidently, he was poisoned, but the murders' identity remains a mystery, as does his final resting place. No less than three tombs carry the name of Robert Leroy Johnson around Mississippi, and they all claim it is Robert Johnson the bluesman who rests there.

Niccolò Paganini (1782–1840) had the reputation of having made a pact with the Devil to gain his virtuoso talent, whilst Giuseppe Tartini (1692–1770) downright stated that he reached a different musical level as a composer and musician after waking up with the Devil at the foot of his bed one night, leading to the composition of the sonata *The Devil's Thrill* and other complicated pieces of music. In Norway, the Devil could give one the power of the fiddle if one knew how to entice him through riddle, trickery, and gifts to gain the Devil's respect. Iberian and Brazilian virtuosos would go to the cemetery to form a bond with a dead musician that in turn would summon the Devil for an ordeal, whilst the Scandinavian guitar player seeking to improve his art went to a church of repute where there they would locate a hole in the wall and place their hand inside so that Devil would crush it to give the gift of the virtuoso.

In the Avesta, we find the crossroad sacred to Sraosha, the Watchman of the Night, who, flanked by the rooster and the dog, protects the world against the demonic and destructive retinue that surges over the world at night.[30] The rooster was attributed the gift of seeing the invisible realm, and the same with dogs. Not only this, but dogs were also creatures who possessed anti-demonic properties, hence the presence of dogs weakened the presence of the demonic. A similar idea is found amongst the Kongo and Bantu, where the dog was considered to possess four eyes, able to see equally well in this world as in the other world. In some Kongolese districts, the penalty for killing a dog is the same as if one would kill a human being. The status of the dog is equally high amongst the Avestan people. The crossroad is for the Kongolese, as for the central African Azande people, a place where spells are made and also dismantled.[31] Prayers to the Watchman of Night were better performed at night at places like the crossroad or where a river ran deep—places considered to be filled to the brim with sorcerous potentiality.

In the Yasht 14 of the Avesta, we learn of an oracular ritual that takes place at the crossroad. In this ritual, the diviner uses the feathers of falcons and interprets how they fall within a crossroad as the basis of interpretation. It was also possible to make a protection ritual using four feathers to summon the protective powers of the falcon for the sake of a person, a family, or a situation like gaining victory in war and conflicts.

In the Aeneid, Hekate was said to be "howled by night" at the city crossroad. People buried at the crossroad, commonly criminals and strangers, would automatically join her in the underworld. Her connection to the crossroads is further affirmed in Hippolytus of Rome's *Philosophumena*, better known as *Refutation of All Heresies* dating back to the third century AD:

> *Come infernal, terrestrial, and celestial Bombo, goddess of the crossroads, guiding light, queen of the night, enemy of the sun, and friend and companion of the darkness; you who wander among the tombs in the hours of darkness, thirsty for blood, and the terror of mortal men; Gorgo, Mormo, moon of a thousand forms, look favourably on my sacrifice.*

---

30 Maneckji Nusservanji Dhalla, *History of Zoroastrianism* (Oxford University Press, 1938).

31 Wyatt MacGaffey, *Religion and Society in Central Africa* (University of Chicago Press, 1986).

These three names given to Hecate represent her basilisk stare given in her triple serpentine form of Bombo, Gorgo, and Mormo, which are lascivious spirit attendants that roam cemeteries like ghouls, hungry for the flesh of wayward wanderers in the night. They are similar to the shapeshifting djinn *al'ghul*—a spirit that possesses fangs, is in league with the Dead and the night, and has anthropophagic and erotic inclinations toward human travellers lost in their realm. Similar themes are also present in the Venusian Duke Murmur's seal, which is depicted below. In his seal, we see the double crossroad and the influence of the Moon is poignant. The necromantic potency of this duke, along with Venus as the planet that watches over the djinn in Muslim lore, speaks of a common resonance across time and space, from Greek antiquity to the Arabic Renaissance.

The importance of night as the realm of cunning activity is demonstrated by the ethnographer José Miguel Barandiarán, who writes about the *gabazkuak*, the "nightwalkers" found in Basque lands.[32] The "nightwalkers" were said to take their power from Gauko, the personification of darkness or night that uses the crossroad as a point of rest, focus, and manifestation. Hence, it is often at the crossroads where the work of nightwalkers is seen to take effect, and even during

[32] Josè Miguel de Barandiarán, *Selected Writings of Josè Miguel de Barandiarán* (Center for Basque Studies, 2007) p.86.

the Sabbath, congress can be witnessed at times in the form of dancing lights or as shining fern seeds and otherworldly music which serve as the terrestrial anchor for the given activity taking place within a specific realm within Gauko—the night.

Concerning fern seeds and crossroads, in her book *Plants of the Devil,* Corinne Boyer writes that fern was used for invisibility, to obtain great strength, or to find hidden treasure, and would be harvested on Midsummer's Eve, or on All Hallows, Winter Solstice/Christmas, or Michaelmas.[33] Similar practices are found in Northern and Eastern Europe as well as in the British Isles and they reveal a constant association between fern and "Small Folk," fairies, and ghosts.[34] One of the procedural uses of the fern entails that you would then look for the fern at midnight at a crossroad where a corpse had been buried, and you would recognise the magical fern exactly by its glowing or shining properties. This magical fern would be able to enchant in various ways, to attract, to bewilder and to confuse. In this search, snakes were said to guide—or misguide—the seeker. Once the fern had been located it had to be gathered on a white cloth or a pewter dish while staying vigilant all the time—guarding the prized seeds and plant because the Devil was said to be able to snatch it away should you be distracted from your vigilance upon the plant. The fern is not the only botanical that we find shining magically at the crossroad: we also find the lore of the mandrake, which has a sinister reputation overall, but the mandrake root found at the crossroads growing from the corpses of criminals was considered to be the most potent variety of the root one could harvest.

Just to add a final comment to this, the deva Rudra, a wrathful aspect of Siva that is given attributes like the noun *ghora,* meaning "extremely terrifying," howls and roams around at night. He is also said to dwell at the crossroad, where he can either help or hurt travellers, very much in the same way many West African stories speak of the involvement of Èṣù in the world.

Power is found at the crossroad which has a reputation of being a place of diabolic congress and compacts. Since the Devil is also of night, he will naturally also be tied to the crossroads, but in a wider sense than the physical place. In Nordic folktales, the idea of the crossroad holds

---

33 Corinne Boyer, *Plants of the Devil* (Three Hands Press, 2017) p.128–129.

34 Richard Folkard, *Plant Lore, Legends and Lyrics* (Cornell University, 1892) p.332–333.

a visceral sense of choice and encounter, a moment of decision. This happens often during the cunning encounter; hence, the Devil is found as a traveller, a musician, a blacksmith or a wanderer of some form or the other. You can meet him on or under bridges, at bodies of water, in desolated places, at groves, under trees, in dreams, and in nightmares—basically in every place that signifies a meeting and parting of "this" and "the other," and thus also at churches and other holy houses. Hence, every crossroad is in itself a diabolic meeting. Deities like Hecate speak of the importance of night and crossroads in relation to spirit denizens ghoulish and sensual, whilst the Devil embodies the darkness in a different way.

The beguiling image of the Devil remains an image of threat, blessing, beauty, and opportunity. Where we find the Devil, we find immediate danger, unpredictability, and chaos. If he approaches for a deal, we know we are in for a complicated bargain. Actually, all of these ideas attached to the Devil indicate that he is opportunity and chance more than anything else. The Devil says that change is good, that we need movement in order to progress—and in this way, his world is the land of cunning and ordeal entwined like serpents of past and future on the pole of constant ascent.

If we turn to the Balkans, Radomir Ristic gives us evocative imagery of the nature of the witch as someone who has a relationship or liaison with nocturnal spirits and denizens of the night—diabolic in every sense of the word.[35] The connection the witch or the cunning one held with these spirits would enable night-flight, marvels and wonders, and behaviours considered otherworldly, such as possessing double sight and the ability to watch the visible and the invisible world with equal intensity. They are someone who could gaze beyond the veils of day and night and see the occult or hidden matrix of creation and the invisible worlds. Ristic is adamant in disclosing that at the root of the idea of the witch we find a Bogomil theological concept. The Bogomils believed in One God, but they also believed His emissary and vicar on earth was Satanael, whilst his celestial vicar was Michael. Hence, we have the concept of the two tzars: the golden Tzar of Heaven and the silver Tzar of Earth.

This field between Heaven and Earth is significant, as it is here that we find the witch as the keeper of the two keys that make them liminal,

---

[35] Radomir Ristic, *Balkan Traditional Witchcraft* (Pendraig Publishing, 2009).

forbidden, and illuminated—an accursed blessing it is, but the witch and the cunning one stood strong between two worlds and in the heart of the invisible world with a foot in Hell and the other in Heaven. Mikael Häll comments in his doctoral thesis:

> *...the pre-modern world and its inhabitants existed in a field of tension between God and the Devil.... The magic of common folk, for instance, was explained as a deviation from the right faith that would lead towards God and instead directed the practitioner towards the Devil....*[36]

The Devil, the Davul, the Man at the Crossroad, the Coal Blacksmith, the Stranger, St. Nicholas, St. Peter, the Sum of Your Fears, the Inconsistent One, the Dragon, the King of Earth, the Man at the Bridge, and many more are the names referring to this icon of "the Devil" as the gate to the other side that would welcome only a select few. Old forms of cult and religion have no worth for the witch unless it adds to her Fate as the odd one out and thus a landscape is explained. The witch is a force of nature that stands at the crossroad of its own wild being and who, in amoral ways, gives reverence to the owner of the "golden key," as much as to the owner of the "silver key." This stance is diabolical, at least from the perspective of religious dogma in Christendom. The witch will always be the cunning outsider who refuses dogma but adheres to the doctrine that makes the world a plethora of enigmas that we can follow to all seven corners of the world. Roper Lyndal recounts the following:

> *In 1670, Regina Bartholome confessed that she had lived with the Devil as man and wife. Aged 21 when she was interrogated by the Augsburg Council, she had met the Devil five years before. She recalled that the Devil was clad in silken hose with boots and spurs and that he looked like a nobleman. They enjoyed trysts twice weekly at a tavern-bakery in Pfersee, a nearby village where Jews lived. The Devil ordered lung sausage, roast pork and beer for her and the two ate with relish alone in the inn parlour. He promised her money, but she had received barely 6 Kreuzer from him, and even that had turned out to be bad coin. In return for this meagre reward, Regina*

---

36 Mikael Häll, *Skogsrået, näcken och djävulen* (Malört forlag, 2013) p.72–73.

> *had signed a pact with the Devil for the term of seven years. She had forsworn God and the Trinity, and she had taken the Devil—her lover—as her father in God's stead.*[37]

A similar account is reported by Isobel Gowdie who confessed in 1662 in front of Scottish judges that she indeed had met the Devil. This encounter seems to have been partly moved by a deliberate search for the Devil on Isobel's part. She told the court how she had been traveling from farm to farm following some ghostly shapes moved by the wind. At some point, she met the Devil, a noble-looking man, dressed in grey whom Isobel gave herself to shortly after meeting him. Their communion was performed in the church of Auldearn where the Devil met her, his black book in hand, and asked her to renounce her Christian faith in the presence of other witches. This done, she received the Devil's mark on her shoulder followed by a baptism composed of the fusion of her own blood and the Devil's saliva. Following this encounter, the Devil taught her about magic, shapeshifting, and how to use the witches' familiar—the fetch.

As we saw in the previous chapter, Elias Ashmole reported in his writings about encounters with denizens of the other side that shared with him secret knowledge which he used for his advances in the studies of alchemy and the theurgic arts. Another notable record of a witch tutored in forbidden knowledge is found in the case of Bessie Dunlop and her otherworldly friend, Tom Reid, whom she claimed was the source of all her knowledge.[38] Her diabolic communion with her familiar and possession of occult or forbidden knowledge led to her conviction for the practice of witchcraft and she suffered death in 1576.

Besides the overarching accusation of heresy, the element that stood out most for the tribunal of judgment was the alliance the cunning ones and witches held with the Devil, the enemy of the Church. This we see from Thomas Aquinas in the parts of his Summa where he addresses magical acts like astrology and the manufacturing of talismans. For Aquinas, the matter becomes problematic when a preternatural—and not divine—source is actively summoned to consecrate and empower objects. This deliberate summoning of preternatural forces was complicated as it encroached upon the realm

---

37 Roper Lyndal, *Oedipus and the Devil* (Routledge, 1994) p.228.

38 Emma Wilby, *Cunning Folk and Familiar Spirits* (Sussex Academic Press, 2005).

of order controlled solely by God; hence, the essential crime of the cunning one was not unlike that of Satan or Lucifer: an invasion of forbidden and divine territory. Naturally, since the transgression was similar in character, the cunning one and the Devil joined forces in a realm of commonality where the cunning one was taught the secrets of God and creation by the Divine Opposer. Instead of guidance through angels and saints, the Devil offered fetch, familiar, and demonic helpers—powers that opened a nocturnal understanding of nature and night, of cursing and blessing, of wisdom, of influence, and of clairvoyance. The perspective of the Church didn't always make much sense to the cunning one who had no problem revering Jesus Christ as the golden tzar of the celestial domains and Satanael as the silver tzar, owner of terrestrial affairs. The Devil meets the witch and generates a crossroad, a point where the vertical and horizontal meet from where marvels of nature are as possible as Sabbath flight.

Being stationed at the crossroad, we can experience the descent to the Land of Death and the ascent to the celestial fields of angels. The crossroad is the realm of communion, and from the crossroad we embark on any journey towards lessons and blessings. There is nothing else. The vast resistance towards change amongst humankind has generated the Devil's bad reputation. Together, his enigmatic ways of securing growth and movement have created a whole array of negative terms to define what we can understand, often using terms that are morally challenged—but morality is no field for the Devil. The choices we make that do not bring us toward destiny and that bring lessons instead of blessings are of the Devil's making.

Returning to the Yoruba Èṣú, we find the belief that Èṣú Yangi (the spirit of the laterite rock) lives at the crossroad and that rocks that appear to grow up from the Earth manifest him in the world as a natural point within a greater crossroad. Èṣú is the power of transformation and movement, and this particular Èṣú is associated with the red and worn dust often found at the crossroad. This dust is said to carry the power for making good decisions, and in the face of challenge, provoke the better choice. So, people go to the crossroad or they take this dust and through ritual acts and words of power they elevate its indwelling properties and its spirit. They ignite the presence of the fire of transformation. The Yoruba see bad decisions as a result of being out of alignment with destiny. When the heart and mind are not in alignment, it clouds one's understanding and it destroys one's happiness. The lessons the Devil gives have the power to help us with this alignment. His ways are of the night—of enigma and challenge. He is the factor that facilitates any form of growth and movement. He is the double-edged dagger, the blade that cuts both ways. The dagger in the ground stands as a cross itself thrust beneath our feet, and by contemplation of this simple imagery, the twain nature of what we call the Devil becomes more accessible and understandable.

The intersection of two or more lines, a track that suddenly reveals one more secret path to take shape at this very enchanted moment, the fairy-footsteps in the pastures marking the ley-lines, the axis of the world tree—these are all symbols of sacrifice and wisdom. The world tree and the polar axis can both be understood as crossroads. At the centre is the point of ascent and descent that creates movement at the crossroad. Still, with of all powers associated with the crossroad, we find the Devil and the unruly powers that challenge what we believe to be true.

Like crossroads holds pluralities, so does the Devil himself. He consists of legions of devils and diabolic forces and entities. For instance, in the period of persecution of social outcasts, people tried for witchcraft and sorcery were often understood to be in allegiance with some devil.[39] At times the Devil was seen as Satan, Ashtaroth, or some other demonic entity—other times as fairies, undead ones, or the spirit of dead people seeking to help someone. The idea of the Devil grew to include a whole host of various diabolic forms. It is clear that the persecutors displayed an understanding of the Devil as a plurality. In cases where the Devil was perceived as a singularity, he was attended by a host of demonic servants that he could send forth to do his work and bidding. While the Kingdom of God was signified by unity, order, and purity, the Kingdom of the Devil was its reversal—a reign of immorality, diversity, and chaos.

It is not uncommon to see these ideas in motion, as shown in the trials against Father John-Baptist Girard in the middle of the 1600s. We find here a case of the exorcism of Miss Mary-Catherine Cadiere, where the Jesuit priest Girard was accused of incest, abortion, and sorcery. The priest had exorcised devils, but in spite of this he had invited in

---

[39] Julian Goodare et al., *Demonology and Witch-Hunting in Early Modern Europe* (Routledge, 2020).

even more devils—particularly of lust and obsession. Likewise, in a trial in the same period, Joan Peterson, known as the Witch of Wapping, was hung in 1652 for the practice of Witchcraft, in the sense of magic aimed at harming others. Here we find another set of witchcraft beliefs attached. The prosecution was particularly occupied with the outlandish visitors and shapeshifting involved in this case. Several people reported that they had seen the Devil taking various forms, such as a dog and a squirrel, and Joan herself taking the form of a cat trying to harm children. The prosecution was particularly interested in the many accounts of the Devil coming to "suck her." We see here the motif of the familiar in the guise of a vampire, and we should also mention that her danger to the children was caused by her powers of bewitchment or *fascinatio*, a phenomenon we shall look closer at in a later chapter. It is curious however that the power of *fascinatio* has also been ascribed to saints, sages, saddhus, sheiks, and other wise people—even Rabbis were reputed to be able to dissolve people by fire with a glance from their eyes. This would indicate that the source of the power was more important than the nature of the power itself. We might see a parallel today with the phenomenon of the herbalist who prescribes plant remedies for the cure of an illness being accused of charlatanism, meanwhile, doctors who use synthesized drugs based on the properties of the very same plant never suffer the same allegations. The formal and orderly society claims authority based on the grounds of its institutionalized schooling and stability, while we have learned to fear the unruly powers in the wilderness that create a dynamic contrast to this order.

Other researchers, especially Norman Cohn, have been focused more on the clear elements of fear and paranoia in the witch trials of the fifteenth to seventeenth centuries in Europe.[40] In the above-mentioned trial of Joan Peterson, we see how irrational observations generate some sort of paranoid truth. One of the fiercer testimonies was of a baker who swore that he was taken in by such unnatural fear when seeing a particular black cat—such an irrational fear that it could only be explained by a witch skin-leaping into the shape of a cat! These elements of fear, both rational and irrational, contribute to an understanding of the more absurd allegations—but fear remains as a steady imprint.

---

[40] Norman Cohn, *Europe's Inner Demons* (St. Albans, 1976).

If we turn to Vodou in Haiti, we find a highly successful conglomerate of various impulses: African powers transformed in this particular soil, aided by French Cunning Craft and, later on, Masonry. We find a faith based on a dynamic interaction of elements according to a natural feeling for the natural hierarchies and a cosmology that is able to divulge tradition in a purer form than is found in many of its sister religions in the diaspora. It is interesting to see how the idea of the crossroad as an inter-dimensional portal has been integrated into Vodou from both French sorcery and African cosmologies. The crossroad is understood from mutually enriching angles, both from French craft traditions as well as those found in African-derived traditions and faiths—together these impulses have forged a deep and dynamic understanding of the crossroad as the creator of the intersection of all-possibility.

In Vodou, both from Benin and Haiti, we find Èṣù takes a myriad of forms under the form of Legba. Legba can be the old wise one Atibon, the highway between the visible and invisible in the shape of Gran Chemin, the monkey on the other side of the mirror in the form of Miwa, or Legba Petwo who is a youthful fiery spirit, fierce and dangerous. In this way, both Èṣù and Legba represent the crossroad and the Man at the Crossroad at the same time. At the Vodoun crossroad, we find Legba and his more unruly counterpart, Kalfou. We also have Baron Samedi who is represented by the cross. Lwa Legba has a variety of manifestations significant for the Crossroad, he is not only Atibon, the form of Legba that most people meet early on in their Vodoun path—he is also Gran Chemin—the Highway denoting the importance of ascent and descent that takes place at the crossroad. Legba Kalfou is perhaps even more reminiscent to the murky image of the European Devil as he presides over the art of sorcery and can send out legions of his three horned bull-shaped devils to execute his tasks for him. A host of vévés, the spirit signatures of the various Lwa, are structured around the basic form of the crossroad, as this is the natural point of congress between this world and the other. In the point of the crossroad, we realize unity, and it is with this realization that we move forward while miracles are made possible. Legba is all-possibility, and he is the Master of Chance and Change as well as doors and gateways. It is with Legba that we can walk within the fields of Gran Bwa, the Owner of the Leaves and the Forest and Baron Samedi, the Lord of Death and Sex, who typifies the enigma of life itself. In the crossroad we encounter the powers that follow us on whatever track we choose to pursue.

The sometimes-radical consequences that are encountered by entreating the crossroad and its powers are evident also in the Cult of Exu, known as Quimbanda in Brazil. Here, we meet the Lord of the Crossroad in classic diabolic imagery as a prankster and a foul-mouthed adversary that feeds on peppers, tobacco, and spicy drinks. In times of need it is Exu that people turn to for advice, to gain the necessary power to effectuate spells—and it is in the Kingdom of Exu, the crossroad, that people can experience the irony of life's problems and find the answers and solutions they need in order to be at ease. It is of interest that when one enters the crossroad it is at times spoken of as entering the "kingdom" or "realm" of Exu, not too different from how witches and shamans transition to the other side in dream, vision, and cunning encounters—yet with the additional element of possession or incorporation by a spirit being, at least in the written accounts we have to our disposal, that is less commented upon in relation to cunning folk and witches.

The demonic in the sense of "vile and hateful powers that are up to no good" also live at the crossroad, and books of sorcery in any culture advocate the use of the crossroads. The temperament of these beings has a long tradition of becoming demonized and shall be discussed more in-depth in the next chapter. The demonic has, at least for our Western occult culture, become linked extensively with the part of the Solomonic tradition referred to as the *Lesser Key of King Solomon* or *Lemegeton,* which is largely modeled on the practices of the necromantic experts in Greek antiquity. The text called *The Testament of Solomon* dates to somewhere around the second century AD and is the blueprint for this tradition as it was forged throughout its development in the West. Basically, the text tells of a vampiric and aggressive spirit that seeks to devour a young boy and King Solomon defends him by gaining a ring from the Archangel Michael. The book also catalogues a number of spirits signified by their unruly and chaotic nature. The main spirit here is Ornias who is said to have many spirits in the crossways, as in the fourty-fourth verse we read about this spirit:

> *And he answered me: "I, O King Solomon, am wholly voice, for I have inherited the voices of many men. For in the case of all men who are called dumb, it is I who smashed their heads, when they were children and had reached their eighth day. Then when a child is crying in the night, I become a spirit, and glide by means of his voice.... In the crossways also I have many services to render, and my encounter is fraught with harm. For I grasp in all instant a man's head, and with my hands, as with a sword, I cut it off, and put it on to myself. And in this way, by means of the fire which is in me, through my neck it is swallowed up."*

Ornias is found under the name Orias as a marquis in the *Lemegeton*, and like all marquises, he takes his powers from the Moon. Orias is said to hold two hissing serpents in his hands and rides a horse while his form is a hybrid of a lion and serpent, imagery that is quite interesting considering the iconography of a devil. Contrary to the passage in *The Testament of Solomon*, the *Lemegeton* depicts Orias as a reconciler and a teacher of the virtues of the stars and especially the mansions of the Moon. It is also interesting to note that in *The Testament of Solomon*, there is a reference to the critical seven days prior to circumcision found in rabbinical lore. This period is said to be presided over by the Demon Queens such as Lilith, Mahalethm, and Naamah, suggesting the importance of Hebrew folklore for this study. It is also here that we find the emphasis on these types of malevolent spirits being many, they being "legion." These forms of spirits, vampiric seizers, also occur in *The Testament of Solomon*. Further, the seal of Orias here reproduced carries a distinctly forked stave, reminiscent of the witches' foot in its centre in reference to the crossroad as a place where roads meet and part and where the visible and invisible realm crosses over into one another.

The Crossroad is also where the pacts are made. In a Book of St. Cyprian from Norway dating to 1780, we find the following formulae:

Go to the crossroad three Thursday nights in a row and say three times:

Lucifer, Ac, Ac, Ac.

The third night, he will come silently to ask you what you want.

You then tell him what you want. He will answer that if you sign this contract in your own blood, he will do everything you wish and accomplish all what you demand.

The contract is as follows:

> *I, N.N. demand your Service, you young Lucifer and the warden of Lukemborg, by the Living God. As long as you are obedient, I will be yours with life and blood—until eternity, Body and soul and in death, I will be yours—in eternity, and I will not myself touch a hair on my head. No change or exorcism will you hear from me, as long as you accomplish all what I demand from you. And to these ends I sign with my own blood, that I renounce to serve the Creator and the Holy Trinity neither in word or sacraments, neither in life or living, night or day, asleep or awake, young or old, until my time of Death. Then it will all be yours, by the blood of the one who have signed.*

This contract the Devil will present for you and it will be sealed by your name.[41]

This is, however, not totally correct if we compare this with the host of procedures for renouncing God dating back to the same time. Apparently, the renunciation of God is a prerequisite for engaging with the pact. Also, on the same day as the renunciation, a declaration to the universe is made. You will need to rise up from your sleep in the name of the Devil, dress in your clothes in the name of the Devil, and so forth. The whole day prior to the encounter at the crossroad shall be a "hallowing" in of itself, a period of altering the consciousness to receive and see the Devil, the dedication said in words and shown by action will then be noted by the Devil, and he will see that you are firm in your heart. Make the following renunciation in which you call "the angels of the pit" when you awake on that morning, and then follow the procedure of doing whatever you do that day in honour of the Devil. Interesting that in the renunciation procedure below is the importance of reciting *The Lord's Prayer* after each act of devilish praise. This would then serve as an aid of transmitting a great power, as found in *The Lord's Prayer*,

[41] Anton Christian Bang, *Norske hexeformularer og magiske oppskrifter* (Ka forlag Oslo, 2005).

to its adversary. Therefore, during the day of blasphemy, the "Father" referenced in the prayer would be associated with the Devil:

> *I renounce you, my God that created me. I renounce you, Jesus, who redeemed me. I renounce God the Trinity that made me Holy. I will never more worship thee or serve you anymore after this very day, this I swear by my body and blood as the Young Lucifer, the greatest of the angels of the pit and Chief, I swear my loyalty under his reign. He will therefore serve me in all what I demand to do and then I will sign this with my own blood as a safekeeping and security of my word, on the condition that he is carrying out all what I command and demand, then I will sign this contract with my own hand and in my own blood.*

The Synagogue of Satan and the Lord of Greenwood

Given the Manichaean stance of ecclesiastical doctrine, the Devil of the Church, Satan, has been with the Church since the apple was first consumed in the Garden of Eden. He has been there as a tempter of future saints and the Son of God, as a force that tested the faithful and offered his earthen kingdom of hedonism and pleasure in place of the celestial kingdom of Jesus. Looking aside from the redemptive qualities of the divine adversary in Sethian, Ophidian, and Bogomil Gnostic traditions—the lack of grayscales in Christian faith made this spiritual realm into an "either-or" binary domain. Choosing Jesus excluded walking with the Devil as the Devil also demanded that his votaries forfeited key elements of the Christian faith like the Trinity. In return, the priest, upon his ordination, had to foreswear the Kingdom of Satan with all its pomp and temptations. Naturally, for the cunning one who worships with both hands (also known as dual-observation), there is no doctrinal conflict between Jesus and Satan, and what is viewed as heresy from a Manichaean perspective is, from a Bogomil angle, seen as a mystery of hierarchies in which it is more about *not* confusing the thrones and principalities, but adhering to their rightful place and station.

It is only natural that several forms of Satanism use the Roman rituals in some form or the other given the importance that the diabolic element has for presenting as the mirror-image of God and the Church, as the classical summoning of the Devil by reciting *The Lord's Prayer*

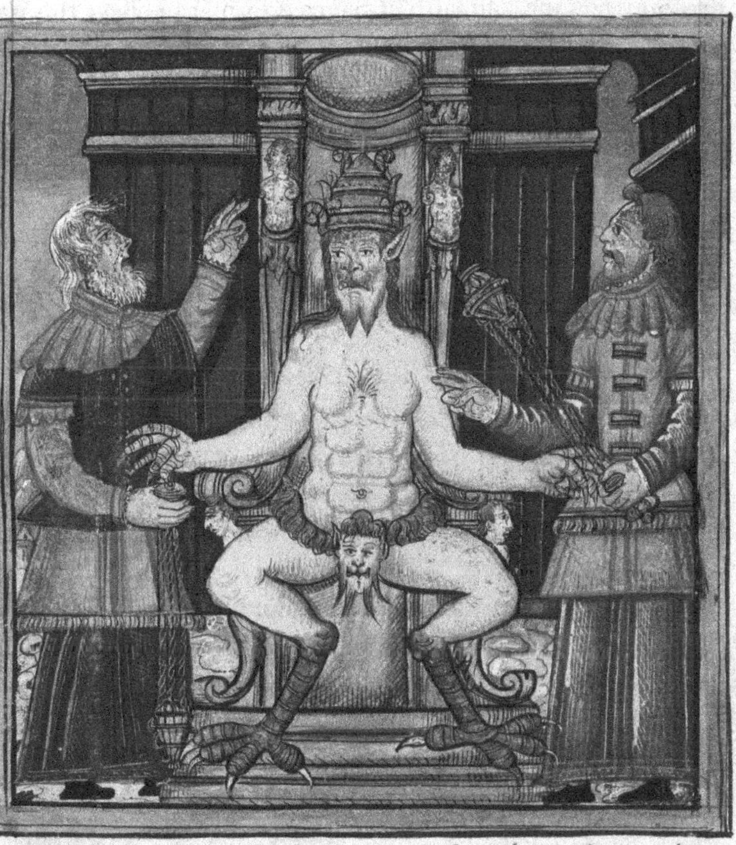

COMBIEN que Sathan depuis ſa creation du Monde ait exercé son regne & tyrannie par toutes les prouinces de la terre, & ſe ſoit faict adorer à vne infinité de peuples, ſoubs diuerses eſ-

peces

backward. The Devil is the embodiment of both God's mysterious darkness and the limits of unfolding. The proximity the Devil has with the Church became even more evident with the Lutheran Reformation and the rise of Protestantism that chiselled out the Vatican and the Catholic faith as the "Synagogue of Satan." Hence, in the modern vernacular when the "old faith" is referred to, many believe this is some pagan pre-Christian religion, but this reference to "the old faith" was a reference to Catholicism. This is evident in the anti-papal propaganda that became widespread in the sixteenth century that arose side-by-side with the increased focus on witchcraft as a criminal offense. One fascinating piece of art from 1597, found in Poierre Boaistuau's *Histories Prodigieuses*, shows the Devil on the throne of St. Peter crowned with the papal tiara and attended by a cunning man and a deacon, emphasizing the strong link perceived between the Catholic Church and heretics of every variation and tone.

The idea of Satan as the Arch-Devil continues to fascinate and intrigue. In 1999, the Vatican revised their liturgical procedure as well as the theology for understanding Satan in the modern world, and accordingly added various aspects of possession and obsession as being caused by spirits or having a psychological cause. All forms of perceived moral decay are ascribed to the Devil in the guise of Satan with his herds of demons that seek to corrupt humanity. The truth is that a personified Satan has always been the dodgy emissary of the Church, the Holy Scapegoat, and the personification of dread that scares people into remaining in the embrace of the Church, and thus by the aid of Satan they are thwarted into becoming loyal servants to a ruthless God obsessed with moral purity.

The merging between the Lord of Greenwood and Satan, as the adversary of God and the enemy of mankind, was completed with the publication of *Malleus Maleficarum* in 1486. This compendium written by, according to the French historian Jules Michelet, the imbecile monks Kramer and Sprenger, came to set the standard for demonological beliefs which rose in the popular imagination. Basically, it was a work that systemized the contents of Johannes Nider's *Formicarius* with some additional material from mostly German and Italian sources. It is in this compendium of witch-finding and the nature of *malefica* that we find the theological foundation explaining the reasons for Satan's power clearly spelled out as a consequence of the fall of some of God's angels, the Fallen Host, which became devils of all forms of seduction. By extension, the difference between devils and demons became blurred as the division between the Devil and Satan became fused into one. Yet, regardless of nuance, the message would be the same: everything pertaining to the other side was vile, dangerous, and would for sure lead to no good for those wandering into this realm. Those who convened with the powers of the other side were, therefore, up to no good, and there was theological reason to assume that these people were witches in the sense of *malefici* and *venefici*. This result came partly as a consequence of the apocalyptic interest within Christian denominations in the aftermath of the Ecclesiastical schism of the year 1054, that separated the Church into the Eastern Orthodox and Western Catholic Churches. The theological debate was concerned naturally with the possibility of unity of God in a church that was not finding unity amongst themselves. This led to a feeling of apocalyptic despair as seen in the recurring theme of Christian iconography from the twelfth century, where the Final Judgment in all its sublime horror found its form. It is in this time of change and turmoil that we find the seeds of the image of Satan as he came to be seen as a grotesque mimic of God's holiness, and the tribunal of the Inquisition was soon to take form as a tool for "cleaning the Church" from its heresies. Satan was a very living reality for the clergy: the power of separation and adversity, the power that threatened to break God's unity. The passage in the Gospel of Matthew and the more eschatological parts of John's Apocalypse were subject to theological speculation and artistic rendering in Christian iconography. It is here we find references to the separation of the goats and the sheep, the reference to the right and the left hand, and that the Devil and his angels preside over hell, often understood as a fiery realm within the Earth. This imagery made such great imprint on the heritage of Christendom that it led to a complete acceptance of the apocalyptical separation of goats and sheep as a reality.

The goat as the representative of the Devil and his kingdom is evident in the XV trump of the tarot, as well as Eliphas Levi's famous depiction of Baphomet which surfaced as imagery in the witch trial confessions of central Europe toward the end of the 1600s. The modern segmentation of Left Hand Path and Right Hand Path also owns its classification to an acceptance of this predominantly Christian classification. This segmentation also found its way to Brazil, where spirit work along the lines of Umbanda is parted into "workings on the right side" and "workings on the left side." This form of segmentation, however, has a long historical precedence as the historian Julio Caro Baroja writes about heretics who already refer to themselves as Luciferians in thirteenth century Germania.[42] The account tells of how they venerated a black cat, whereupon conclusion of the veneration, the candles were extinguished, and an orgiastic feast was celebrated. Upon completing the feast, the candles were again lit, and a dark or "black" man was summoned to appear from the corner of the room. This man was said to have a body that shone like the Sun while his lower part was furry like a cat. Nigel Jackson recounts a similar theme in *Call of the Horned Piper*, where he reminds us about the Ashton-Upon-Lyne processional, where the prosecuted one was said to be "Riding the Black Lad," a spirit-form said to possess "burning eyes."

This repeating theme is striking. Countless testimonies can be found in which the wild and untamed are presented together in uniformity with the light. Already in the twelfth century, we see the Devil depicted with cloven hoofs, horns, and a tail—a bestial mimic of the human form. This form was striking for the people adhering to the peasant craft, as the Lord of the Wild was certainly a figure that kept nature, virility, death, and sex within its representation. That the goat was seen as a representative of the Devil, with its notorious devilish eyes, strength, virility, and strong smell of wilderness, also summoned the imagery of Satan through the sacrifice of the goat known as Azazel in Leviticus 16, the scapegoat that was taking the sins out in the desert and who Jesus meets again in his forty days of temptation walking around in the desert in Matthew 4 as Satan. Prior to this segmentation into good and evil, left-handedness had been subject to skepticism in cultures across time. The whole idea of left as sinister is often distorted and shortcuts are taken in order to identify it as something averse in the sense of evil or chaotic. In astrology, a sinister movement of planetary bodies signifies a motion towards a position or aspect, while dexter signifies a movement away from an aspect of position. This means a planet in a sinister movement warns about an influence that is about to emerge, whether it has a good or bad influence depends on the nature of the planet and the aspects it is making.

---

[42] Julio Caro Baroja, *The World of the Witches* (University of Chicago Press, 1964).

The idea of Vama Marga as the sinister path is also famous, while in reality, the name denotes the placement of the woman in the tantric *panchamakara* ritual, where her sinister placement is seen as crucial for the ritual's success. Looking at the many meanings of the word *vama* itself, it can signify everything from "vomiting" or "casting out" to a whole range of facets related to the role of woman in the *panchamakara* ritual as well as "snake" and "adversity" as well as "misery." This ties the idea in with the Sakti and tutor of the path of witchcraft, Nivritti, mistress of the *Yathu-marga* and thus the well-known theme of women as the vessels for unnatural or supernatural powers are indicated. Dadaji Manhendranath, the Guru of the Nath succession in the West, comments about this in his article *Sinistruversus:*

> *The other division in Tantrika is known as Vama Marga or Nivritti Marga. Vama means left or opposite-turning because Dakshin means normal, sun wise or clockwise. Vama is not a religion but a spiritual esoteric path for those who have the basic qualifications. It is the path of return, left-turning or sinistroversus. Return to what? First it is the path of return to the natural life of natural relationships and therefore differs from the restraint patterns and rules required for the slaves. Slaves must serve and not enjoy; they must worship and not attain. Vama Marga is also known as Bhukti Mukti Karnika—The Path of Enjoyment and Liberation. The path is not for everyone. To escape from the world, the rounds of rebirth and the miseries of life requires a way whereby one tastes the Microcosm in all its aspects. Without this experience, one can hardly have the capacity to reject. This is the way of the Gods and the way of the Masters.*

Another recurring theme in the descriptions of the Devil through the historical records relevant to our disposition is the reference to his "blackness." Richard Cavendish recounts several episodes carrying this theme such as one account from Orleans in 1022. The account tells us about a group of heretics that were executed for worshipping the Devil, who first appeared to them as Ethiopian, a Black man, and later as an angel of light—we might see here some grim caricatures of the development of the Satan-Lucifer theme in conjunction with the Luciferians in Germania of the 1300s. Much later, in 1587 in Soissons, France, Cavendish writes concerning Catherine Darea who beheaded two girls with a sickle—one of them her own daughter. She explained the act, saying it was the Devil in the shape of a Black man who had appeared to her, given her the sickle, and ordered the killings.[43] Naturally, an event like that would likely be an expression of a psychological condition of the criminal than anything else. The blackness of the Devil was related to his realm, the night, and by the seventeenth century the witch became a conglomerate of all sorts of forbidden arts and practices—such as those seen in the drawing from Nicolas Rèmy's *Demonolatry* from 1693 reproduced here. The witch is in a circle with a book of black arts, a skull at her feet, and accompanied by animals nocturnal like the mice, owl and snake. A triad of witches are carrying the goat headed Devil whilst another witch is flying away on her broom to the Sabbath. The drawing really captures the totality of the imaginary symbology believed to be the witches' world, even a musical priest looking more like a Jack O'Lantern is found there—tying the church, music and poetry to the witches' art.

The Wilderness as the Crossroad

The wilderness as the crossroad has become firmly affixed as the dwelling of the Devil. During the era of Romanticism, it was the woodland deity Pan that became the recurring icon for poetic renderings of the untamed powers. Pan himself was the Greek Lord of the Wilderness, a guardian of shepherds, and a muse for the flute-players. His form was bestial with horns and the lower part of the body in the form of a goat. He was a reputed seducer of fair women and a great lover of nymphs. The Roman equivalent, Faunus, was one of the *di indigetes* deities, meaning that he belonged to the oldest heritage of Roman spirituality. Similar to many other deities, he was also seen as having once been a divine king of Latinum, known as Fatuus, related to fate, divination, and prophecy. It has also been suggested that Faunus was actually the original Lupercus, which ties him in with a rich ancestry of the Romans as a people born from wolves. The spirit-herd attending to Faunus were known as Fauns, nymph-like *genii locorum* of the woodland, just like the Satyrs were the attendants of Pan. The similarities in terms of ancestry are well worth mentioning as similar themes also occur in fairy-lore in the North of Europe. The fairies, or Sidhe, were said to have their habitat in woodlands with the legends and fairytales speaking of a Queen of this otherworldly

43 Richard Cavendish, *The Black Arts* (Perigree Books, 1967).

LUD. LAVATERUS
vande
Spooken
en Nachtgeesten.
tot GORINCHEM
By Paulus Vinck 1680

realm and also about a horned man-like creature associated with the serpent power that runs like a fire through the earth—and in humans. The *kundalini* is the same type of fire as the telluric fire ascribed to Old Nick, and it is this fire that rises in the *volva* when she travels out through her ecstatic *seiðr,* the word itself a reference to the cooking fire. Faunus is the serpentine fire that runs through the woodland and creates the specific prophetic upsurge along ley-lines. The Lord of Untamed Wilderness, given that he is the original Lupercus, is then retraced by its imagery to the famous sculpture displaying the twins suckled by a she-wolf.

This wolf is either their mother or foster-mother, she is Larenta, mother of Lares whose feast day was around the winter solstice during the Saturnalia. Another interesting observation is that the Latin word *lupa* can mean both wolf as well as "sex worker" (*lupa* was a common slang for "sex worker" in Roman times), which is significant for the month of misrule itself, as the wolf is the walker between. She is also associated with Fauna who had a shrine and an oracular priestess close to the Aventine Hills. As Fauna, she was also given the names Luperca, Dea Dia, and Bona Dea, but this association seems to have been a reference to the virginal daughter of Larenta and Faunus who gave birth to Bona Dea and whose worship was by "wine and myrtle" —clearly Venusian references. The similarities between Bona Dea and the Sabine goddess Ops are of interest to note and might suggest the assimilation of a "pagan" deity into the existing deity or the adoption of a deity vested in a new name given the abduction of the Sabean women by Romulus' during the founding stages of the Roman Empire. The wilderness or the woods seem to be crucial here as it was the women of the wild regions in particular that Romulus and his warriors had sought out to be the mothers of their children.

Lupercalia and Saturnalia likely contributed to the form, myth, and function of the modern-day witchcraft revivals. The festival of Lupercalia was originally held on February 15 but was moved to February 1, and thus coincided with Candelaria. Candelaria is a festival with quite an interesting origin and was at some point celebrated in honour of St. Valentine, the saint that lent his name to Valentine's Day, February 14; thus the frank expression of love and affection might reflect a ward against malefic influences. Varro states that Lupercalia was a pastoral festival older than the founding of Rome. The original purpose of Lupercalia was to purify the city and exorcise the perimeters of malignant spirits and hostile beings. It is interesting in this scope to see that Justin the Martyr identified Lupercus as "he who wards off the wolf," with Faunus, which gave form to the attributes of Pan as hailed by the poets of the Romantic era. This is remarkably reminiscent of another deity, the Etruscan Culsus, who seems to have traits in common with Faunus, Apollo, and Hermes—which we shall look closer at shortly. Let us first look at one of the most frequent references to the spirits of the crossroad, namely the tricksters.

Tricksters of the Crossroad

The Devil is reputed to be a trickster. But what does it really mean to be a trickster? Deities reputed to be tricky include Oðin, Loki, Prometheus, Èṣú, Hermes, Set, Anansi, Aphrodite, Cupid, and animals such as the fox, raven, coyote, and others that share a reputation of being deceptive, elusive, enigmatic, and prone to generate problems for the human wayfarer at times. The word itself "trickery" is derived from the Old French, *trique,* meaning "cheat" or "deception." This is probably from the Latin *tricae,* which was used in a variety of circumstances. One meaning was "to shuffle," and another referred to certain complicated conditions of life in the sense of a "tangle of difficulties." That the word was used in medieval France as well as in Latinum to designate a specific condition related to games of chance is evident, but the latter interpretation is also significant as it denotes the condition people often find themselves in when they go to the Kingdom of the Crossroad. It is also possible to combine the idea that life is a game of chance with the tangled conditions we are at times confronted with. The player who holds the dice in their hand and is about to lose all or gain all is taking a chance. They are in the crossroad. The lovelorn woman that goes to a consult with Exu or Pomba Gira to enflame the spirit of love in her object of desire is in the same way placing herself in the crossroad—the game of chance is on, for better or for worse. From the perspective of Ifá, the reason why Èṣú tricks people into complicated situations is to force them to walk toward their destiny. In the Ifá context, destiny is not a preordained fatalism consisting of limited choice and free will; on the contrary, the idea of destiny is related to the "way we came to earth," the astrological engraving or imprint caused by our birth if we refer to the alchemists and astrologers from the Renaissance. Hence, to follow one's destiny is to make choices in life in alignment with our unique "way we came to earth" which in turn leads to an increase of good fortune. It is in this realm that Èṣú steps into the equation and aids through either advice or by creating situations caused by one's own life choices that lead to moments of contemplation of where their road of life should go.

We also see in typical tricksters that they all possess wisdom and hidden knowledge, but they rarely make access to this easy. While the reputation of, for instance, Oðin is that his adherents are consequently followed by "bad luck," as stated by one informant of Germanic Hexencraft, there are other deities, like Prometheus, that are almost altruistic in their trickery. Indeed, the Devil is a trickster, but he represents an idea that is quite different than a cheap bluff at a card game or senseless confusion. In many lineages of Traditional Witchcraft, this condition is referred to as "being in exile," subject to an ordeal or test from which the natural result is renewed knowledge and wisdom. It is the repeated theme of finding light within the wilderness. In essence, the situation is as follows: you come to the Crossroad entangled in confusion and you want direction—or you come to the crossroad in search of the wisdom only "the Devil" can give you. As such, the more potent example of the journey through the crossroads of the worlds is found in the myths and imagery of Oðin and Lord Cain, two carriers of the witchblood that earned their divinization through the path of ordeal.

If we turn to Hermes, he is not only a psychopomp, but also the guardian of doors, gateways, merchants, alchemists, and thieves. The recurring theme is the one of change, opportunity, and fluidity, and as such, the role of the trickster is typified by the spirit and temperament of the planet Mercury. Crucial for an understanding of Mercury, according to traditional sources such as William Lilly, is that this planet takes on the properties of whatever stellar body it is conjoined to.[44] This means that he is good with good and ill with ill, male with male and female with female. It is interesting to note that Mercury in himself is considered cold, dry, and melancholic, and is said to rule the spirits of animals. Oðin is depicted in the same format—cold, dry, and melancholic—but with his mistress Freya, he blossoms, just as Mercury blossoms in a dignified

44 William Lilly, *Christian Astrology* (Regulus, 1985).

conjunction with Venus. If we continue to recapitulate Lilly, we find that animals under Mercury's domain are the hyena, ape, fox, squirrel, serpent, and spider.[45] He is also reputed to be the vehicle for divination with the muses and is close to herbs like vervain, anise, and dragonwort, being especially fond of nut trees. In Islamic lore, nut trees are seen as particularly dubious or downright dangerous places, as they are reputed to be a resting place for djinns.

We must understand the function of trickery as ordeal, chance, and opportunity as the tools the warden of the worlds uses to stimulate our growth in such way that we can reach our pearl of great wisdom and understanding. If the Mysteries of the Crossroad are approached like Oðin, who sacrificed himself to himself on the *axis mundi* in order to gain the wisdom and understanding necessary to understand his Fate, we will be rewarded with a clear understanding of mission, purpose, and destiny. It is in nearly every culture that this motif meets us when we venture into the crossroad to commune with the Devil in one of his many guises and masks. Surely, the Devil will come, and he will open the game of chance for you and ask you to choose—and you will take the consequences, be they the road of ordeal or be they the sanctity of blessings. From this, we have the dictum used amongst some traditional conclaves of the Craft, when they say: "May the Curse, Cunning and Blessing be" —a direct reference to your interaction with the powers of the Crossroad.

Betwixt the Horns

The Devil has horns—but so does Michelangelo's Moses. It has been commonly accepted that the horns refer to lunar domination, which is the symbolic property of the bull's horns or the "horns of the moon" as a symbol of dominion. Horns are also given to the son of Jupiter, Ammon, Apollo, Janus, Isis, Pan, Faunus, Cernunnus, Pasupathi, and others. This ties The Horned One together with the two gates of the solstice, the gate of gods and gate of men, represented by the two horns giving and closing access to the Golden Age. René Guénon addressed the importance of the horns in relation to the crown through the shared linguistic root *krn*, emphasizing the deities or kings elevated status. He brings the attention to the Celtic solar deity Belen, who also was identified with Aplun or

45 William Lilly, *Christian Astrology* (Regulus, 1985).

Apollõn among the Greeks.[46] Apollo is thus found to possess horns through his epitaph or quality as Apollo Karneios, from Cernunnos, sharing the root *krn* which gives rise to words meaning "power" and "elevation." The same root *krn* is also found in Kronos. This generates a link with Saturn as the power of elevation in reference to his earlier station as the Lord of the Golden Age and the relationship with Janus as the Herald of this Golden Age. What is also interesting is that the same root, *krn,* also forms the words *cornus, corona,* and *Karneios.* We see here a relationship between horns (cornus), crown (corona), and power (Karneios). *Karneios-Karn* also means "high place" as a symbol of the Polestar and the sacred mountain, a term also used to describe the pile of stones (cairn) in its reference to *tumulus,* or tomb, and the *omphalos* of Delphi, the oracle of Apollo, who rose on the inner planes as the fumes from the underworld filled her nostrils. The Land of the Gods becomes the Land of the Dead when the spiritual centre disappears, which explains the transition of Kronos as a God of the ever-shining Golden Age to the Lord of Death. We see here opposing life-giving and death-dealing attributes of this power signified by the horns.

Following this thread, the Devil's trident becomes like Siva's *trishula,* and thus denotes supremacy and ascent to the summit, as we find in the crown of thorns placed upon the head of Jesus Christ. We might even notice the pointed similarity between the thorn and the horn—thus the thorns on the crown denote multiple insights.

The Greek word *Keraunos,* meaning "thunderbolt," also seems to have derived from the same root, and we see a most interesting theme surfacing related to horns or a crown as related to the summit of the mountain—for it is here at the summit that lightening is most likely to strike. We can therefore say, for instance, that Moses with his horns has been understood to represent a lunar balance and power that can also be a direct reference to luminous rays—evident signs that he reached the summit of the mountain on his own pilgrimage to receive the law, which can be understood as receiving destiny.

We cannot escape the significance of Alexander the Great in this section, the son of Ammon, The Master of the Double Horn according to *The Egyptian Book of the Dead.* Let us turn to *Megas Alexandros* as our icon to symbolize the understanding of magic and witchcraft during this period of cultural transition because it is in the imagery of Alexander

---

46 René Guénon, *Symbols of Sacred Science* (Sophia Perennis, 1995) p.185–190.

the Great that we find the greatness of the Arts coming together. He was born in July 356 BCE and died in 323 BCE in Macedonia. His name in Aramaic and Arabic is particularly interesting for our study. In Aramaic, it was *Tre-Qarnayia,* meaning "two-horned one," and in Arabic his name was *Dhul-Qarnayn,* also meaning "the horned one." It is quite interesting to note that in the modern-day revival of Wicca, this is one of the names given to the "horned master of the craft." Alexander also imprinted an image on coins of himself with the horns of a ram in the likeness of the Egyptian god Ammon.

Alexander is considered by historians, in general, to be the breaking point between Greek and non-Greek cultures due to his friendly attitude towards migration and cultural exchange. Through his teacher Aristotle, he developed a taste for philosophy, including what later would be termed "the liberal arts" by clergy in the Middle Ages. He was considered a hero by the people, his lineage stretching back to Achilles on his mother's side and to Heracles on his father's side. By birth, he was the son of King Philip and his fourth wife, Olympias, who was reputed to sleep in a bed of snakes. The night she was impregnated with the child that was to be Alexander, Olympias had a dream where a spirit came and sealed her with the image of a lion. She went to a seer in Telmessus who interpreted this to indicate that the child would have this characteristic. Another historical curiosity is that the temple of Artemis in Ephesus burned down the night Alexander was born. When he was still a young man, he went to the Oracle of Ammon at Siwa, and the Oracle revealed that Alexander's father was no other than Zeus himself. In Alexander's time, Ammon was considered a chief deity, a mixture of Ra and Horus with features similar to Sol Invictus, and we might be able to stretch this into his presence in the cult of Mithras cultivated by Roman soldiers as a secret legacy of Dhul-Qarnayn—at least it is a possibility. We also see that Egyptian heritage entered Europe through Alexander, not to forget much of what would be termed "paganism" later. The Egyptian connection was of course strong, not only with Alexander, but generally until the decline of the Roman Empire as is evident from the son of Venus, Julius Gaius Caesar, and his infatuation with Cleopatra of Egypt. With Ptolemy, the geocentric worldview entered the world.[47] The Ptolemaic worldview was one of organic and natural interaction,

---

[47] J. L. E. Dreyer, *A History of Astronomy from Thales to Kepler* (Dover Publications, 1953).

a holistic connectedness where the formlessness of The Beginning separated itself into heaven and earth as representations of mother and father. One started to see that the earth as the centre of the cosmos was marked by a sacred mountain, hence the gods lived on Olympus, the *omphalos*, the navel of the world. This cosmic centre designated the importance of the four cardinal points extending from it and the idea of the axis mundi that linked the zenith and nadir of the cosmic realm, creating a perfect geometrical cosmic harmony. This indicated that mankind needed to be in a "geometric" relationship with the gods in order to be subject to nutrition and protection of the divine. In Ptolemy, we find Babylonian and Egyptian astronomy and astrology meeting each other in the richness of Greek thinking as expounded on in his treatise on astrology, *Tetrabiblos.* Of this holistic and geocentric worldview, Martin has the following to say:

> *From a geocentric perspective, the Moon was the closest of the planets to the Earth and Saturn the most distant. Mercury, Venus, Sun, Mars, and Jupiter occupied positions two, three, four, five and six respectively. The terrestrial, sub-lunar realm was sharply separated from the celestial super-lunar realm by an abyss of cosmic space populated by elemental and demonic powers. These powers controlled the terrestrial realm, even as they in turn were controlled by the celestial deities... at the same time, an earlier chthonic (from the Greek chthon meaning earth, of the underworld, and its spirits) evocation of sacrality began to flourish in place of the relocated celestial sacrality. The ancient festival of Demeter, goddess of grain, celebrated at Eleusis, enjoyed renewed popularity in the Hellenistic world and survived well into the period of Roman decline, and the orgiastic frenzies of Dionysus, the very embodiment of chthonic spirit, swept the Hellenistic world.*[48]

Roman religion was based upon absorbing neighbouring cults and gods, with the Sabine and Etruscan deities particularly subject to assimilation. In contrast, Celtic deities were recognized as wilder manifestations of the Roman deities. One Etruscan heritage of particular importance

[48] Luther H. Martin, *Hellenistic Religions* (Oxford University Press, 1987) p.7.

that we shall turn to again is Janus. It has been suggested that Janus was the very same as the Etruscan deity Culsans who was also a deity of doors and doorways. An interesting detail is that Culsans had a female consort, Culsu, who presided over the same domain but was particularly related to doors and doorways of the underworld. Her emblems were scissors and a torch, suggesting a relationship with Hecate and Diana. Her torch and domain, such as the door and the crossroad, also intersect with Dame Fortuna who presided over Fate with her wheel and scissors. Keeping in mind that the cult of Fortuna and Diana were imported by the Etruscan king Tullius, we might see the probable configuration of the later role of Hecate as the Queen of witches and sorcerers. Reading the accounts, historically and scholarly, about Roman religion due to the process of assimilation, or the Roman interpretation, it looks like Culsu drifted away from Culsus. Where he became more and more identified with Janus, Culsu with her torch, scissors and affinity towards necromancy became a prefiguration of Hecate. If we take a moment to think about this trinity of Culsans, Culsu, and Lady Fortuna, we see that such organization of deities fits very well into the comprehension of the world and being, both mundane and spiritual, what we could see as a "witch-consciousness" in which the Dead, the otherworldly, and the celestial interact at all times and points. Emerging from this we have the necromantic and oracular element, the relation with Fate—which in turn is needed for the oracles to be useful, and the opener of ways, both in a feminine and masculine manifestation.

The role of Janus is of note for the further historical understanding of witchcraft via its partial fusion with Mercury-Hermes, an assimilation probably done through his praise name Janus Geminus or Janus Bifrons, thus paving the way for eventual correspondence with Mercury, the planet ruling Gemini. Originally, Janus was depicted with one-half of his face shaven and the other half bearded, holding a key. This iconographic representation symbolized the powers of Saturn and its secrets held by him. There are also those who say that the dual face symbolizes the Sun and the Moon, but it is perhaps best to interpret this in a Saturnian fashion and thus see it as a manifestation of transition in multiple senses. It is, in the Saturnian sense, interesting to note his relationship with the nymph Carna who aided Janus in his ability to control timelines.

As a reward, he gave Carna the dominion of the door hinges; thus she is the possibility of turning back and forth through time. Carna is a minor and obscure deity, particularly related to pig flesh and beans, and by name related to the Saturnine origins of *carna-val.*

Returning to the historical anecdote of Romulus' men kidnapping the Goths or Sabine women, we see that Janus caused a hot spring to gush forth and thus hinder the attack of Romulus' men. From the perspective of the legacy of wise folk, it is interesting to note Janus' relationship with fire and hot springs, thus relating him to water nymphs and the element of Fire. The relationship between Janus and Hermes is perhaps a bit of a stretch, and it might be more correct to say that Hermes took on some qualities of Janus, while Janus himself followed a quite different development, turning more to the Pan-like Culsans and finally being recorded under such names as Jack in the Wood, Robin Goodfellow, and names from similar myths found in large parts of the world—a lover of nymphs represented by the serpentine-fire of the woodlands. When considered, this makes sense on a mystical level and subtly marks the reasons for the importance of Hermes in magic and witchcraft from the Middle Ages and in particular during the Renaissance as we shall see in a later chapter. From the cunning perspective, it seems that the Wise Art is related to the woodlands and the kingdom of Faunus. It is the untamed gods and spirits, the spirit of trickery and possibility, the powers of frustration and radical change found in the undiluted and pagan (as opposed to civilized) order that is the home of the craft.

St. Peter's Cross

The motif of reversal, in terms of humility, is found in the cross of St. Peter: the inverted cross. St. Origen commented that Peter felt it was not right that he should be crucified in the same way as the Master and thus he asked to be hanged upside down as a sign of his unworthy state; thus, the symbol of St. Peter is the inverted Latin cross with two keys crossing, an effective symbol that hearkens back to Janus himself. Pierre Puget's painting from around 1659 makes the keys stand out greatly. The Lord of the gate to past and present, the herald between ages, and the one with the keys to the celestial spheres and the realm of the netherworld.

In Christian theology, the symbolism of the keys was related to Judgment Day. It was St. Peter that you met upon death, and he was the one who opened the doors to Jerusalem or Purgatory. We find the inverted cross in the Church of St. Peter. Pope John Paul II drew the attention of conspiracy theorists who suggested the Pope was a Satanist during a visit to Israel when he had the inverted cross marked on the front of his vestment. Eugene Vintras (1807–1875), who founded the Church of Carmel in France after a revelation of the prophet Elijah, came to be accused of both witchcraft and diabolism because of the many miracles he performed and had the habit of wearing vestments with a similar marking as the Pope, the inverted cross. For Vintras, this was as a symbol of humility in the manner of St. Peter. However, the French Occult revival also came with its own Satanic sub-stream. St. Peter was the first one to assume the inverted cross as his symbol, hence the inverted cross also becomes a symbol of misrule, of turning the tide, of going against the grain. And it is this mystery that is associated with the two keys, they key to Hell and the key to Heaven, the infernal realms and the celestial realms. Just like Kronos was entrusted with the keys to Above and Below by Janus, the Devil holds the very same keys entrusted to St. Peter.

At the closure of this chapter the mysteries held by the Devil and the importance of the Crossroad will be illustrated through ritual. This ritual, called *The Masquerade of the True Cross,* was used by the Traditional Witchcraft conclave Via Vera Cruz in formal celebrations, and is presented here with kind permission of the magister of the group, Azazayin Shin'Ar. The ambiguous and enigmatic parts of the ritual are left to their own mystery, unexplained.

The intention of this rite is to enjoy the night of Free Doom and light the Saviour's sacrifice offered to us. Upon giving up blood and breath, he gave this to the marked ones, the brood of Cain, and this night we, as his rightful ancestry, can reignite the spirit and flame of the divine blacksmith. A large part of the rite is done by Cain's tutor, the cave-dwelling wisdom himself. Given the sabbatic nature and crooked design of this rite, we must enter the rite in union with Nature, which means with our patron—chosen for the occasion or by Fate. Each participant needs to exercise their patron as it is their patron that will enter the circle, with or without its human hue. Furthermore, this rite also aims towards a merging between patron, holder of the patron, and the land as it is mirrored both in the Mother below and the Saviour above. This must be the objective of the rite because it is where the heart of this mystery is found.

As seen upon going through the rite there are empty spaces which should invite the direct merging with spirit and the pure expression of mystery into a complexity of being. So, with this I say, read this rite and read it again and throw it upon the pyre—for by memory and night alone shall the blood take life in the Night of Sacrifice where Ecstasy and truth shall reign!

The Masquerade of the True Cross

The Magister goes to the centre of the circle while the Chancellor stands at the circle's gate and greets all by giving each one a coin that is crossed. At the gate, on the Stone of Peter, they will place a clock, and the Hammer of Cain is given to each participant to break the clock upon entering. This being done, the participants will go to their quarters.

With the path of the Moon everybody will chant *sahr,* which is a call of Saturn to bind the wolves to the circle's edge. This being done in seven cycles, the circle turns in the path of the Moon chanting *tor a hu,* which calls upon the holy owl (Lilith) to watch the circle. Libations are given to the eight corners and the gate.

The Devil adores the cross and throws twigs and sticks upon the pyre burning in front of the cross. He will then set the cross aflame and produce wine and sacraments (mushrooms) as the power of the Saviour is stolen and given to the convent. Before giving this, he will appoint the younger Lilith, Na'amah, to ignite the rite and the elder Lilith to guide the rite. The Sun at Night will be appointed to cease the rite. This election is done in the moment, so everybody needs to be aware that they can be elected.

The sacrament is distributed by the Devil to those elected.

This being done, the Devil will give each a charm to be buried under the stones marking the circle. This will give earth to the call of the angels.

The summoner will lead the convent in the call of the faithful retinue while the Devil stays in the pyre adhering to the dragon and make her soft.

The oath-bound ones enter as the gods of men are called.

Those in the circle call the supporting angels in a state of tranquillity and stillness.

This being done the circle follows the path of the Moon, left leg stamping the ground by each step as each call their patron. When under the influence, the people lay down and go to the dreaming Sabbath.

As the people conclude, they will take the coin given at the entrance, cross themselves, make a personal prayer, and throw it in the pyre.

This concludes the Masquerade of the True Cross.

The Masquerade Proper

Everybody is given a coin at the gate of the circle by the summoner.

The summoner will give a special coin to the Chancellor, who will enter before all others in a unique act of veneration.

The smashing of the sand clock by the Hammer of Cain occurs.

The Chancellor takes the hammer from the circle's centre, saying:

Oh Old Tubal, Master of the Nail that never cools,
In fire I take your token
To stop the Wheel of Time
Doing this I take you as the author of the path towards return
I shall break time in your name and doing this
I will be bountiful as the sand upon Peter's rock
Amen.

The sand rushes out on the rock and the convent enters as they gain the coin.

Adoration of the Cross

The Devil will be seated at the North looking at the cross declaring:

This is the night of Free Doom
The path has been made
By the blood of salvation
Through his acceptance we can all return
And become whole
You are the Way and you are the Life
And in this moment it hath been made free
For the kin of Cain by honour of the mark
This Blood and this Life we shall now take.

The Offering of Nature

The Devil goes to the pyre and gives twigs and sticks to the cross chanting the spells upon each gift of Nature given.

The Devil enters the Crossroad:

In this Night I am your Shadow of Comfort
And your dying Breath is me
Stretched out on the four corners of the world
Zenith and culmination
Point and restriction
I am you and you are me
I am He and I am She
The Sum of the Wisdom the Stone holds
In this Night the stone of betrayal shall give forth your blood
And in this cup shall be the living life
Of Saturn's golden nights
The gift of eternity
Taken from your bleeding body
In this Holy night where you give
Life everlasting to the kin of Cain.

The Devil brings the "blood" to the congregation.

The Devil takes the sacrament and calls the congregation to enter. As the proper ones enter, he appoints the rulers of the rite.

Moon is appointed by the Devil's hand to rule the rite with the words:

Changeable you are Lady of Absence
Take this token and rule this rite well
Tonight, we adore your presence
Keeper of silver gates you are
And let good abundance flow in this sacred Night
Be who you are
And fill the emptiness in the witches' heart
Be the constant flow
Amen!

The Sun is appointed to end the rite by the Devil's hand:

Steady you are
Daughter of Helios flashing rays
May you burn the eyes of Night if need be so
May you break the blood at the golden gates
If need be
Be vigilant Sun and be present
Be the one that allows the blood to flow
Be the one that allows the heart to flow over
Be the edge of the circle's delight
Amen!

The circle is marked by a charm given to each that the Devil decides, which are placed at or under the stones that mark the circle. The circle is thread with the call as told at the beginning of this text, with charms, Moon, and Sun.

The infidel is called "the oath-bound ones." A calling to the Lady of the Birds of Silver is made by the Maid who directs the gathering of the infidels. While this is being done the Maid shall direct the rite in accordance with her patron spirit or familiar.

The complete circle gathered; the infidel being granted entrance by being given a coin. The faithful ones are called with the witch's cry done by the summoner.

The supporting angels are called by the Maid and wine is offered at the quarters as they are called.

East: *Cor Leonis, ruler of the triple flame (Leo) VERCHIEL*
Great messenger who lives at the heart of the Lion
Protector of the arc
Voice of prophecy
Great protector of Mystery
Hear us and be with us
Great VERCHIEL (repeat until being filled with the angel).

South: *Aldabaran, ruler of the triple earth (Taurus) HANAEL*
Author of beauty and grace
Protector of earth's wonders

Lustful and stable one
Great protector of Mystery
Hear us and be with us
Great HANAEL (repeat until being filled with the angel).

West: *Formalhaut, ruler of the triple airs (Aquarius) CAMBIEL*
Great Angel that moves thoughts
Steamy one who knows discernment
Moveable yet steady you are
Great protector of Mystery
Hear us and be with us
Great CAMBIEL (repeat until being filled with the angel).

North: *Antares (Cor Scorpio), ruler of the triple waters*
(Scorpio) BARBIEL
Great Angel who moves the Heart of Men
Great One who makes us protect, defend and keep
Poisonous One, Giving One
Great protector of Mystery
Hear us and be with us
Great BARBIEL (repeat until being filled with the angel).

And this we pray in the name of the winds of the four corners,
St. Michael, St. Gabriel, St. Raphael and Most Holy Uriel,
Lord of the World!

The circle is made secure by appeasing wolves and snakes by pouring milk and cider at the eight corners and giving a piece of raw meat to the four main quarters. See the instructions on how this is made.

Ama is called so all will be in their centre with the following words:

Good Mother
Dragon below
We step on your scales and leaves
We pour unto you wine and milk at the circles heart
You are She that will ever be
And we greet you as we step upon your domain
Without you, we will never be.

Everybody goes to the end of the circle stamping their left leg walking widdershins and calling the devil in whispers in conformity with the mantra given:

IE-U-SA-SA-SA-U-IE.

Joining at the centre, each devotee makes a personal appeal to their patron at the pyre and enters the edges of the circle for the Sabbath of the True Cross. The Wine is given as much as the Sleep is given....

When the rite is over, the coins are, with a personal prayer, thrown on the pyre and the celebrants leave the circle.

CHAPTER THREE

SERPENTS OF LAND AND STAR

The ancestry of witches and cunning ones is frequently understood to be different from the ordinary human strain, bringing a dimension of "otherness" to the design. Paul Huson starts his *Mastering Witchcraft* speaking of such witch-history and reminding us of the legend in Leland's *Aradia, or The Gospel of the Witches* that speaks of a great primordial darkness known as Diana. Diana divided herself and became night and day. From her day side surged her brother, Lucifer the Sun, who was given rulership over the day, whilst Diana ruled the night as its Moon. The Moon became fascinated by the Sun, and so it happened that Diana and Lucifer found themselves in a passionate and sexual relationship which gave birth to Aradia, also known as Herodias, who became the primordial witch.

We find another form of otherness in the design of ancestry in the Arthurian legends of Merlin and Morgana La Fay who were of elven decent, hence her name, "of the Fairy." In Balkan witch-lore, we find both of these ideas tied to the bloodline of the witch. A witch or cunning one was always someone with a strong link with dragons or fairies. Dragons are seen as serpentine fiery celestial beings who, in the guise of meteors, fell to earth and took up residence in specific trees. Fairies are seen as female dragons, hence we speak of the cunning ones and the witches as "dragon-people." Ristic comments that the transmission of power to create a "dragon-man or woman could be established from the mother sleeping with a dragon, the father with a fairy, or one was nursed on fairy-milk as an infant."[49] If we look at popular folklore in the world, the seventh son was often considered as someone who possessed particular gifts or abilities. If a child was birthed still contained within the placenta, it was like being embraced by the other side, and special abilities would be possessed by that child. In Norway, there is a belief that people born on Thursdays at twilight are born naturally *trollkynnig*, or magically gifted.[50] In addition, as we already discussed, we have the avenue towards power through the cunning meeting with fairy spirits and diabolical pacts.

Witchcraft and the craft of the cunning ones, no matter the method of transmission, is something "other," something that came to humans through a fall or a descent or meeting with non-human beings. In some instances, we see that the idea of witchblood is something that is passed on through a fairy or dragon that will then generate a specific type of cunning one, like the *strigae*, a hybrid—someone who is both human and "other." But this is not the only avenue for becoming a cunning one; as we have seen, the possibilities for transmission of the witchblood can come through blood as well as through other forms of conveyance. The qualitative difference between being born a witch and what takes place through rituals of ingress does not impact the existence of the cunning arts and the cunning folk.

Dragons are, by all measure, kin to snakes. Balkan witch-lore suggests that a particularly old and powerful six-winged snake who lives in lakes, the Snake Czar, becomes a dragon if they live until very old.[51] In a similar fashion, in Nordic mythology, the world serpent, Jormundgandr, is sometimes described as a large snake, other times as a dragon.[52] Of interest in relation to the Serpent Czar and his six wings is the angelic class of angels known as the Seraphim, who also have six wings and whose name, *seraph*, means both "fiery" and "snake."[53] This imagery is found as early as the eighth century on stamp seals from Judah. Hence,

---

[49] Radomir Ristic, *Witchcraft and Sorcery in the Balkans* (Three Hands Press, 2015) p.33.

[50] Nicholaj de Mattos Frisvold, *Trollrún* (Hadean Press, 2021).

[51] Radomir Ristic, *Balkan Traditional Witchcraft* (Pendraig Publishing, 2009) p.202.

[52] Nicholaj de Mattos Frisvold, *Trollrún* (Hadean Press, 2021) p.43.

[53] Benjamin D. Sommer, *The Bodies of God and the World of Ancient Israel* (Cambridge University Press, 2011).

this suggests that angels were imagined as fiery serpents, which would also have been defined as dragons given the age and wisdom of these seraphs. We also find this idea of age turning a serpent into a dragon in the Bible, such as in Revelation 20:2 where we read that: "He seized the dragon, the ancient serpent." In the Garden of Eden, the serpent communes with the first couple, and it is the serpent that mates with the first and second women, Lilith and Cheva. Thus, the human strain is inoculated with this specific diabolic, yet angelic, pedigree through the Fall of the heavenly host. In chapter 21 of *The Ethiopian Book of Enoch,* we learn that the fallen host was understood to be stars under the rulership of Uriel the Archangel, and in chapter 23 and 24 the angel Raguel explains to Enoch how these stars or luminaries, upon falling, became burning mountains.[54] These fallen luminaries then sought out women to beget offspring, the giants or Nephilim, whilst they taught their women the magical arts and witchcraft.

The idea of the Fall is not unique for the Western Mystery Traditions as we find similar themes also on the African continent. Yoruba myths tell about how Osanyin, the lord of herbs, fell from the sky and sunk within the earth in the city Iràwò on the border of Benin and Nigeria. Interestingly, the name of the city means "star." Oduduwa, the founder of Ile Ife the sacred city of the Yoruba, is said in some accounts to have fallen from the heavens. Other myths say he came from Mecca, others that he came from Egypt, and yet others that he fell from the heavens and the place he fell was Ile Ife. Oduduwa had sixteen sons and these sixteen went out to found kingdoms on the African West coast, and still today traditional kingdoms trace their lineage back to Oduduwa.

Basically, in Yoruba/Ifá metaphysics is the idea that we are all divine beings who are going through a human experience. Likewise, the Dogon of Mali, the Fon of Benin, the Ewe of Congo, the Yoruba and Hausa of Nigeria, the Vodusaints of Haiti, and several other mystical traditions related to the great monotheist religions of the world suggest such a heritage. Just as the Vodousaints of Haiti speak of Danbalah and Aiyeda Wedo as the parents of Aizan, the first mambo or priestess, the Yoruba speak of a descent of celestial beings to earth. This is also evident in the salutations done at the *potau-mitan,* the central pillar in a vodou *societé* that is envisioned as the tree on which the cosmic serpent Dan

54 Paul C. Schneiders and Robert H. Charles, *The Books of Enoch* (International Alliance Pro-Publishing, 2012).

or Danbalah descends upon. This imagery is identical to the serpent in the Garden of Eden, but with the absence of the problem of cosmic evil. It speaks about how the owner of Heaven, after making the Earth a habitat, sent Obatala, the creator deity, to Earth from Heaven along a chain of gold. Upon arrival, the first human beings were created, and they were called *eniyan,* a word that can be translated into "an angel made of earth." It is said that these beings lived in harmony with all living beings on earth, but at some point, they touched the supernatural powers and started to be destructive. The owner of Heaven allowed water to rise and most of the *eniyan* died, but some were saved, and it is these beings that passed on the witchblood. The eniyan likely survived because they went to the mountain where the children of Seth, "the upright one," dwelled—and from here came the line of royal witchblood. I find reason to suggest that this light-seed that is often referred to as "witchblood" came through both Cain as well as Seth, Abel's replacement, who represents the perfection of the seed of power. We should note that the Mark of Cain was given by God like it was given to Seth, which, in the *Book of Raziel* and in Masonry, become the pillars of wisdom that secure occult knowledge for humankind.[55] Seth represents the continuation of both the fallen seed and the upright seed, the totality of angelic wisdom, and he was marked by this seed of light because nothing was corrupted in him. In Seth, we find the royal and the sacerdotal initiation conferred by God himself, and thus Seth is the great unity itself that his name expresses—The Appointed One. His name adds to seven hundred, the value of the Hebrew letter *Nun* that is sacred to *akrav,* the scorpion, a great protector of sages and wonderfully wise in its own right. The *akrav* is also the protector of the Rav, the Master who ventures within the fields of *keshuph,* the nomadic sorcery of the Hebrews whose goal is a form of reintegration of the sage along the line of mysterious disincarnated ravs or rabbis. According to the *keshupherim,* Schemesh ben Yethro, in the tradition of *keshuph,* the scorpion is seen as a guardian of the accomplished master who is in deep union with the Moon and her mysteries. The master sees himself as a descendent of Seth through Moses, and his magic brought to him through his wife Zipporah's father, Jethro.[56] These mysteries along with

---

55 Michael Howard and Nigel Jackson, *The Pillars of Tubal-Cain* (Capall Bann, 2000) p.118.

56 Personal correspondence.

the secrets of the seven planets and how they were under the jurisdiction of the angel Uriel brings interesting threads into a crossroad of power that for the Hebrews was reminiscent of witchcraft.[57]

Animals like bats, scorpions, owls, crows, toads, serpents, and dragons have become associated with ideas like witchcraft, the night, and danger. Certainly, these animals share the common trait of igniting some level of fear and fascination in some of us, but this fear and fascination some of us experience is actually a response to the otherworldly cunning quantities these animals possess and represent. Considering an outlandish descent from on high, a fairy-race, or an Elven bloodline, the serpent of dragon is appropriate to focus on and we can take the claims of Nicholas de Vere to be a living descendant of such elven bloodline, the dragon kings and queens associated with the Frankish Merovingian dynasty (450–751). This dynasty claimed to be the successors of the progeny of Mary Magdalene and Jesus Christ, which counted legendary men like King Arthur, son of Pan Dragon. De Vere states that this "Grail bloodline" is antediluvian in origin and was represented by red-haired Grail or Dragon Kings that gave rise to the concept of "royalty" in the world. He comments that this Elven race originated with the offspring between angel and woman, known as the *nephilim* or *anakim*, and as such the Grail bloodline is understood to come from celestial dragons or angels. De Vere also points out how heraldic representations of the serpent was, at times, given the wings of a swan or of a bat. He further comments that people who possessed this bloodline were seen as gifted, "people of the powers," "people of the stars," and "wise ones."[58]

What is interesting in de Vere's presentation of his bloodline is the consistency of theme found in myths all over the world about Draconic or serpentine influences involved in the creation of a bloodline that was passed down through human history. These themes are found not only in Middle Eastern and European heritages but also in African and South American legends of descent, how an outlandish race ascended to a mountain or to the top of trees to escape some sort of catastrophe.[59] What we understand to be witchblood is actually one of many ways of expressing this particular pedigree. Those who are truly witches, so to

57 Joshua Trachtenberg, *Jewish Magic and Superstition* (Atheneum, 1987) p.120.

58 Nicholas de Vere, *The Dragon Legacy: The Secret History of an Ancient Deadline* (The Book Tree, 2004) p.42.

59 Nick Liguori. *Echoes of Ararat.* (Master Books, 2021).

speak, are touched by the blood of this race, so rites of ingress solely serve to quicken the seed that already flows in the blood of the witch. De Vere says about this:

> *The word "dragon" is derived from the Greek "edrakon," which is an aorist of the word "derkesthai," which means "to see clearly." The Dragon, therefore, is the inherited Dragon archetype and that archetype is the conduit of clear sight through which racial knowledge flows. Clear sight also and principally refers to transcendent consciousness.*[60]

A seed is just a seed, and if it does not receive nutrition and attention, it will not sprout. Likewise, if the culture that it is planted in is full of corruption it will likely not sprout, or if it does, it may grow into a deformed hybrid. The recurring theme of this is that what we understand to be fairy blood is a bloodline that imparts the special sensibility and powers we ascribe to witches and has a supra-human origin. This means that witchblood can be transmitted even today by forms of faerie intervention.

The Angels of Witchblood

The fallen host found amongst the angels were given the epitaph *grigori* in the Slavic *Book of Enoch* and *irin/iyrin* in Aramaic, meaning "wakeful," "watchful," or, more commonly, "watchers."[61] The watcher angels were largely involved in annunciations, prophecies, and apparently spreading their seed. The most famous example of this in the Bible is when Gabriel the Archangel announced the pregnancy of Mary by revealing that a divine seed was planted in her. Gabriel is an Archangel who is the ruler

---

60 Nick Liguori, *Echoes of Ararat.* (Master Books, 2021) p.41.

61 A linguistic curiosity here is that the name irin is also found in Yoruba, defining aquatic angelic beings who guard the secrets of the owner of the ocean, Olokun, and they take the form of swords or sword wielding forces. Yoruba, Aramaic, and Hebrew share some common linguistic roots, so similarities are found all the time, but in the case of irin it is interesting to see the function is similar: the irins are watchful guardians of Olokun's secrets.

of the fixed star Formalhaut in the constellation of Pisces. This star is also known as the Watcher of the South.

As seen in the beginning of this chapter, the witch-lore from Tuscany, Italy, as retold by Leland states that Lucifer is the angel of witchblood, an idea that we also find in the work of Andrew Chumbley and in the work of Madelaine Montalban's Order of the Morningstar. Montalban saw Lucifer as similar to Asael/Azazel, Dionysius, and the Serpent in the Garden of Eden whose name is more correctly called Lumiel. She writes:

> *The secret tradition also teaches us that Lumiel/Lucifer does not just seek to help us from the higher planes, but descends to earth and incarnates as a great teacher from time to time. Jesus of Nazareth, it is said, was one such incarnation.*[62]

Montalban also saw Lumiel/Lucifer as the spouse of Lilith, who then by association becomes the progenitors of the race of witches via the birth of Cain, the first murderer and journeyman. Expounding on these ideas, Michael Howard brings Lumiel and Lilith to the craft as the angels of witchblood. His vision of the attributes of the angel of witchblood is of an ageless man in a shining white robe with a blazing white star on his brow, his neck adorned with a silver Tau cross entwined with a serpent. He is considered a teaching angel with a preference towards instructing women and can be resorted to as a source for help when all else has failed. His colour is said to be violet, and his stones are emerald and quartz crystal. Deities that reflect some of his traits are Osiris, Ptah, Adonis, Tammuz, Attis, Mithra, Balder, Lugh, Dionysus, Pan, Krishna, and Christ. All of them are deities related to sacrifice and mystery and are from whom teaching emerges. Of these related forms we might say that it is the mysteries of Osiris—Tammuz—Mithra—Dionysus—Christ that depict Lumiel's essence more accurately, as we see within them both the celestial descent and the terrestrial sacrifice. It is through such descent that the Archangel of Earth was set to watch and illuminate the world.

Several Craft myths give great importance to the account of the sixth chapter of Genesis, which speaks of the Fall of the Watchers which

---

62 Madelaine Montalban, *Book of Lumiel* (1982) p.11.

has many various interpretations of its meaning. The accounts in *The Books of Enoch* are valuable resources for understanding the celestial mysteries and how the angelic host "fell" or descended, but the angelic corruption is summarized in an interesting way by the cleric, novelist, and historian Daniel Defoe in his 1660s treatise called "A system of magick; or, a history of the black art: Being an historical account of mankind's most early dealing with the Devil; and how the acquaintance on both sides first begun":

> *But tho' he suffer'd Martyrdom for his Scheme (having been expell'd the Parliament of two Kingdoms for it) we do not find he has yet had the Benefit of his Project, so we must wait till he is pleased to make the Experiment. But to return to the Antediluveans: The old World, I say, as wicked as they were, had some shadow of Good in them, and for some Years, nay some hundreds of Years, they maintain'd the Character of the Sons of God, before they were debauched by the Daughters of Men; that is to say, before they blended the Race with the corrupt Seed of Cain, and mingled Blood with Idolaters. Where, by the way, we have an accurate Description of the Times, I mean in those early Days, of the Race; 'tis evident 'twas just then as 'tis now, the Ladies were the Devils of the Age; the Beauties, the Toasts, the fine Faces were the Baits; the Hell lay concealed in the Smiles of the charming Sex, They were the Magicians, taking the Word in its present Acceptation and its grossest Sense: There lay the Witchcraft, and its Force was so irresistible, that it drew in even the Sons of God.*[63]

Similarly, we see in Craft myths found in several places in Europe the same basic themes as we find in strands of Italian sorcery and cunning traditions known as Stregoneria, and related witch-lore, even published in Leland's *Gospel of Aradia* and Paul Husons' book, *Mastering Witchcraft*. As mentioned earlier, the beginning is described as a vast darkness whereupon Diana creates night and day through dividing herself. She retains rulership of night herself and gives the rulership of day to her

[63] See https://quod.lib.umich.edu/e/ecco/004843566.0001.000

brother, Lucifer, the Sun. Diana, in the form of a cat, meaning that she would behave seductively like a cat, seduced her brother and gave birth to Herodias/Aradia as a consequence. A similar theme is found in the interaction between Mesopotamian Na'amah the seductress and Azael, repeating an even earlier theme of Lilith's seduction of Schamash, where he becomes the Sun in the Kingdom of Night—the Realm of the Dead. A similar idea is expressed in the tension between Tubal Qayin and Na'amah and it is here we find the seed to fall and redemption. It was Na'amah that brought the fall into effect. There are many explanations and ideas of what this legendary fall actually was and what motivated it. If we allow morals and theodicy to stay in the background then the fall caused a proximity between the celestial and terrestrial and affected hierarchies and harmonies, as Dionysus the Aeropagite comments in his *Celestial Hierarchies:*

> *Hierarchy is, in my opinion, a holy order and knowledge and activity which, so far as is attainable, participates in the Divine Likeness, and is lifted up to the illuminations given it from God.*[64]

This would suggest that the Fall led to a dislocation from the spiritual centre, but at the same time it opened the road for conceptual ideas like pantheism and animism to find a root and expression—the idea that the divine or celestial is to be found everywhere. A dislocation from the spiritual centre causing a disruption in the established harmony would mean that the Fall of the Watchers was simply a movement away from their harmonious station when a new relationship took form. Dislocated from their own stations, the Fall ignited in humankind a thwarted seed: a seed that was seen as corrupt by the doctors of the Church, a seed generated by the misplaced desire of angels could only breed anomalies and danger. It was a completely different order that the angels fell from, surely not an inferior and terrestrial moral order that has the tendency of imposing upon the angelic host. The word used in Hebrew to denote the corrupted seed in Genesis 6:11 is from

---

64 See http://shrineofwisdom.weebly.com/the-celestial-hierarchies.html

the root *shachath*, meaning "decadence," "destruction," and "damage." It is the same root found in the word *chamath*, meaning "crime," that is also used in the sixth Chapter of Genesis to denote the corrupted ways. Rabbinic authorities have also seen the explicit sexual tone in this word as related to perversion and, given the violent connotation of this word, I find it reasonable to believe that the perversion we speak of was the violation of women. Genesis says that the Nefilim took whom they wanted of women. The commentary on the Torah, *Yalkuth Me'am Lo'ez*, edited by the late Rav Kaplan, points out that the word *nefilim* can also be written *nefalim*, meaning "aborted infant."[65] It is crucial to note here that this similarity cannot be arbitrary, as it was common amongst the Hebrews to give an herbal philtre to provoke abortion in cases where the woman had suffered rape or became pregnant with the child of a man other than her husband. Rabbinical doctrine suggests that mere fantasy of a another being during coitus, particularly during the moment of orgasm, would influence the child with qualities of that person. The Nefilim were reputed to be stunningly beautiful and capable of provoking lust and erotic thoughts in the mind and heart of women. This factor has also been ascribed to the reason why the Nefilim were called *Anshey Shem*, "renowned names"—interesting that the word *shem* is also found in *shamam*, "to destroy," and shares the root with Schemesh in one of his variant spellings.

The Nefilim were called by seven names, one of them being Eymim, which refers to fear, the condition arising when we are confronted with something that is life threatening. They are also Refa'im, because their voices made the heart turn into wax, Gibborim and Zamzumim, which refers to a strong physique and the attitude of warriors at all times ready to battle, Anakim, from *anak*, the Sun, and Avvim, a word borrowed from Aramaic, *avviya*, simply meaning "a snake" in the sense of "something that lives of the dust." Bringing into the equation that the root of seraphim, "burning one," *seraph*, meaning "snake" should illumine the nature and origin of this "other blood" as being angelic and "fallen."

The origin of the witchblood is related to the Fall, it is related to the other side, but the Fall itself is clearly misunderstood. Let us again return to the Celestial hierarchies and see what the nature of the third

---

[65] Aryeh Kaplan, *Jewish Meditation* (Moznaim Publishing Corporation., 1988) p.326–327.

order of angels is, the Thrones from whence the Fall occurred. As can be read in *Celestial Hierarchies:*

> *In the third rank are those who, from their unity, simplicity, constancy and firmness, are sometimes called Thrones, sometimes Seats; who themselves also are wise and loving. But from their simplicity, they have the attributes of unity, power, strength, fortitude, steadfastness. Which very attributes the Cherubim and Seraphim also possess... steadfastness comes from simplicity, simplicity from purification. For when each object is purified back to its own simple nature, then, being uncompounded, it remains indissoluble through its unity. Whence it is clear that purification is assigned to the Thrones. Moreover, when a thing is purified, it is illumined, and after it is illumined, it is perfected. This last office is given to the Seraphs, the other to the Cherubs.*[66]

Also of some interest in this regard is the number three, the number Pythagoras thought was most perfect. This perfection was also adopted by the early doctors of the Church through the importance of the Trinity. This number is also found frequently in fairy tales when the protagonist is supposed to make some heroic undertaking, often involving three ordeals to accomplish the goal. Hence, it is not without interest that the third order of angels holds a specific correlation to the third heaven, the *Shehaqim*, where the secrets of the Fall are found.

The third heaven is described in the *Second Book of Enoch* (also called *The Book of the Secrets of Enoch*) as being the original location of the Gan Eden. It is here we find the Tree of Life. It is a curious heaven though, called *Shehaqim*, as it has a dual quality to it. To the north of this heaven, we have the gate to the hell where sodomites, witches, sorcerers, and other people that commit "sin against nature" are sent. It is also reputed to be the crossroad between corruption and incorruptibility. Seeing the third heaven as a geometric outline of the original Paradise, we can also understand the profundity of the meaning of the Fall as related to angels and watchers. It is also significant that Hell is in the North, one of the epitaphs of Lilith is "The Northern One," Islamic angelology says that it was to this heaven Jibrail took Mohammad and showed him Paradise. It was also in the North, the land of Nod, where Cain's exile was located. It is

---

66 Aryeh Kaplan, *Jewish Meditation* (Moznaim Publishing Corporation, 1988) p.326–327.

interesting that the angel Anahael is ascribed dominion here by rabbinical authorities and Christian mystics, while in Islam this is the heaven of Azrael. Actually, it is in accordance with the topography of the third heaven with which we can understand the very nature of Gan Eden and what a fall and exile actually mean. The angelic origins of the witchblood are ascribed to the mysteries of this heaven. This is clearly presented in the following passage from 2 Enoch, or the *Slavic Book of Enoch:*

Of the assumption of Enoch to the third heaven.

1. *AND those men took me thence, and led me up on to the third heaven, and placed me there; and I looked downwards, and saw the produce of these places, such as has never been known for goodness.*
2. *And I saw all the sweet-flowering trees and beheld their fruits, which were sweet-smelling, and all the foods borne by them bubbling with fragrant exhalation.*
3. *And in the midst of the trees that of life, in that place whereon the Lord rests, when he goes up into paradise; and this tree is of ineffable goodness and fragrance, and adorned more than every existing thing; and on all sides it is in form gold-looking and vermilion and fire-like and covers all, and it has produce from all fruits.*
4. *Its root is in the garden at the earth's end.*
5. *And paradise is between corruptibility and incorruptibility.*
6. *And two springs come out which send forth honey and milk, and their springs send forth oil and wine, and they separate into four parts, and go round with quiet course, and go down into the PARADISE OF EDEN, between corruptibility and in corruptibility.*
7. *And thence they go forth along the earth, and have a revolution to their circle even as other elements.*
8. *And here there is no unfruitful tree, and every place is blessed.*[67]

It was here in this heaven the serpent found itself, between corruptibility and incorruptibility, in the heart of the crossroad whose arms became four rivers, and as we see, the Garden of Eden was first situated in a celestial sphere, and it was from this sphere from which everyone fell to Earth.

[67] See https://sacred-texts.com/bib/fbe/fbe115.htm

The Denizens from the "Other Side"

Through the Earth and the land by way of veins and subterranean rivers, the blood of our ancestors run in streams along with the memory of all other beings that were birthed, lived a life, and passed away. The memory is kept by trees, rocks, and winds while the tales are spun and sung through legends of myth and remembrance. The land and the stars flow in our blood as much as the memory of many worlds flows through the sap of trees that stretch their roots down deep within the caves of forgotten memories, nurtured by the wisdom resting in the bones of our ancestors, celestial and carnal. Our familiars, be they dog or toad, bird or snake, cat or boar, live in witness to our ancestry and embody our sense of kinship with nature, our cord of blood that stretches through time and creates the circle of being. The "blood" is described by Chumbley as a "Serpent's Fire within" that is born from a "cunning seed," the "wiseblood."[68] This is the seed of Lumiel who is the serpent who makes the circle of the Royal Art, a seven-headed great Dragon described as the "Angelic soul of the Master Cain." This speaks of the cunning seed revealing itself in a distinct form, and with that comes a perception of the world, the *derkesthai*, the dragon-sight. The blood of Lumiel flowing through Master Cain sees the Blessing and the Curse as equally meaningful and necessary for establishing the Cunning, and it is with this attitude and aptitude to do what is necessary with the realization that the Cunning Craft made by the blood of Cain is hard and painful work, a work with hostile forces, with snakes and dragons, the fire within and darkness everywhere.

Staying with the concept of witchblood, but expanding a bit on the possibility of different broods, we find stories about how the Fay, or fairies, mated with men, and also the many stories about the "changeling," the substitution of fairy children for human infants.[69] From north to south, we find legends and fairytales about spirits from the other side who take the shape of comely men and women to seduce mortals. The Sidhe, the fairies in the British Isles, could marry some handsome man and the child begotten from these unions would have a foot in each world. At some point in their life, the call from Anwynn would be so great

[68] Michael Howard, *The Book of Fallen Angels* (Capall Bann, 2004) p.183.

[69] For a great resource of fairy tales and changeling stories: https://sites.pitt.edu/~dash/britchange.html

that, in many cases, they left to stay in the Realm of Death. Likewise, in Amazonia, we have legends of the Boto, a pink dolphin that lives in the sweet waters. Legend says that on moonlit nights this dolphin can take the shape of handsome men and seduce—or rape—women in order to generate children.[70] Here we see similarities with what was actually the fault of the Nephilim straying outside their circle. Similarly, mermen have generally a more aggressive reputation as seducers than mermaids, indicating that they take on martial qualities in their activities. This peculiar pedigree naturally creates a yearning towards something lost: the root. For the witch, the land itself is a constant reminder of life and death as a cyclic eternity, change and transition, and naturally the other side. Whether this is spoken of as a flight, a crossing of a river, the doors of the castle, or the direct avenue of feeding the land itself to honour and reconnect—the Witches of the Land carry the same message: that we are the living link on a vast cyclical chain of being, and by reconnecting with this peculiar ancestry, the memory of the mighty deeds of the Witches of the Land before us will enflame our blood anew.

Fairy beliefs are quite universal, and legends about beings and settlements hidden from the gaze of ordinary sight are found in the mythical heritage of many cultures. We can here speak about a theme that goes back to the epic of Gilgamesh, with Inanna journeying to the throne of Ereshkigal to suffer death by the hand of the queen, to Orpheus' attempt to rescue his beloved from the realm of death and to the Scottish ballad of Tamlane or Tam Lin who is also abducted to the fairy realm. In all these instances there are found encounters with otherworldly beings. We have Orpheus with his nymphs, Tamlane with his fairies, the legends of Proserpina, and other themes as already discussed, hence, let us continue a bit further with the serpentine motive.

The serpentine motif is continued in the cult of household spirits, nature spirits, genii locorum, and even djinns. The connection between genius and genii loci is rarely reflected upon. The Romans often depicted the genii loci in the form of a snake. As seen on the next page in the fresco from 50 AD showing the genii loci in front of the *lararia*, the shrine for the household spirits and ancestors of the house. The *lares*, from the word *lar* meaning "home," were protective spirits that could be ancestors of the city itself, the people, the family, or even prior owners of

---

70 Luís da Câmara Cascudo, *Dicionário do Folclore Brasileiro* (Global Editora, 1952).

the house given the person or family was of some renown. It's imperative to understand that the *lares* were cultivated within a precisely defined geographical location, they were bound to the land.[71] The serpent form of *lares* is usually interpreted as a fertility symbol by historians, but the fertility of the land is just one part of this mystery. The snake in Roman culture brings memories of the Pythoness at the temple of Apollo, hence the *lares* in the form of a snake suggests their capacity to be oracular and thus guide the household. Further, the snake is of both dirt and of the subterranean tunnels, so it had access to what was hidden beneath the dirt and soil as the ancestors do. The words *genius* or *genii* represent the spirit of ingenium that engraves the unique mark than makes each and every one of us stand out as different from one another. For women, this spirit was often called *juno.* But Juno was also a goddess, daughter of Saturn, wife of Jupiter, and in her annual celebration, a vital element that fed the sacred snake barley cakes. It might be that this observation was done in order to maintain the connection between the genii of a person and the genii loci through the protective nature of the *lares.*

The serpentine imagery is quite stunning in many ways, and we see the same imagery appear in the lore of the Djinn, the fair denizens of the Arabic deserts, oases, and gardens. Actually, if we look closer at these mysteries, it can widen our perception and understanding of the ambivalent reputation of the fairies.

It might appear that the word *djinn* or *jinni* is, due to their phonetic similarities, etymologically derived from *genii* or *genius,* the Latin word for a tutelary spirit. However, it seems that this etymology is speculative, designating a Latinized idea of what the fairy beings of the Arabic people were, be they a form of genii or nymph-like spirits. So, while the idea of the manifold nature of the genii or daimon corresponds in meaning with the nature of the djinn, the word itself is from a quite different origin; nevertheless, the connections are quite interesting in themselves. The word *djinn* has been suggested to originate from the Semitic root *jnn,* which is the root found in the word *Jannah*, "garden," or simply

---

71 Robert E. A. Palmer, *Roman religion and Roman Empire* (University of Pennsylvania Press, 1974).

"Gan Eden." The word describes an oasis or garden that is hidden or veiled and not attainable by ordinary perception, rather it is the open and clear eye of the heart that is needed to gaze into Paradise. Similar ideas are reflected in our perceptions about the Fairy Land or Elphame. Like the fairies or the Scandinavian elves, the djinn can be the malevolent aide of the sorcerer or be an influence towards the good, akin to a daimon or guiding spirit of the cunning one.

Ambivalence is also found in different classes of djinn, like the Ifrit and Marid. The latter is said to dwell at the coast and are masters of the weather, the Ifrit are seen as vile and fiery djinn that live in desolated places and can appear in serpentine forms.[72] Iblis is said to be the King of the Ifrits, but has been intimately linked to another class of djinn, Shaitans, that in turn is the class of djinns more frequently associated with the fallen host in Islam. These djinns are full of resentment, delighting in intrigue and deception, counting every enslaved human as a victory. They can take a number of forms ranging from a serpent or jackal to a beautiful woman, yet the serpentine form appears to be a constant along with the humanoid form, to emphasizing their ambiguity and tendency towards both good and evil found in their wisdom.

Serpents represent wisdom and fertility, but they are like the watcher angels, with a gravitas towards what is either constructive or destructive. The serpent represents a conduit between the worlds and can open for wise spirits as much as malevolent ones. Turning to Vodou lore in Haiti, we find the big celestial serpent Danbalah and his spouse Aiyida Wedo. The serpent-rainbow represents snakes like the python and boa constrictor, whilst vipers are owned by other lwa, like Kalfou, the owner of the "other side" of the crossroad as well as various Simbi lwa who are reputed to possess deep magical knowledge and capability for sorcery.

Witch myths like those quickly looked at in this chapter attest to the significance of snakes and dragons as ancestors, as well as a symbolic form of the first power falling into their given places. In discussing the phenomena of the fall of these celestial dragons and snakes,

72 Robert Lebling, *Legends of the Fire Spirits* (I.B. Tauris, 2010) p.22.

Ristic points out how many of them fell into trees that consequently became sacred, which is the case of the Cult of Danica, also known as Lucifer, in Serbia.[73]

We will close this chapter with a ritual that enacts these complex mysteries of the Craft, a celebration of the dragon-man, Master Cain's transgression, designed to be performed either on the first Monday of April, which is, according to fisherman lore, the day this deed was done, or according to some Roma people, on the eighth or ninth of April, or, alternatively, the winter solstice. The ritual was the subject of a yearly celebration over a cycle of seven years by the Craft brotherhood Via Vera Cruz and is offered here as a further way into this mystery of the Royal Art.

The Supper at Midnights Table

You will need for this ritual a cup, a dagger, a hammer, and a skull. Further, a bread baked using grains and fruits and nuts of the earth should be presented along with red wine. The ritual uses the double circle or the double chamber. The first chamber being the Blood Acre proper, the act of calling to the Opposer is done at the Blood Acres edge before one enters into the Chamber of the Sabbath to feast upon the flesh and blood of the All Profaner.

The Oracle of the Rite

From the circle's northern gate, the Magister will intone the decree of this ritual and raise the attention of the rite's purpose:

Hekas Hekas este bebeloi!
Biloi biloi hua!
By One Step the Path is Thread with a Million not even Begun!
Listen, ye Spirits resting in fire blue
Listen to this Call you have heard before and
Yet will hear again!

73 Radomir Ristic, *Witchcraft and Sorcery of the Balkans* (Three Hands Press, 2015) p.22.

Before the Gods of Mortal Man the Elder Race, the Dragon's Children who stole the Fire, who churned the Ocean, who discarded the Clay, who turned away from the Tree of Good and Evil, who crossed the river of death and forgetfulness and placed themselves at the crossroads under the stars. With the back to the One. And in his Shadows to become the circle entire. As my left hand stretches back to take again what is mine so my right hand goes forth in becoming. I am the Moment always born anew. I am the circle and its ever-moving point. In the Moment I am the Child born by the horns of the flaming torch and the lightning bolt. To be the Keeper of my Fateless Fate. To rest in the embrace of Al Shujah. This shall be the Design. To rest within The One of Many Names. The Many of One track alone. And as I turn against the hand that made me, I am faithful towards my oath of eternal Self becoming. May I be tested by ordeal and curse on the forge of Cain. May I always drink deeply from the poisonous cup of the Hidden One. All I cast on the fire to be created anew. And by fire the Wheel shall be turned once again. And as it was in the beginning it shall ever be. Now and forever more.

The Rite of the Void

With ash and water make a double circle. The one in the path of the other.

Recite Psalm 68 and enter the circle. The assembly will go in a clockwise direction armed with their Athame in their left hand with the calling Al Shujah Al Kabil while the Magister is going deosil calling the faithful ones of the Retinue of Bha. A bread should be presented in the centre of the circle. When the call has been completed, the Magister should position themselves in the centre of the circle and silence shall be exalted in this moment. With Athame and hammer, they shall stand over the bread and say:

God, creator. It is time to commemorate those who have walked the one Path Unique. The time has come anew. And I saith unto Thee Lord as It was said and done unto Cain our father that unto Cain and his offering you had no respect! Cain was angered and your countenance fell and you said unto Cain, "talk with thy brother," and you told him that if he had done well his offer should be accepted. And Cain had done well. So he went with his brother into the field and tried to reason with him. But the blood of the Great Dragon rose in Cain and he slaughtered the profane one. And the Lord saith unto Cain that the blood of his brother screamed to him from the ground. And the Lord spoke with Cain and cursed him into Exile and closed the gardens of Eden for him, but he also placed his mark on his brow and feet so he could rest in his Exile by the Lord's blessing. Those who killed Cain would be seven times accursed. And so it is that I, the One True Sorcerer of the Dragons Brood again is here with my gift of the earth and hear me as I call forth the profaner! Hear how his blood is screaming from the earth! Hail Abel! I call you, Son of Clay, Son of Mortal Man, All Profaner, rise from your grave so I can slay you again! In this, the commemoration of the Dragons race and its legacy I send you to Hell! By calling you. By slaying you. And again, let your blood scream to the Lord I take my oath anew and plough the ground to make thy grave. All profaner, hear me! I am the forger of crude metals, I am the nail that never cools!

Here, stab the athame and hammer in the bread.

And by this my deed is done once again. My oath taken once more and the mark received yet again.

Then, the rest of the brethren will enter from the Northern gate and stab their athame into the bread.

When all people presiding have performed this act, one should turn their back to the fruits of the earth and turn outwards, showing the sign of the pentalpha upward and downward. The Magister should remain in the centre but with their back turned to the bread and say:

With body, mind, and speech we give this Mortal Clay to the Shadows. To all Otherness we present this Clay in order to pave the way for unique Self becoming.

The attention should be directed towards the black void, the Exile where powers rests. Exile, the Gan Eden of Cain. The Magister will then leave the circle through the northwestern gate into the second circle or the next chamber.

The Rite in the Suppers Chamber

The Offering of Flesh

In the gate of the second circle, the Magister should stand with the skull of Cain, bread and oil. The bread should be dipped in the oil, used to make the earth sign on the skull, then on the forehead of the participant, and then eaten. As people have eaten the body of Abel, they should gather behind the Magister and again chant Al Shujah Al Kabil. When everybody is gathered in the second circle, the Magister will turn to the covin and say:

We have stretched back to be here in futurity. On the bones of our father, by the blood and flesh of the deed, by making it all anew yet again we turn the wheel of the season and put to rest the profane in a constant ordeal of self-overcoming.

They will now call forth both the Two Eyes and the Tongue (Liliya Mahazhael and Draku Ezhu). The skull should then be taken to the banquette table and positioned in the centre. In front of the skull should be bread or earth, and the wine should first fall upon the ground in front of the skull as it was in the original act where the earth feasted upon Abel's blood first.

The Offering of Blood

A jar of glass filled with wine should be presented to the skull.
Take the jar and bless.

This is the blood of Abel, the first profaner,
Who served as the sacrifice at the entrance of transgression
This is the body of Abel,
For upon the first death wisdom was born
As it All was born to Die,
So mote also this be
Make me strong in the embrace of my fate
Make Destiny and Dignity
My constant companions

May the remembrance of the first
Shedding of human blood be celebrated
Always as an honour unto me, saith Thy Lord
Cain, cause I swear that I will test and twist
You by flame and Poison
To enter my Nest is to enter within the fangs
Of the Dragons Mouth, by poisonous fangs
By the needed transgression I will inflict pain
As the means to remembrance and
the measurement will be all Otherness.

Pour the blood within the chalice and say:

Blood and Flesh, Spirit and Soul
with this Death is set in Motion
By nocturnal flight and angry Ghoul
The world gets colour and emotion

As Angels, Fallen or Broken
We will rise in the Cunning Art
By the Lord Cain's many token
We will forge Thy burning Heart

In Flame and Death we stretch out
The Exile opens up, a garland of roses
By the foot and hand, we take the Oath
Pastures open up to rider-less horses
And the Word is said and taken
I am the One, eternally begotten
For Love, I see all things forsaken
I take back what is mine as I drink
This, the blood of my Deed!
And this shall be my Creed!

This is a matter a million times true!
May the Curse, the blessing, and the Cunning be
It All unto Me!

The banquette will be performed, by feast and laugher and by any kind of pleasure that one who is about to be thrown into Exile will partake of.

The Consummation of the Rite

Psalm 68 should be recited backward and concluded with the words:

As it was in the beginning it shall ever be.
Now and forever more.
This is a matter a million times true.

By the Bloodied Graal so shall this Mystery become!

CHAPTER FOUR

THE MOUNTAIN OF LADY VENUS

The earliest accounts of the Witches' Sabbath are found in 1430s Europe, recorded in the Western Alps roughly where France and Switzerland meet from Lyon to Lucerne.[74] The symbolic importance of the mountain is also found in the trial of Cossandeir Maugetaz in the region of Lausanne in 1438, where he partook of the diabolic erotic festivities of the sabbath at a "certain mountain behind Gruyeres."[75] In his work that predated *Malleus Maleficarum,* Johannes Nider's *Der Formicarius* or *Anthill,* composed in the years 1437–1438, used material from this very region, especially from the university cities of Basel and Lyon, hence material gathered around this province was archived in these cities. The mountain of the Sabbath, called the Venus Mountain, was popularized by Nider in this work, but it was in *Malleus Maleficarum's* question six in part I states: "All Witchcraft comes from carnal lust which is in women insatiable." Witchcraft had, until the 1430s, been seen predominantly as a melancholic suffering, which in that time meant not only the suffering of sadness and depression but more than this one suffered from delusions. Hence, it is here in the work of Nider we find the witch becoming a Venusian figure, not solely a Saturnine one.

---

[74] Michael D. Bailey, *Origins of the Witches' Sabbath* (Penn State University Press, 2021).

[75] *Ibid,* p.116.

This transition was probably heralded by the evolution of the Wild Hunt through the succession of Diana and Herodias as the leaders of the wild ride of the Ladies of the Night. This transition of beliefs became solidified in the twelfth and thirteenth centuries through the writings of John of Salisbury (1110–1180) and William of Auvergne (1180–1249), who fused the ideas of *lamia* with the night-flying host of Diana and Herodias.[76] In Bavaria, the leader of the host of *lamia* was described as being led by Perchta by Bertold of Ratisbonne (Regensburg) (1210–1272).

It is also worthy to take into account William of Malmesbury who, in 1125, recounted the legend of Prosper Mérimée, a young man who offered his wedding ring to a statue of Venus. This created complications similar to those that Asmodeus caused Judith in the Book of Tobit, where Asmodeus, by murdering her seven spouses in a row, hindered the consummation of marriage. In the legend recounted by William of Malmesbury, a consummated pact is only broken by the intervention of a nigromancer who can orient Prosper Mérimée into learning how to dissolve the pact. The nigromancer gives him a letter he needs to read to Lady Venus and gives him an orientation on how to meet her. He does as he is told and ventures out in the night along crooked paths until he meets her. She is described as volatile with her hair flowing freely across her shoulders, naked, riding on a mule. These themes we find in the more famous thirteenth century legend of the travelling troubadour Tannhäuser, who spent a year venerating Lady Venus on her mountain. These Venusian elements flowed with ease into the imagery of the witch forged in Germanic territories in the late fifteenth and sixteenth centuries, which marked the beginning of the witch-hunts.

The priest Johann Geiler von Kaysersberg (1445–1510), who was instrumental in Protestantism taking hold in Strasbourg, handed over large amounts of material to Nider that detailed the sexual and ecstatic nature of the sabbath flight.[77] Keyserberg's vision of witchcraft is found on a woodcut from 1517, reproduced on page 90, made in Baldung Grien's workshop and used to illustrate one of Keyserberg's pamphlets. This woodcut demonstrates the Venusian anxieties ascribed to witches

[76] Lamia and strix were seen as similar entities by Pico della Mirandola (1463–1494).

[77] Charles Zika, *The Appearance of Witchcraft* (Routledge, 2007) p.246 n.7.

in a difficult historical time on the continent where we find death, the demonic, the erotic, and the ecstatic finding its visual harmony depicting the outlandish and dangerous witches.

Von den Unholden oder von den Hexen.

It is of importance to comment on the historical backdrop of the emergence of the witch as a product of Saturn and Venus in the formative twelfth to sixteenth centuries. The church started to define witchcraft only in the ninth century via the *Canon Episcopi* and later Burchard of Worms (950 or 965–1025) in the tenth century through his *Corrector*, where we find a section named "Concerning Women's Vices" in which sorcery, Fey, ancestor veneration, adultery, and abortion are all spoken of under the descriptor of "malefica."[78] However, in 1054 we see the great East-West schism of the Church that generated theological debates concerning dogma and belief and out of this the idea of heresy took on a renewed importance. This period of religious unrest gave way to The Great Famine that, from 1315 and a couple of decades, made life complicated on the continent until it gave way to the Black Death in 1347. The plague roamed Europe with force and brutality until 1352, but in truth, the plague didn't go away as such, and for centuries the plague rippled across the continent.

---

[78] John Shinners, ed., *Medieval Popular Religion* (University of Toronto Press, 2008) p.467.

As if famine, plague, and economic instability were not enough, we also find social tension generated by the great Papal Schism that unfolded during the years 1378–1417. The schism naturally gave way to more theological unrest and the rise of anti-papalism, finally leading to Martin Luther nailing his ninety-five theses of theological disputation to the Church door in Wittenberg in 1517, instigating the Protestant Reformation. It is interesting to keep this backdrop in mind when we seek to understand the ideas of witchcraft that were established in these centuries. The witch that was seen as a delusional saturnine figure in Burchard's *Corrector* (1008–1012) became transformed through the late Middle Ages into a dangerous and wanton vixen under the rulership of Venus in 1437 with the publication of Nider's *Formicarius.*

In the same historical period, we also find the therianthropy of the night-flying witches, that from the tenth century spoke of wild Night Rides headed by Diana, Herodias, or Lady Habondia.[79] Habondia held a long association with witches as their leader through her Roman name Abundantia, the "Dame of Abundance," that Pierre de Lancre defines as the "Queen of the fairies, witches, harpies, furies; and ghosts of the wicked" in his *On the Inconsistency of Witches* from 1612.[80] In Germanic territories from Switzerland to Bavaria and Austria, Habondia was known under the names of Perchta and Frau Holle, depending on geographical region. Interestingly enough, Jacob Grimm (1882) comments that Frau Perchta was, since the tenth century, envisioned as a white-robed deity, and like Frigg, was the owner of spinning and weaving and a leader of the wild hunt. Frau Holle is a hag in the Grimm fairytale, but in folklore she is a voluptuous seductress, a perfect fusion between Saturn and Venus, reminiscent of the relationship between Frigg and Freya in Nordic mythology, who both represent two different qualities of Venus. The name Holle or Holda finds its origin in the old Norse Huld or Hulder, which in their Germanic and Scandinavian variants, all contain the idea of "gracious" and "loyal." The spirit being, *hulder*, is a bit more complex. Norwegian folktales speak of hulder as a spirit that inflames lust and who can seduce her victim to disappear in her eroticism as much as vanish into the "other side," to be fairy-taken.

---

79 Canon Episcopi expresses a great discomfort concerning women who ride with demons, a sentiment Burchard of Worms expands on in his *Corrector.*

80 Arizona Center for Medieval and Renaissance Studies, 2006.

The other side is represented by mounds and hollow trees, as the wanton Huldra's saturnine side is found in her description as a being similar to a hollow tree trunk. In the Balkans and in Sweden, these beings are more commonly called "wood-wife" or "wood-lady," and according to Nigel Aldcroft Jackson, these beings hold a deep connection to Oðin.[81] The Hulder people themselves live within mounds, together with a host of other chthonic spirits tied to trees, farms, families, vegetation, and death. This means that they were seen as the caretakers of Jord/Mother Earth who was venerated at hills and mounds, these formations seen as her womb. Huldra, taking the shape of Frau Holle or Perchta, is described as living at the bottom of a well, like the Roman Lady Veritas, where she spins threads made from flax and linen. She is both the dark grandmother, the hag in Grimm's fairytales, and the wise Forest Lady dressed in white. Frau Holles day is the twelfth night, sixth of January, the day the Three Magi visited the saviour. Hence, the days from Christmas until twelfth night were also known as "the crooked days" in memory of the wild hunt that rode free on those nights.[82] As Jackson writes:

> *Frau Holda is the feminine counterpart of the Master of the Wild Hunt, and she is essential to a balanced appreciation of this area of pagan spirituality. The night-travelling witches of the Northern Lands, far from being demonically deluded as ignorant and vindictive churchmen said, were in reality the preservers of a hoary Wisdom Tradition...*[83]

This Wisdom Tradition is what the inquisitor Fra Beltramino de Cernuscullo in the 1380s called *Ludus Dianae,* or the Games of Diana. He equated Diana with Herodias, and Nicolas of Cusa (1401–1464) also brings this association to Lady Fortuna (Richella quasi Fortuna), Dame Abundia, and Frau Holle or Hulda.[84] The Games of Diana were composed of the participants dressing in the shape of animals and led by Diana-Herodias who took them to wine and dine at various houses under the banner of the "good society." This "good society" brought blessings to the houses they visited. However, Lecouteux points out that

---

81 Nigel Jackson, *Call of the Horned Piper* (Capall Bann, 1994) p.18.

82 *Gardenstone 2011: Goddess Holle: In Search of a Germanic Goddess* (Books on Demand, 2011) p.110.

83 Nigel Jackson, *Call of the Horned Piper* (Capall Bann, 1994) p.19.

84 Claude Lecouteux, *The Pagan Book of the Dead* (Inner Traditions, 2011) p.159.

in this self-same region of Brixen that lies between Italy and Austria, the Games of Diana, also called the "Good Game," is mirrored by the "Zogo del Diavolo," the Devil's Game, which focuses on the mysteries of Anima Sola and the souls in perdition.[85] The elements present—the wine, the bread, and the food—were the gifts of Lady Abundia/Habondia and the way of travel was through fetch and dream, hence the Wisdom Tradition ascribed to Diana, and, by extension, Venus, in the form of the voluptuous Frau Holle and Huldra, is of trance and abundance, of spirit-flight and sabbath-congress.

Diana is herself represented by the crescent moon as well as the sickle, and with this, she holds the memory of Saturn as a secret unveiled. At her sanctuary at Lake Nemi, she was attended by the water nymph Egeria and the woodland deity Virbius, both of them having a significantly marked Latin history—Egeria as consort to Numa Pompilius, second King of Rome, and Virbius' resurrection by Asclepius after being trampled down by Poseidon's horses who took care of Diana's sanctuary under the name of Rex Nemorensis. The woodland associations are rich in the imagery of Habonida, possessing several traces associated with dryads. The wood, the night, and "the lantern of Diana" create the atmosphere from where abundant Venus unfolds her secrets, one of those secrets being her relationship with Lucifer, the Son of the Morning, who is his daughter, also known as Lucifera. Agrippa comments the following about Habonida/Lucifera:

> *...and she is called Lucifera, i.e. bringing light, bringing the years of the Sun to light; and she is called Hesperus, when she follows the Sun, and Phosperus, because she leads through all things though never so hard.*[86]

As seen earlier in this work, Lucifer is of great importance for the true persuasion, and in particular, for sabbatic modalities of the Nameless Art, as he provides origin, legacy, and fate by virtue of blood. Lucifer/Lumiel as the witch-father evolves within a greater cosmosphere than the crude and erroneous anti-Christian qualities he is so often ascribed. Lucifer/Lumiel as witch-father means that his particular brood are people of a similar disposition, marked by a fire that reveals itself in vision,

---

85 Claude Lecouteux, *The Pagan Book of the Dead* (Inner Traditions, 2011) p.160.

86 Cornelius Agrippa, *Three Books of Occult Philosophy* (Llewellyn Worldwide, 1993) p.427.

perception, sensualism, and the numinous clarity only the Empyrean Fire can bestow. This pseudo-diabolical farce is, perhaps, most evident in how the number 666, the number of the Beast in the Book of Revelation, says in Revelation 13:18: "Here is wisdom." This Wisdom rests in 666 being a number of the Sun, more specifically of Sorath, the Genius of the Sun, which reveals the Solar Logos embedded in the mystery of Lucifer as consort of Diana, father of Herodias-Lucifera. Yet, Lucifer has also been equated with Venus herself, partly due to the wantonness and desirous disposition of the Fallen Host.

The Roman Venus is the goddess of sex, desire, charms, enchantment, all things venereal, and the amatory arts. She also presides over victory, prosperity, and she is considered to be the ancestor of the Romans through her offspring Aeneas. The importance of Venus is seen in the shared linguistic root of the words "venereal" and "venerate." The imagery of Venus is not only about desire and the erotic, for she is also related to Fate and Fortune, found in Venus Caelestis and Venus Felix. Agrippa refers to her as a mother whose tender affection always saves her children from misery, and that she also humbles the high and the low, the strong and the weak, the noble and the vile—rectifying and equalizing all things for she is the power that moves *nous*/spirit. Agrippa also comments that she is said to be the first parent of humanity with a particular bountiful disposition towards mortals and by the power of love and delight joins lovers and creates unions.

The Venusian theme as manifested in the crafts and arts of the countryside focused mainly on Venus as the bringer of light from the Moon, yet she rests in the Gardens of both Sun and the Moon, night as much as day. The Moon, or the Nightwalker, as she used to be referred to, is the speculum that filters the various lights from planets and stars to the Earth. It means that, in this relationship where Venus brings the multispectral light from the Moon to spread across the Earth, we find a wide array of love, beauty, and fortune taking place. So great is this variety of manifestation of possibility that, at times, Venus in her form of Lucifera, tends to generate herself as the experience of a female response to the Man at the Crossroad.

Returning to Holda, at times she is also seen associated with Hel through the relation they both have with aspects of death, dark, winter, and the night. I believe we find here an initiatic motif that should not be confused with the powers themselves. Ishtar's meeting with Ereshkigal is of similar significance and power, as well as those stories that tell of the Maiden of the Woods meeting with the Mistress of the Earth, for we see through the myth of fairytale an initiatic drama playing itself out. The same motif is found in the myth of Proserpina's seduction and descent. In the Norse myths, it is also clear that Freya and Hel cannot be the same deity by looking at simple ancestral heritage. Freya is a Vanir, while Hel is a daughter of Oðin's blood brother, Loki, a Jotun. What they have in common though is the Venus Mountain, and thus they enter into a symbiosis where the one opens the gate for the other and we move within the Mountain. Certainly, this Mountain is related to ascent along the axis mundi, and it is Venus in her great capacity as a teacher, lover, and distributer of Fortune that leads the witch to their ascent, noted by the seduction found in and night-walks taken through the oneiric realms of the Witches' Sabbath.

The Witches' Sabbath

This nocturnal convent of witches, known as the Witches' Sabbath, is heavily influenced by Venus, the Moon, and the Crossroad. In a specific aspect of the Moon the spirit goes out to the Crossroad of Night to meet the Devil. We might perceive Venus as the power that animates this possibility, as well as the Queen of the Venus Mountain herself. The usual testimonies of what went on at the Sabbath were largely accounts of obscenity and excess in all forms of earthly delights, lust, wisdom, elevation, and joy. The witches travelled by air in the night to meet their master and initiator, linking this mystery intimately to folklore all over the world, such as the Varcolac in Romania, the Vetalas in India, and not to forget the description of night battles in Carlo Ginzburg's analysis of the Craft of the Countryside in Northern Italy.[87] Ginzburg is particularly occupied with the areas of Trieste and Friuli, and interestingly enough, they border the Slavic regions where the legends and myths of night-flight are many and more richly detailed than most other corners of the world. This specific association between witches, lycanthropy, and vampires will be further discussed in the sixth chapter.

In her study about the cunning folk in North Europe, and in particular the British Isles, Emma Wilby comments that: "The Sabbath was more commonly described as occurring in churches and churchyards, or out

---

87 *Ecstasies: Deciphering the Witches' Sabbath* (Penguin Books, 1992).

of doors." She further comments that in 1661, a Janet Hewitt claimed to attend Sabbaths at a place called Muryknowes where they celebrated with ale, bread, and meat at the nocturnal gathering. Likewise in the same year, Helen Guthrie claimed that she and nine other witches gathered in the churchyard of Forfar where they sung "the old ballads" and danced with the Devil who she describes as a "black iron hewed man." Yet, another interesting account from 1665 is told by Elizabeth Styles, where she claimed she had consumed wine, cakes, and meat at these gatherings. This bounty of gifts was brought to the gathering by the Man in Black, whereupon they danced and made merry, and when they left the gathering, they greeted each other with the words "merry meet, merry part." As some of you might be aware of, this greeting was used amongst the early Freemasons and is still used in quite a few lodges. If we can see the timeline here showing the convergence of common ideas in seeming separate subcultures, things indeed take interesting turns.[88]

We should take note that the term "Witches' Sabbath" is of a fairly recent provenance, and it seems to have originated from Trent, Germany where, in the fourteenth century, the papal inquisition thought they had discovered a new heretical sect of devil-worshiping witches. Since they were considered to be a cult, they naturally needed to convene as well as possess some secrets to convene about. As Kittredge points out, witches have always been the subject of hatred and disrespect by the majority, both because the lack of conformity to cultural rules and regulations, but also because they were so much in tune with Nature that gifts of apparent supernatural power were gained and inherited by them. We see this even today: how people who have a problem with conforming to social regulation are subject to accusations of various kinds, as society in general has a problem trusting what does not conform to it. As told the idea of an organized witch cult of devil-worshipping witches was not seen as anything real until the fourteenth century. Kittredge suggests that this was purely transference, since the Church managed to destroy the Cathari heresy, the Synagogue of Satan was partly fashioned by the Church, substituting the now destroyed Catahri into a new form of heresy. The *Canon Episcopi* was subject to a reinterpretation and its

---

88 *Cunning Folk and Familiar Spirits* (Sussex Academic Press, 2005) p.86.

contents understood in the growing demonological theories that were spreading amongst the clergy. There was a great difference found in these views on the continent and England. For instance, the witch trials reveal that it was in Germania that the idea of witches organized as a cult grew. In Britain, witches were tried for criminal acts as individuals, and if a group was involved, each participant was tried individually. These accusations were tried by civil court until the 1540s, as the Inquisition was mainly occupied with heresies within the confinements of the Church itself, a part of the work of Reformation. There is not one single trial concerning the Witches' Sabbath during the reign of James I. Only on the continent, in the areas we know as Germany and France, do we find these accusations and trials. In England, witches confessed to having familiar spirits, such as dogs, toads, and cats, and to performing malefic magic; however, no reference to the Sabbath is found and, indeed, there are no references to the Witches' Sabbath as late as the Chelmsford trial of 1589. All these trials and confessions resulted in a tract written in 1593 by the Reverend George Giffard in which he details witchcraft beliefs found in Essex in their entirety, but yet again, there is not one single mention of a feast, a sabbatical orgy, or the like. What we do find are references to beliefs where Giffard describes shapeshifting into wolves, whereupon the witches fly to a banquette in the night. The first time the issue of the Sabbath surfaced in the British Isles was in Scotland, in the confessions of Newes of 1591. Even if the demonic pact was a reality, the Witches' Sabbath was not. The witch was considered to be a loner. She might have other companions, but they were hardly organized. In a few years this changed dramatically.

The first account of the Witches' Sabbath in any British trial is the trial against the Lancashire witches in 1612. Here, Anne Whittle confesses to having been admitted to the witches' circle by the witch Elizabeth Southerns. She said that the Devil came to Elizabeth's house after midnight and they went out to meet him. They partook in a meal and later their familiars took the remains. Elizabeth's daughter was also charged in this trial who reported that, at one point, some twenty witches came to their home—only two of them were men—with the purpose of naming her familiar and to also plot the murder of a man named Thomas Lister. Elizabeth's daughter said that they dined and wined, and after the party, the witches left in human form, but when they were away from the house, they took on the shape of horses, fowl, and other animals, and then disappeared. However, it was the conspiracy to murder Mr. Lister that was of concern for the court, and it was on these grounds that these women were convicted. This is the first of quite a number of accounts of the 1600s that refer to Sabbath like meetings that include night-flight, shapeshifting, and malefica. But as Kittredge says: "There is not the slightest evidence that they were organized at all. Some of the accused were innocent, some were guilty in intent. Now and then, like other criminals, a few of them may have met to eat or to plot a murder. But "covens" and devil-priests and Satanic orgies are, for England, out of the question."[89]

Ginzburg is particularly detailed in his account about night-flight and shapeshifting amongst Italian and Slavic witches. His research demonstrates similar points as expressed in the remainder of this chapter. The themes the Witches' Sabbath consist of were crystallized in the middle of the fifteenth century, along with the paranoid compendium *Malleus Maleficarium* setting the standard for the witch's nature and her beliefs. For instance, the phenomena of skin-leaping became demonized as late as in the fifteenth century. Prior to this, those who suffered from this affliction were considered innocent victims, often subject to a hereditary condition that affected the psyche or soul. Already in the fifth century BC, Herodotus spoke about people who were periodically transformed into wolves. Likewise, in Africa, Asia, and Scandinavia, are accounts of these bestial metamorphoses of people turning into felines and canines, mainly: jaguar, wolves, dogs, leopards, and the like. In 1555, Olaus Magnus, Bishop of Uppsala of Sweden, described how werewolves in Prussia, the German area, broke into people's homes, drank their beer, and slaughtered the people. Here, we see another common motif of the Sabbath: the accusation against the witches of a type of banquette, in this case, a feast of stolen beer and human flesh. Considering this shift in cultural perception of the witch, Ginzburg says:

> *...during the same period the hostile image of the witch crystallized. This is not a mere coincidence. In his Formicarus Nider speaks of male witches who transform themselves into wolves; in the Valais trials, at the beginning of the fifteenth century, the defendants confessed that they*

[89] George Lyman Kittredge, *Witchcraft in Old and New England* (Oxford University Press, 1929) p.275.

> *had temporarily assumed the shape of wolves when attacking the cattle; From the very first evidence about the Sabbath, the connection between witches and werewolves therefore appears to be quite intimate.*[90]

The same motif is found in sixteenth and seventeenth century Friuli where the term *benandanti* was given to women who participated in the procession of the Dead, but also referred to other individuals, many of them males, who declared that they went out at night to fight for the fertility of the crops with fennel stalks against other types of witches, the *malandanti*, who were armed with canes of sorghum. They further said that they took on the shape of mice, butterflies, hares, or other animals in their night flights or to journey in the procession of the Dead. It is a bit unclear in Ginzburg's account whether we are encountering here two different classes of witch or if these terms refer to the same witch, but what's actually of importance is recognizing both their aggressive and hostile aspect as *malandanti* and the more purging and benevolent Christian manifestation as witnessed in the funerals as *benandanti*. As such, this ambivalence is in itself interesting and probably reflected the growing social tension concerning witches in the fifteenth century. Without going too deeply into the many details found in Ginzburg's rich account of the *benandanti*, we can list the following repeating themes:

- They took on a different shape at night while their bodies slept in a death-like state in their beds
- They went out to fight for the fertility of the land
- The fight was against malevolent witches or malevolent dead
- The *benandanti* were intimately linked with the mysteries of death, even the night flight they often describe as a state of lesser death
- The presence of herbs such as asphodel is reputed for its connection with the underworld, fennel for exorcisms, and rue for protection
- The presence of the mark, usually the caul of birth
- The reference to "devils" as their lovers and deities of power

It is interesting to note that these same elements are still found amongst practitioners of the Art in many areas in Italy: the sabbatical encounters by oneiric means; the importance of deities such as the

90 Carlo Ginzburg, *Ecstasies: Deciphering the Witches' Sabbat* (Penguin, 1992) p.154.

Grigori or Watchers who were condemned as fallen and diabolic in a theological development that began with Augustine before becoming full-fledged in the Reformation; the importance of certain herbs, often understood to be the unique property of the family; the belief in the Mark; and amoral trafficking with Saints as well as pagan deities. What seems to be absent is the sexual and cannibalistic element, and certainly, by the simple fact that the Craft was commonly preserved by families, there were no sexual rites within the family. Therefore, sabbatical and sexual encounters pertain to the nocturnal Sabbath, and as such, it should be understood as spirit congress or sexualized encounters with the familiar. This being said, since the variety of practices and beliefs are so wide, it is not fruitful to give more detailed accounts of any more common references than this. I know personally about traditions with roots in Italy that vary from complex theology and ritualization based in astrology and classical magic to other lines that are quite simple which lack this rich philosophical foundation and function and are more based on devotion to Saints and congress with their familiars.

The motives discussed by Ginzburg are found in the larger theme of the Witches' Sabbath and are given a more diabolic colour. They consist of the following elements:

- Nocturnal flight to either an imaginable or physical location
- The presence of a devilish creature with initiatory power
- The guidance and presence of animal familiars
- Sexual rites and antisocial behaviour
- Blasphemy and denial of faith with the successive pact

Witches, Toil, and Trouble

What we are left with is the presence of familiar spirits, night-flight, shapeshifting, charms, cures, curses, spells, divination, even pacts with spirits, but this was always a thing related to the individual or families. In the Lancashire trial, Elizabeth's daughter referred to these people, these witches, as members of her family, such as aunts, cousins and the like. From this we can conclude that the developments to come from more organized conclaves of practitioners, such as the horseman's word in the eighteenth century and other groups of traditional craft, most likely developed from what we today refer to as hereditary witchcraft—that which was practiced in blood-families. We can assume that some of these familiar traditions came to initiate people who were not of the blood as a way of securing the "old faith" or simply because they had common interests. To some extent this is partly the origin of what we today call Traditional Witchcraft, but not its totality. Other groups probably organized themselves on a more Masonic model, but in what direction the influences flew is quite impossible to verify, as we saw in the example in the previous chapter with Elias Ashmole and how he perceived the world. We are left largely with myths and legends pertaining to the Craft lineage in question.

What is of importance here is to note that any Craft lineage I have had the pleasure to know to some extent, being from the various parts of Europe or England, do share some basic features in common as an irrevocable fundament, in spite of a rich variation of elements and teachings. Some do possess quite complex mystical teachings while others are quite simple and related to practical spell craft and magic associated with rural people, such as cord magic and wortcunning. What seems to be common is the importance of ancestry, reflected in the importance of lineage, the need for silence both related to the art as well as to certain spiritual points of power. Further, there tends to be marks of Christian elements and ultimately there are quite a few similarities with Roman paganism—regardless of language used in order to refer to these same principles and powers. It seems to me that what we today refer to as "traditional craft" is the result of harmonious and cunning interactions between cunning folk, hereditary witches, and, at times, more scholarly practitioners, such as Freemasons or adepts of other magical arts.

Beliefs ascribed to the witches' power were basically focused around three areas: spirit communion, fortune telling, and the power of the word—be they words for curses or blessings. Even this belief was a remnant from the ecclesiastical precedence. Now this has largely gone into the forgetfulness of time, but the Church in the Middle Age possessed the power to utter the "curse of God" when extreme conditions provoked such action. Papal letters quite commonly carried with them an anathema on those who failed to heed the letter's contents with a final malediction on them. Likewise, as Keith Thomas records:

> *...four times a year the general sentence of ex-communication by bell, book and candle was pronounced against all thieves, murderers and enemies of the Church. Laymen could also avail themselves of this ecclesiastical power of malediction.*[91]

It was not uncommon that members of the church contacted their vicar or priest to help them with maledictions of thieves and the like. One example is the theft of ecclesiastical artifacts from a church in Barcelona in 1628, whereupon the bishop placed a curse on the land around the church that caused the crops in the circumference of the Church to be completely ruined. For Protestants, this was all wrong—to be able to do wonders or make effective curses would indicate that the cleric could manipulate the power of God Almighty. It was a short road to walk from this to being accused of diabolism.

Similarly, some people were understood to be gifted with the same power to cure or to bless. Quite often these people were Catholics, and those who were to be found in Protestant countries retained a distinct Catholic format in their spellwork. A practice like fasting had magical use in what was known as the Black Fast, a practice of starvation and intent to inflict illness and death on one's enemies. Likewise, wine, hosts, candles, bells, incense, and many other items were used to bless or curse people, animals, or crops. Naturally, if a person could bless, they could also curse, and not all churchgoing people considered it natural that the priest alone would possess magical power—leading to the theft of sacramental bread for protective usage. This bread could be crusted together and placed on doorsteps for protection or fed to sick horses to regain their health of body. The Black Fast was forbidden by the Bishop of Durham in 1577, which would indicate that this practice was indeed alive and well—and considered effective. Keith Thomas writes:

> *The most common maleficent technique was the use of image-magic, by making a model in wax or clay of the proposed victim and then sticking pins or bristles in the part which was to be afflicted. That this*

91 Keith Thomas, *Religion and the Decline of Magic* (Penguin, 2003).

> *kind of magic was extensively practiced there can be no doubt. It had originated in ancient times and was well known both to the Anglo-Saxons and in the Middle Ages.*[92]

Given the extent of malefic magic using images, tablets, and dolls, we might assume that there was some reason for the general fear of witches. In the whole Tudor reign, these types of props seemed to surface all the time, likewise during the reign of Elizabeth I. Most of these practices were defined as "natural magic" and it is in the first book of Agrippa's *Occulta Philosophia* that we find references to these types of workings, such as taking a pig's heart and nailing it with pins and broken shards. In a recent edition of the same work, we find a quotation from *Secrets merveilleux de la magie naturel et cabalisitque du Petit Albert* from 1722. The work is ascribed to the natural magic of the friar Albertus Magnus and fuses natural magic with Kabbalah—which is quite interesting for the time in which it was written. It is in this manual of natural and kabbalistic magic that we find a well-known formula—the hand of glory.

The raw basis for making the hand of glory is to take the left or right hand of an executed criminal, the fouler the better. Make sure to press out all blood from the hand and place it in an earthenware pot where it shall be pickled for fifteen days. During these days the pot needs to be subject to heat, either by Sun or furnace, in order to extract all fat from the hand. This fat is collected and mixed with the oil of sesame seeds (which would indicate Arabic influences) and virgin wax. The taper is then fixed on the top of the fisted hand, between the ring finger and the longest finger, or the candle is cut in five pieces and placed on the top of each finger. These preparations need to be done under the influences of Sirius, most likely applying some benevolent aspect between Sirius and Mercury. Once it is ready, bring the hand with you to the house you plan to rob and you will not be discovered.

It is interesting to see that Kabbalah and natural magic became fused as we entered the 1700s. This would indicate that natural magic, mysticism, and ritual magic (primarily the Solomonic tradition) were not separated in such a way as is common today—low magic and high magic being performed by "low people" and "high people," respectively. Rather, it referred to different layers of the magical universe. I believe that it was in this time that we saw the upsurge of learned witches, or cunning folk, who

---

92 Keith Thomas, *Religion and the Decline of Magic* (Penguin, 2003) p.612.

knew a little bit of many things but were basically focused on using their gifts in good ways, to be helpful to their local community. But this created a certain ambiguity in the community where people sought out the cunning folk when something was radically wrong, while also fearing them—or in paranoid cases went as far as to blame them of being a "witch" if something went radically wrong, especially if feared on a collective level. I believe there is reason to understand that the typical Magus during this time, and as far as Francis Barrett, was a person who worked within the world as a whole, which made natural magic possible—from astrology to wortcunning, simple spellcraft to complex theurgical ceremonies, curses, and divination.

We can see this as a natural progression from the preserved ecclesiastical mysteries of the Middle Ages that were quite often under the protection of royalties and aristocrats. Naturally, this was continued by people with education, status, and opportunity. It is also interesting to note how the influence of Kabbalah, popularized by Pico, took such a hold on Western mysticism and magic. It would be naïve to believe that the kind of universal Magus exemplified in the person of Ashmole was a unique occurrence, as the knowledge and practice of the cunning folk were of such varied nature that it would indicate that people drawn to magic and mysticism did meet and discuss matters of the Art and Craft, unconditioned of their main orientation whether they be strategies for healing a cow from a strange disease or the realization of divinity. It was quite often an issue of need and opportunity. Rather, the disputes were between organized magical orders, and it is indeed quite ironic how the attempts to establish magical orders consistently led to disorder and schism. From Ashmole to Barrett, we see a particular kind of universal Magus that I suggest is the healthy fruit of the cunning one together with skills and greater social and financial opportunities than what was common. So, certainly, all this dissent within magical orders led to many with knowledge just giving up and engaging themselves in more fruitful conversations with solitary practitioners instead. Also, as commented on by Keith Thomas, in the British Isles a natural meeting point was the pub; on cold nights in good and cunning company with the fire burning and a pint too many, secrets were shared and alliances formed. My personal conviction is that this was the way of meeting and forming small circles of the Art, that there was never a formal organization of witches who agreed on creed and dogma as some believe in the modern day.

So, here we are, at the crossroad of a world where humanism, rationalism, the Era of Enlightenment, fairy belief, and the Protestant Reformation contributed to radical change in people's religious and magical perception. In reality, there was little difference between those who were referred to as cunning folk and those called witches. In fact, these terms were commonly used interchangeably, depending on the client. The spiritual constitution was similar, but the problematic point was not as before with the issue of necromancy and the problem with ambiguous spirits. We might see this as a crude continuation of the debate during the Renaissance concerning spiritual and demonic magic. As Keith Thomas has demonstrated in his voluminous study, the social climate changed after the panic ridden paranoia concerning witches and the skeptical works of Reginald Scot influenced the perception of more and more learned men who saw in witchcraft nothing more than "women's toil" and a blasphemous and impotent meddling with fantasy and delusion. There was however a segment of society referred to as cunning folk that we should look at closer. Owen Davies says these cunning folk were "just one of several terms used in England to describe multi-faceted practitioners of magic, who healed the sick and the bewitched, who told fortunes, identified thieves, induced love, and much else beside."[93]

The Witches' Foot

Many are the Avenues of Night, Hel-way, Wild Hunt, Venus Road, spirit track, all of it related to a journey along a road. The witches' foot, as we find in the rune Algis, is clearly the imprint of a bird's foot and denotes that the track we use is one of birds. This is further exemplified in the sagas associated with the mystery of this rune, its deep association with Freya/Frey, and the consequences when love turns into obsession. This rune tells the story of how Frey sacrificed his sword to conquer the love of the beautiful Jotunwoman named Gerd. It was this act that indirectly unleashed Ragnarök and caused the death of Oðin. Because the sword he sacrificed was supposed to aid the Aesir race in Ragnarök, but ended instead up in the hands of Skirnir, the Jotnir, as payment for the love spell he helped the Vanir with. Not only this but, deprived of his magical sword, Frey himself also died at the hand of Surt.

---

93 Owen Davies, *Cunning Folk: Popular Magic in English History* (Hambledon and London, 2003) p.vii.

ᛉ

Not only is the rune marked by the timeless trinity, but it truly manifests the totality of Venus' strength and empowerment, exaltation and fall. In *Skirnirsmál,* we learn that Skirnir was trying to use all forms of bribery and flattery to convince Gerd—deciding in the end to resort to the magic of the rune Algis:

I score troll runes, then I score three letters,
Filth, frenzy, lust:
I can score them off as I score them on
If I find sufficient cause.

If we pursue the Venusian theme even further, we find that the extreme variety of her powers is also the girdle around Orion, the starry hunter forging the form of Oðin, Semyaza, and Cain, the Three Marys. The central star in his belt is called *Alnilam,* meaning "string of pearls," and has the power to convey public honour to the one who gains its influence. Alnitak is the lowest star and is associated with nuts and grains, nuts being a delight of Venus in antiquity. The upper star is called Mintaka and is reputed to bring good fortune. In Roman literature, in the time of Varro, we see these three stars are referred to as "the Vagina." This leads us to the conclusion that Venus is the power of possibility, and it is through the *Via Veneris,* the power of the Holy Spirit itself, that the craft of the witches takes on power and potency.

The Rite of Taking Flight

The mystery of night-traveling is disclosed in the silent world of the herbs of solace as we find in several recipes of *Unguentum Sabbati.* Iohannes Weyer, a student of Cornelius Agrippa, gives the following formulae: Sium (cowbane), acorum vulgare (sweet flag), pentaphyllon (cinquefoil), uespertilitoris sanguis (bats blood), solanum somniferum (deadly nightshade), and oleum or oil.

Another unguentum from traditional sources indicates root of liquorish, root of mandrake, flowers and leaves of datura metel, belladonna, anise and oil. This recipe has also been found to include variants of aconite or monkshood, which I would advise extreme caution with.

Yet another, from Scandinavia, indicates a decoction of dried *amanita muscaria* and then a salve or oil of wolfsbane or monkshood, mandrake, and henbane—yet another recipe that I believe should be used with extreme caution, given the chthonic properties of this mixture that can result in an ongoing and eternal nightmare, coma, and death. Monkshood is a frequent guest in the unguentums, but it is a radical poison that can effectively paralyze breathing and slow the heart, with no known antidote.

For spirit flight to the Master's Sabbath, I would recommend the following philtre: take one teaspoon of mandrake root, three leaves and one flower of *Datura stramonium* or Melli, a tablespoon of ripe belladonna berries, a tablespoon of liquorish root, and a tablespoon of hyssop. Place this in cognac sufficient for it to cover the herbs for a week, then mix this with 1.5 litres of red wine. Let this rest for twenty-four hours and it is ready for consummation. But, still, it is not possible to stress enough to show caution with the intake, even with recipes like this that have the effect of counteracting the toxins that aim to shorten one's lifespan, inviting one into the final journey. It is also possible to add one flower of lily to this simple philtre. It must also be said that these herbal mediators can be called by name only and thus the flight commences with the Green Allies as spirit to spirit.

Crafting of the Staff of Flight

From a piece of rosewood, blackthorn, fig, or hazel, cut a wand in the shape of the witch's foot. You will do this when the Moon is growing and in Taurus, Cancer, or Libra, or alternatively in a good aspect with Mercury. You can also do this on a Mercurial day in his first hour of night. Then, in the hour of Hermes, you will leave an offering of ground coffee, milk, wine, three coins, and honey in gratitude to the spirit of the tree that will oversee the work. Agrippa says about the Moon in her exaltation:

> *From the operations of the Moon, they made an Image for travellers against weariness, at the hour of the Moon, the Moon ascending in its exaltation; the figure of which was a man leaning on a staffe, having a bird on his head, and a flourishing tree before him.*[94]

---

[94] Henry Cornelius Agrippa, *Three Books of Occult Philosophy* (Llewellyn Worldwide, 1993) Book II, ch. XLIV.

You will take the staff to a river in an hour when Venus is rising, and with red wine and milk, pray to the fairies observing you, declaring this wand as your ladder to the Sabbath. Prick yourself and anoint the top end with your blood.

The next day, when Venus rises in the sky, you will take a cord of leather the height of your body and you will strike nine knots on the cord, one knot for each of the Three Fates and their threefold placement in time and space. You will then tie the cord around your staff.

The third night you will bring the staff to the same place as where you washed it, and you will bring a knife with you. You will carve in the lower end of the ladder the rune Hagal and chant with the words of otherness Hel-Hagal-Hela while carving. You will then carve the witches foot on the top, at the heart of the roads parting and chant, in the language of the birds Algiz—Algiza-Holda-Algiz.

In the centre, you will carve Laug and chant with the voice of fertile water, Laguz-Freya-Laugar. Anoint the staff with breath and oil and let it rest in a dark cloth until the full moon in a dark place, avoid exposing it to the Sun.

On the appointed night, when Venus rises take your staff and your *vinum sabbati* or *unguentum sabbati* and you will position yourself to the north and wait until the Moon surfaces in front of your eyes. You will then make a petition to the Moon to take you on her wings so you can travel to the Hidden Convent and anoint yourself.

Take the ladder and stab it to the ground repeatedly, shouting:

Sator, Falcifer, The Witches of the Land
The Moon is full and fertile and I bid you Mighty Dead to rise
From Grave and Alcove, From Pound and Woodhouse
Rise from your slumber and come to the ladder's steps!

You will then feed the earth with wine and almonds and hold your left hand to the ladder and see in your minds' eye the skull-faced legions rise from the ground.

You will then say:

Of Masters of the Skull and Wine, Blade and Cross
By your blood I call upon He who rideth Out in the Wild Hunt
Hooded master of Grove and Pyre
Dark One at the Door and Crossroad
I beseech you to open the Witch way to the Sabbath

By the Fates so fair, and the Sisters Wyrd
Throw the silver thread across ladder and mount
Ninefold Mother, Hel, Herodias, Holda
Queen of Elphame, Queen of Venus' mount
Take me to the Hidden Convent!

You will now recite the runes of journey, focus on the witches' foot, and ascend to the sacred place behind the Moon, through the well of thorns, and let the Witches of the Land, Faunus himself, or your famulus take you through the ladder and into the Sabbath Circle.

When you seek to return from the Nocturnal Conclave in the Fairy Hill you will again grip the ladder and shout:

Sator Rentum Tormentum. In Nome Patri, Filii et Spiritus Sancti,
by the Skull of Wisdom and in the Master's name!

On returning, you will leave an offering of fig, apple, and water to the genii loci and fair folk of that particular place.

By using the same spot for the Sabbatic flight, you will manage to generate a portal at this place, and with greater and greater ease you will be able to traverse between the Kingdoms.

CHAPTER FIVE

SORCEROUS DIMENSIONS OF THE CUNNING CRAFT

Witchcraft and sorcery are ideas so related that we might state that the Craft of the Witch is Sorcery. According to the Online Etymology Dictionary, as early as 1300, sorcery has been equated with "witchcraft, magic, enchantment; an act or instance of sorcery; supernatural state of affairs; seemingly magical works."[95] The word itself is ultimately from the Latin *sors,* meaning "lot, fate, fortune," which gave us *sortiarius,* someone who could read—or manipulate—people's fate and fortune. As such, we can understand that a sorcerer is someone who has the ability to manipulate the world and create their own Fate, someone who possess the occult or forbidden knowledge that enables him to access "source."

Sir Edward Evans-Pritchard, when he studied witchcraft amongst the Azande in Sudan in the 1930s, presented an observation that concerns the use of sorcery which might hold some merit. He comments that the Azande believe that witches gained their power either through inheritance or through training. Witchcraft was largely understood as the capacity to do harm, *malefici,* through the invasion of a target in such way that the witch would have total control over it. This suggests a difference in quality or nature between those who operated witchcraft or magic through their innate power from those who resorted to the use of paraphernalia, tools, and substances—the art of the latter more frequently being classified as "sorcery." The impact was similar, the difference was found in the use of external agents in relation to the

95 https://etymonline.com/search?q=sorcery

exercise of innate qualities and powers.[96] This understanding of sorcery is in harmony with Western ideas of what a wizard or a sorcerer does.

Modern dictionaries give a wider field of interpretation of what a sorcerer is, common themes being enchantment, incantations, and thaumaturgy. The words "black magic" and "nigromancy" are frequently used as synonyms. In Old Greece, the art of sorcery also held a deep connection with the *pharmakeion,* those skilled in the use of herbs.

The word "sorcery" is currently used in a variety of ways to define a practice that is experienced as forbidden and occult, with a focus on the manipulation of reality through pacts, enchantments, and incantations in close rapport with the spirit denizens of the world. We might go as far as suggesting that sorcery implies a manipulation of something connected to the source. For instance, the Haitian *bokor* or *bòkò* is commonly referred to as a *sorcier* due to their capacity to manipulate the world in such a way that can bring harm or healing to whomever they wish. The bòkò is often said to work with both hands, in reference to working both with God and Satan, practicing their craft outside the religious confinement of traditional Vodou, hence a sorcerous practitioner and not a religious one. A bòkò, like the original idea of a sorcerer, is someone who has the reputation of manipulating Fate, who can traffic with malefic spirits, and who is versed in the use of poisons.[97] We find the same ideas that are transposed on the bòkò, as on the sorcerer, as on the witch from Medieval days—namely maleficent magic, from the Latin *maleficium.* The term simply just referred to something bad or wicked, as we find in words like malignant, malicious, and malice which are traits given to diseases, behaviours, and people. However, in 1398, the University of Paris issued a written condemnation of magic in twenty-eight articles where we find the interpretation of *maleficium* that became associated with witchcraft from then and up to early modern times.[98]

These articles clearly define *maleficia* as "harmful magical acts," and these acts, for a large part, involve the intervention of a demon that is understood to be an adversary of God. These harmful magical acts involve enchantments, the talismanic arts, offering incense, and performing exorcisms aided by a demon. In these articles, even doing good with the aid of a demon is judged harmful, a concept that coloured

---

96 Ronald Hutton, *The Witch* (Yale University Press, 2017) p.18.

97 Jeffrey E. Anderson, ed., *The Voodoo Encyclopedia* (ABC-CLIO, 2015) p.30.

98 Brian P. Levack, ed., *The Witchcraft Sourcebook* (Routledge, 2015) p.50-52.

the divide between licit and illicit magic from the time of Aquinas (1225–1274) who set the standard for illicit magic that involved the aid and assistance of a demon. Demons were understood to be beings that tempted humanity away from God, and as His adversary, he opened the roads of antinomianism and religious rebellion. This is evident in the use of the word *maleficarum* that, since the late twelfth century, was used to describe a varied conclave of individuals that were considered to be against the establishment, their maleficia resting in their hostility towards social order and compliance. We might say that, since the Medieval Ages and up, a free and rebellious spirit always ran the chance of being seen as malefic and therefore a witch.

A last important observation concerning maleficia is found in traditional astrology where Mars is known as the "lesser maleficia" and Saturn the "greater malificia." These epitaphs are related to the destructive capacity of these planets. As the great astrologer Abu Ma'shar wrote:

> *Now as for Saturn and Mars, since excessive cold and excessive heat is found from their activities in the seasons when they govern over them, and whenever these two principles are more excessive the destruction of animals comes to be, for this reason they made them both infortunes.*[99]

One example of a use of the "infortunes" can be found in the astrological timing suggested for effectuating a curse through a Curse Cord.[100] For best results, it is better to use the day and hour of Saturn when Moon and Mars are in opposition in the first and seventh house, as Mars is the ruler of the first and the Moon is the ruler of the seventh. The opening of this ritual uses certain Psalms for attack and there are also versions that use the Lord's Prayer said backwards in the conclusion of the working. This suggests that by the fifteenth century *maleficia* was often found as a term that categorized Saturn, Mars, Moon, curses, and demons or devils. *Maleficia* was the art—and nature—of the witch and the sorcerer.

A sorcerer is not made from nothing but from everything, which is why the attitude of the sorcerer is one of curiosity, interest, and engagement. The more the sorcerer is free of judgments, the greater

---

99 Abu Ma'shar, *The Great Introduction to the Science of the Judgments of the Stars* (The Cazimi Press, 2020) p.225.

100 Richard Kieckhefer, *Forbidden Rites* (Penn State University Press, 1997).

the access to powers will be and the more they will place themselves in a position of learning how the bonds and vinculums of the world work, and thus be able to manipulate these naturally existing rays and vibrations, free from any religion or formal social structure.

It is also crucial to learn and master an oracle as an aspect of the sorcerer's trade, as it is through the manipulation of oracles that Fate shows herself and reveals what lies ahead. In this is found friction between established religious orders and the cunning ones, similar to how it was in Antiquity when someone who threw lots and could see Fate and thus the future would be a threat to the existing priesthood. In both cases, they made themselves independent of the politico-religious structures, convening with Spirit and Fate in a way that generated uneasiness amongst the ruling priesthood, which for the sorcerer, became redundant.

This means that we can understand the sorcerer as an expert of occult philosophy with the aim of manipulating the world, that the sorcerer must possess deep knowledge of how the world and creation works, and that they must get familiar with the techniques available to manipulate order. This means that sorcery is a practical art, it is an occult exercise that uses knowledge to gain more knowledge through the performance of sorcerous experiments. The attitude of the sorcerer is, as such, vital and any good sorcerer will ensure that their spirit is always high so they can rest in constant awareness of the world. This awareness is free from prejudgment, because prejudgment will always be mediated by a reaction to the established socio-religious order of the world. Therefore, the ability to see a thing for what it is—and not through the veils of social and personal conditioning—is of importance for the sorcerer in order to be precise in experimentation and work.

The sorcerer has one significant ally in this work of gaining focus that's free from social and religious disturbance: plants. This means that it is vital for the sorcerer to be lodged into a rapport and symbiosis with nature itself, because the sorcerer, like nature, is not a de facto social being but a natural one. This importance given to nature calls upon another realm of consequence, which is the stars and planets. By understanding these two realms—the kingdom of plants, and the stars and planets in the heavens—above the sorcerer is able to bring heaven to earth and hence the sorcerer will, in the perfection of this knowledge, be the universal human who sees no threshold—only being.

Understanding these two realms that the sorcerer embraces, it is possible to work actively and precisely with the source of creation, and because the sorcerer does meddle with the source, with creation, they also traverse into the realm that the Church states is solely the domain of God. The Kabbalist Arthur Green describes this domain in the following way:

> *Kabbalah teaches that there is a secret unity of all Being, hidden within the multiplicity and diversity of life as we experience it. God and universe are related not primarily as Creator and creature, which sounds as though they are separate from one another, but as deep structure and surface. God lies within or behind the facade of all that is.... We, in fact, discover the Oneness of Being by staying right here, paying as close attention as we can to the present in which we live.*[101]

This invites a certain worldview, and even if we find resonance with this worldview amongst Heraclitus, Pythagoras, and Plotinus, it is perhaps better to condense these ideas into a presentation of the sorcerous worldview whilst leaning on these sources.

Let us start with Heraclitus, who entered history as an atheist philosopher *a posteriori.* For him, the building block of creation was fire, and from fire, he deducted ideas about change and the importance of the word or reason (logos). Heraclitus insisted that the universe was in a state of constant change, hence his famous saying: "We never step into the same river twice." This constant change was generated by a temporary unity of polarities, leading him to conclude that up and down were always the same—yet different.[102] Heraclitus was of the opinion that these temporary and floating moments of unity were moments of harmony that again were subject to change. In other words, a moment of "becoming" was a fixed harmony that, in the next moment, would change.

Plato was both in agreement and disagreement with Heraclitus due to Plato's insistence on the Pythagorean ideal of reality that led to his philosophy of the eternal Forms. Plato found it problematic that

---

[101] Arthur Green, *EHYEH: A Kabbalah for Tomorrow* (Jewish Lights, 2004) p.20.

[102] The post-Platonist philosopher Deleuze addresses this complexity in his work *Repetition and Difference* (1968), and it is recommended reading if you want to delve deeper into these subtle matters.

eternal Forms where subject to change, but Heraclitus never commented that eternal Forms where changeable, just that when something meets another thing, a field defined by change with the quality of fire was established. Plato insisted on a pre-ordered Pythagorean and orderly cosmos that makes mathematics reliable and the work of the Heraclitan fire which generates temporary cosmic situations. We might deduct from these considerations that they both were true and right because constructive and understandable change can only certainly happen in reference to a solid—to something immovable. For Plato, these were his Forms, and for Heraclitus, this was fire. Plato understood Ideas to be a sort of divine heat, stable and eternal that could reveal themselves through images and patterns. Heraclitus invited in the principle of change which he saw as a river, hence you can never have the same understanding of a thing twice. Time changes everything—because of this, timing is vital to the work of the sorcerer. The sorcerer is presented with precise moments where his work can be done.

We know that the Stoics, who greatly influenced Plato and Roman politics, held a fascination for Heraclitus and his idea of fire as the building block of creation and being. Fire was understood by the stoics to be *krinein*, a separator, which invites an interesting thought—namely, that the element which brings unity is also its separator. So fire was, for Heraclitus and the Stoics, both the primordial substance and the agent of change by virtue of its capacity to separate. Now, separation can mean both to discern, or to see what something is from what it is not, and also to generate a view of opposition. This idea is contained in Heraclitus' observation that "strife is justice," which invites the field of the sorcerer to take shape.

If fire is taken as the building block of creation, and we agree that fire is changeable and changes by nature, then we find that fire can etch eternal Forms into something solid. Just as we find that change is typical for the human experience. Hence, the sorcerer must become a friend with fire and understand all its layers in order to manipulate the world. Since fire is the sorcerer's friend and separation rests in fire as a substance, a unifying field must be embraced, which is earth. Earth provides all *materia magica* available for the sorcerer—plants, beasts, and minerals—all of the earth, marked with the insignia of fire. Fire also holds more divine qualities, as we know most heavenly bodies are shaped upon a core of fire and heat, no matter the coldness it radiates. The core of every living thing is fire, whether we notice it or not.

A good expression of this dynamic between fire and earth that's used for sorcerous ends is found in Quimbanda. Here, we are confronted with spirits that hold the memory of earth but are fed with fire, be it tobacco set on fire, fiery alcohol, the fire of candles, or fiery red peppers. At the same time, we are speaking here of the memory of living life encoded in earth—threatened by forgetfulness—but by introducing fire, this memory becomes alive in unique ways. It can never be exactly the same because time is change and the various persons feeding fire to this memory are never the same. The response will always be a variation of this memory encoded and engraved upon earth, as it changes, transforms, and provides opportunities.

These opportunities open up for works or for communion. The sorcerer will value the communion with spirit, knowing that wisdom can be tapped into here, and if the relationship with spirit is tended to, knowledge and guidance can be secured.

This is how fire ideally works. But in order to make fire workable and understandable, we need to work up a foundation and an understanding that enables us to manipulate the fire of change. This foundation rests on the understanding that these bonds are generated through temporary separation and can be worked and understood through the unity of creation. Meaning, the sorcerer is someone attuned to change, because change is typified by the work of fire, but in order to understand how to work these moments of merging and meeting, we need to understand how stars bond with earth and how this generates a technology that explains the magical dimensions of every cosmic network that enables connections—a theory expounded in great detail by the friar Giordano Bruno (1548–1600).

Giordano Bruno and Magical Bonds

Giordano Bruno was occupied with the study of optics and memory, a Thomist by inclination, but ended his life as a heretic, burned for theological error. One of these errors was related to his cosmology and accusations of pantheism, and likewise his repeated attempts to give scientific and rational explanations of spiritual relations and realities, as found in his treatise on bonding. Here, he discusses the basic premise for attraction, and thus gives an outline of the function of what was called "magic," but condemned as "sorcery" by the Inquisition—as it is ruled by very natural principles that belonged to basic physics. Bruno comments on the needed conditions to establish a bond or vinculum:

> *For action actually to occur in the world, three conditions are required: (1) an active power in the agent; (2) a passive power or disposition in a subject or patient, which is an aptitude in it not to resist or to render the action impossible (which reduces to one phrase, namely, the potency of matter); and (3) an appropriate application, which is subject to the circumstances of time, place and conditions. In the absence of these three conditions, all actions are, simply speaking, always blocked.*[103]

Bruno continues with a description concerning *mixis,* or mixtures and blends, that reveals an Epicurean and Stoic influence. It should be mentioned that Aristotle speaks about similar themes in his works concerning physics, stating that not all powers and potentialities can be mixed, and stresses the need for the presence of a predisposition in the bodies that enables them to receive the active agent. Water mixes well with water because of similarity, and water and wine mix well because of a sympathy that makes one disposed towards receiving the other, while water and oil are in conflict and thus do not mix with each other. What is needed is the study of the nature of the matter at hand in order to decide what agent would be effective. For example, medicine for the human body must be of such nature that the pores can absorb it and introduce it to the bloodstream or that it can be introduced to the digestive tract or directly to the blood.

Furthermore, the human animal experiences the world, both natural and supernatural, because of the senses. It is the senses that are the roads towards the soul. It is therefore worthy to carefully investigate both the individual itself as well as humankind at large, which also includes the variety of planetary powers dignified or afflicted in the individual. This form of bonding between the active and passive powers is of a more general type while the bonding caused by harmonies, such as song and poetry, is of a different type. The rhythm of song and poetry is caused by measurements of numbers in sequences of time. The level of effect varies from individual to individual, as some people are more

---

103 Giordano Bruno, *Cause, Principle, and Unity* (Cambridge University Press, 1998) p.147.

moved by the tragic and others more moved by the comic. As Bruno says, "different harmonies bind different souls."[104]

There are also other forms of bonding, caused by vision, imagination, and thought, along with some significant nuances between them. First, the bonding caused by vision where the eyes are the medium, works like this: if we see a thing of beauty, this arouses pleasant feelings within us, and if we see something ghastly, it evokes unpleasant feelings. Bruno describes this process in the following way: "...the emotions of the soul and spirit bring something additional to the body itself, which exists under the control of the soul and the direction of the spirit."[105] Here, he expounds on a central mystery because feelings, like compassion and empathy, are also conveyed to us through the eyes, from where he concludes that feelings are bound through vision.

Then there is the bonding that occurs through imagination. Bruno says that the role of imagination is: "...to receive images derived from the senses and to preserve, combine, and divide them." This can be accomplished by a creative free choice, as is done by poets and painters who combine images in a particular form of order. This bonding can also occur without deliberate choice, such as when some form of inspiration arises in us, producing internal images, whether awake or asleep. Interestingly, Bruno comments that this form of bonding can lead to mental illness, which he calls "the dreams of the wakeful" in which one confuses images for reality, generating mania and melancholy. Today we would refer to this form of bonding as delusion and a symptom of mental disorders. Surprisingly, he also presents an environmentalist allegory here, speaking of the seed that is sown, which responds to its predisposition but also acts upon what is found in its environment, where improper mixtures create disturbances, hindering healthy growth. Bruno even provides a further diagnostic explanation and a suggested form of treatment, as he sees these forms of disturbances as arising from a besiegement of the spirit, where noxious material distorts the world of images and generates fantasies and delusions. The cure is said to be "a simple purgation of humours and a simple diet are adequate to cure disturbed images and then free the internal senses which are bound in this way."[106]

---

104 Giordano Bruno, *Cause, Principle, and Unity* (Cambridge University Press, 1998) p.147.

105 *Ibid.*

106 *Ibid.*

Bruno considers bonding by imagination crucial for the physician, he says: "this is the doorway and entrance of all the actions and passions and feelings of animals. And to that linkage is tied the more profound power of thought."[107] Thought is the last agent of bonding Bruno speaks about. Imagination and thought are intimately related to each other, as imagination duplicates thoughts to some extent. He relates this form of bonding to faith and contemplation, and it is by thought produced by speech that a person is bonded to honour or to ill repute. Clearly, Bruno is touching on the core of rhetoric as presented by Aristotle, and in particular, how it is related to the character of the orator. It is likewise illuminating to see that, in recent years, Lacan perceived similar effects, as he writes in *Ècrits:*

> *It is through the pathway of the complex that the images that inform the broadest units of behaviour are instated in the psyche, images with which the subject identifies one after the other in order to act out, as sole actor, the drama of their conflicts.*[108]

After this, we move into the field of the intellect, the divine mind, memory, and reason; what Bruno refers to as "the spiritual powers of the soul," which relocates us to an order outside of bonding. Bruno is adamant in stating that love or Eros is the most powerful bonding agent because it reveals itself in sympathy and harmony, a cosmic amalgam or amoral glue, if you wish. If so, Eros would be the force that regulated and provoked the four temperaments as the compass of cure for the Renaissance physician. To discover what humour or virtue is in excess, you must bring the excess into harmony with the rest of the humours and virtues so that mankind can experience a state of contentment and balanced fullness of life. This would indicate being turned toward what is good and true, like Psyche was turned to Eros. Bruno comments that the "heroic enthusiast" comes to realize that he can translate everything into the species of his intellect, in a seemingly endless process of actualization. This is due to the bond of love, which elevates him ever higher in this process, eventually causing him to realize the infinite (and thus apparently illimitable) potentiality of his intellect. Knowledge and love are thus revealed as the two cosmic forces which

[107] Giordano Bruno, *Cause, Principle, and Unity* (Cambridge University Press, 1998) p.147.

[108] Jacques Lacan, *Ècrites* (W.W. Norton & Co., 2007).

are apparently separate in nature but which spring from the same potency and source. The slight difference between Bruno and Ficino was that Bruno advocated a form of holistic universalism and saw no difference between the material and spiritual in terms of accessibility which led to a perception of the cosmos as pulsating with the mark of God everywhere and a lesser focus on the inherent order. It was this "spiritual" orientation that towards the end of his life generated a theology that led to his errors as he reinterpreted vital statures of the Catholic doctrine from this perspective. Ficino, on the other hand, kept stricter to the Neoplatonic worldview. This can even be as simple as a difference in focus, and was concerned with mankind's ascent to the Divine Mind—as Ficino says in his Platonic Theology: "God is one for three reasons. Firstly, because He is highest unity. For if whatever is highest is one of its kind, what could be more one of its kind than highest unity?" He explains the ascending and descending scales or sequence of emanations in the following way:

> *To turn now to the particulars, magicians take it as axiomatic that, in all the panorama before our eyes, God acts on the gods; the gods act on the celestial or astral bodies, which are divine bodies; these act on the spirits who reside in and control the stars, one of which is the earth; the spirits act on the elements, the elements on the compounds, the compounds on the senses; the senses on the soul, and the soul on the whole animal. This is the descending scale.*
>
> *By contrast, the ascending scale is from the animal through the soul to the senses, through the senses to compounds, through compounds to the elements, through these to spirits, through the spirits in the elements to those in the stars, through these to the incorporeal gods who have an ethereal substance or body, through them to the soul of the world or the spirit of the universe; and through that to the contemplation of the one, most simple, best, greatest, incorporeal, absolute and self-sufficient being.*
>
> *Between the highest and lowest levels, there are intermediaries, the higher of which have a greater share of light and action and active power, while the lower levels have a greater share of darkness, potency and passive power. As a result, all light in lower things, which comes to them from above, is more powerful in higher things.* [109]

[109] Jacques Lacan, *Ècrites* (W.W. Norton & Co., 2007) p.108–109.

Unfortunately, the theory of vinculums, bonds, or rays is rarely discussed in modern works detailing the sorcerous art. It is this theory that explains why some sorcerous acts work better than others. Considering the various vinculums or bonds that are at play, it is possible to enter the natural flow with an understanding of how to thwart it in our favour. The effectiveness of a spell or magical work is to some extent relying on how well it is integrated into the natural flow and unity of the world in the moment the work is performed. In short, we need to be aware of the resonances, sympathies and dissonances between powers, forces and ideas. All traditional faiths in the world express the same fundamental truth: that Eros or Love is what sustains and upholds the world and creation. Today, when you speak about Love as the critical and fundamental element for the Art, people tend to project the limited ideas of this immense power and belittle it or limit it. Seeing today how people impose various forms of obsession and selfishness, self-delusion, and profane points of view upon Love, it is understandable. When Eros is seen merely as the field of the erotic it limits its primordial power and relegates it to domains, material and restricted. We are the eyes of the Unmovable Mover looking back at itself in the bonds of Love, so by looking inward, we are actually experiencing the vastness of the majesty in all things through its interconnected erotic pulse. Here, so many go astray, looking inward to find a uniqueness that is an oblique pathway to the construct of a possibility of identity, which is often mistaken for being one's selfhood. Our True Self is like truth itself, formless, and it follows from this that the moment you say "I am" or "that is," you will always limit the vast possibility inherited in the I and the thing. When we look inward, we should see the reflection of creation and through this realize our destiny. The realization of destiny and unity will make us see how we are all connected to the same source through an intricate and wonderful web.

Eros, Love, the Erotic, the Sensual, and all forms of Passion are fire. Fire can give heat and life, and fire can make barren and desolate. This is the excess of heat that made Mars into an infortune, a *maleficia.* This power Jung saw as the profound power of bonding, a purely feminine power contrasting the male "logos." Plato saw Eros as that pulse of constant attraction towards being complete, described in the dialogue concerning Eros and Psyche. Eros is that great power that constantly turns our daemon towards the possibility of completeness. When we say we love another person, it is because Eros has motivated us to see our own possibility for perfection in the image of our beloved. From the twelfth century and onwards, instigated by Dante's *Fidelie d'Amore,* we saw the rise of troubadours and the concept of courtly love, an enactment of the lovelorn passionate tension between the lover and beloved. This erotic tension is often ascribed to *vama marg* tantra, where the use of states of excitement ending in spiritual release will have a profound effect on all planes and within the totality of the body's neurological and spiritual circuits. It is the power of longing when our bodies are not met in sensual embrace with our beloved that the mind forges bonds of beauty that encourage the knight and troubadour to see his imperfections clearly, mended and whole in the image of her.

The idea of passionate tension is of great interest in this scope, passionate in the sense of suffering caused by the separation between lover and beloved and also the longing for union. It is the same basic dynamic that makes spellcraft work. It is this which we call the vinculum of Eros—the secret mechanism within all forms of bonding and sorcery.

The Enchanted World

A traditional worldview is primarily an enchanted worldview, one in which we seek to understand oneself and one's place in the vastness of all creation—to find one's proper station in life. The late Rabbi Aryeh Kaplan suggested to start with the simple acts of meditation and contemplation, what is known as *hitbonenuth,* where one focuses on a leaf, flower, or an idea, and with the mind filled with this simplicity, one allows the mind to use it as a mirror for self-reflection. By seeing oneself reflected in the leaf, one can see the divine within oneself, thus enabling communication with the Divine—with the Source.[110] This possibility indicates that there is indeed a sacred centre, a common origin from which tradition seeps forth in the pathways of mystery. This is the world of Nous, the Divine Mind, or *Mundus Archetypus,* a realm quite different from the usage we find in psychoanalytic thought, where archetypes are reduced to subjective structures below the world of divine Platonic forms. Modern psychology, and in particular psychoanalysis, operates completely within this adverse pathway of investigating causes and connections by looking within and downwards. By this perception of the human mind, any connection to origin is strategically severed,

[110] Aryeh Kaplan, *Jewish Meditation* (Schockton Books, 1995).

and individuals become the product of whatever beliefs they choose to import from a dysfunctional world that is severed from Source.

So, the situation today is that when the modern human is "searching for the Self" by turning their eyes inward, they do not see the glory of their happy destiny and their station of prosperity, but a network of tangled choices that leads to nowhere—what we understand to be individuation, a dislocated construction resting solely on personal truths and the emergence of the socially constructed ego. So, certainly, from this point when a self-declared Magus, sorcerer, witch, or whatever tries to work wonders in the world, little happens unless a lucky strike enters now and then. The bonds of Eros are more than anything forged in the sorcerous arts of theurgy, and theurgy is solely concerned with engaging the transcendent vertical spiritual dimension, the domain of the supra-human. The Magus is one who, as Cornelius Agrippa writes, "...doth... transcend the progress of the angels and comes to the very Archetype itself of which being then made a cooperator may do all things...."[111]

It is quite interesting to see how a term like archetype has become mumbled and deformed, as the *Mundus Archetypus* or *Mundus Imaginalis*, is certainly the realm of pure vision, of unmanifested possibility and reality. This is the Sufi Emerald vision that is reflected within the immutable essence known as Ayn al-Thabitah. And it is this realm that is the sacred point of "the return." It is here we find the infinitude of the Archetypical Ideas within the Noetic World, ruled over by Kronos himself, from Koros Nous, the "Abundance of Divine Mind," making it similar to the paradisal Golden Age. It is such elements that provoke Guénon to comment in apocalyptic words on the state of modernity. Modern spiritual humankind is like a troop of spiritual beggars who lost their maps and compasses. But instead of finding the map, they create an approximation of what they believe the world is and follow a broken intuition to an illusory North. This is sadly often the state of contemporary witchcraft as they claim providence by horizontal heredity or spiritual vinculum, while often the effort of actually embarking on the return is never even begun.

From the Divine Mind, a golden Chain of Being is stretched, and this was a common understanding of the world's interconnectedness in the Renaissance or in the Elizabethan world, as we also can refer to the time of the Fairy Queen, perhaps a more proper terminology for our subject matter.

---

[111] Henry Cornelius Agrippa, *Three Books of Occult Philosophy* (Llewellyn Worldwide, 1993) Book I, ch.1, p.3.

The Chain of Being

The Chain of Being was one of the three ways the Elizabethans understood the universal order. The two others were as a dance and as a series of planes corresponding with each other. This idea was intimately understood in connection with virtues being riches of God's abundance stretching from the foot of God's throne to the meanest of inanimate objects. Nothing in creation was seen as useless; everything had its place in a hierarchy as links in a golden chain. This hierarchy assumed that all things had something above them in dignity and something below them in dignity—or virtue. The idea of perceiving creation as a golden chain of divine virtue came from Plato's Timaeus and spread through the schools of Neoplatonic thought during the Middle Ages and until the eighteenth century. The Chain of Being made possible at least two ways of ascent into the divine embrace, as Tillyard says: "The Chain of Being is still a means of spiritual ascent: but only in an ideal interpretation. God has a ceremonial as well as a natural law" which should suggest that the importance of Jupiter as the fountainhead for the Chain is an important observation, given Jupiter's way of providing enlightenment, namely through religious and ceremonial works.[112] The hierarchy of the chain can be presented in the following way:

1. The inanimate class of mere existence, such as the elements, liquids, and metals, varied in virtue and nobility in spite of their common condition.

2. Life and existence where we find the vegetative classes; again, the virtues and degree of nobility varies.

3. Life and feelings or the sensitive class where there are three grades: sensitive beings that have touch but not hearing, memory, or movement, like shellfish and parasites; those who have touch memory but no hearing, like ants; and, finally, those animals that have all these faculties, like horses and dogs.

[112] E.M.W. Tillyard, *The Elizabethean World Picture* (Vintage Books, 1942) p.26.

4. These three previous classes lead to humanity who has all of these faculties, and in addition understanding, and thus becomes the Sun of earthly phenomena.

5. Then there is a class that is spiritual and rational, the angels that are linked to humanity by understanding, but different by their lack of worldly attachment.

This orderly chain creates an interrelated dynamic where everything finds its place and function in creation and the world in harmonious and beautiful ways.

The stars, and likewise Lady Fortuna (astrologically called *pars fortuna* or the "Part of Fortune"), were equally esteemed. The golden chain of virtue that connects the divine throne to all things in creation brings providence, fortune, and good human character as the moving forces of history. Fortune is symbolized by the wheel presided over by Lady Fortuna. The planets were seen as the agents of communication between eternity and creation. Fortune could be both good and bad, thus replicating the cosmic qualities of humanity and life. The stars were generally considered terrors and astrology was applied as a tool to diminish the hostile influence of them. This, however, was a superstition brought into play by a young and growing Christianity. Humanity has a natural tendency towards virtue or vice according to their sympathetic dispositions to given planets. This is evident in how planets shape physical predisposition, the humours, tempers, illnesses, and professions. All kinds of activity were seen as potentially dignified or ill-dignified, the heavens mirroring the earth. This perception was related to the idea of ascent to the divine virtue that flows from the throne of God, mediated by all forms of forces, ill as well as good. The battle between the ill influences of the stars and their effect on one's Fortune was considered, as Tillyard writes:

> *...the pervasive operation of an external fate in the world. The twelve signs of the zodiac had their own active properties. The planets were busy the whole time; and their fluctuating conjunction produced a seemingly chaotic succession of conditions, theoretically predictable but in practice almost wholly beyond the wit of man.*[113]

[113] E.M.W. Tillyard, *The Elizabethean World Picture* (Vintage Books, 1942) p.54.

This leads to the conclusion that each individual is, in reality, in charge of their own destiny and fortune, since suffering is inflicted on oneself by the lack of understanding of one's connectedness with the cosmos.

Coming down to the more crude and large parts of creation, we have the elements. Agrippa, in his Book I of *De Occulta Philosophia,* presents a lengthy discourse on the nature and combination of the elements. The elements were considered parts of a perfect whole, as if God was not divided but rather segmented into a variety of aspects that saw their reflection in different qualities of the one. The elements had a different meaning for the Elizabethan mind than for the modern mind, as they were thought about in terms of their effects. Air and fire were considered as having an upward-moving motion, while earth and water had a downward-moving tendency. Further, the elements were founded upon the notions of hot and cold, dry and moist, so earth as an element was the name for the cold and dry qualities of matter in combination. Earth was considered the heaviest and lowest element due to its cold and dry nature, associated with the dregs in the centre of the world. Surrounding the earth, the waters were found, which were cold and moist. Surrounding the water, matter was regarded as hot and moist and was called Air, which was considered nobler than water. Then finally, fire, which was hot and dry and understood to be the noblest of elements, was associated with divinity in its ability to enclose the Earth's globe. Fire was considered equal to the divine in regard to its invisibility and potency. Devils took their powers from the air, a noble element but still inferior to the fire. The elements were seen as engaged in a constant transmutation with each other, shifting their weight and balance, and thus having a great impact on the world. Ovid says: "Nor can these elements stand at a stay/But by exchanging alter every day."[114] The harmonious interaction of all things is mirrored in the playfulness of the elements and their constitution and interaction. In this, they become a mirror of humanity's mutability, the natural state signified by this dynamic, and constant alteration of elements and the influence of transmutation and change.

---

[114] E.M.W. Tillyard, *The Elizabethean World Picture* (Vintage Books, 1942) p.63.

Finally, we have the result of these influences on the human-made world, the microcosm of the great cosmic vastness that mirrors the divine archetypes and forms. By looking at the world and creation at large, we can see in what ways that perfect and imperfect humanity and its organization mirrors the celestial perfection.

The Elizabethan worldview was geocentric, but not in the sense that it was a belief in the astronomical reality of creation, but because the centre of human affairs and the place where Fortune played itself out was the Earth—the point of reference and understanding for Elizabethans. On Earth, we find the golden chain of humanity which has interesting and conflicting qualities, being a double nature partaking both in the kingdom of angels as well as of beasts, thus being a bridge between the celestial and telluric, partaking in all three worlds—Ideas, Celestial, and Material. In Iamblichus' *Life of Pythagoras*, we read that: "Man is called a little world not because he is composed of the four elements but because he possesses all the faculties of the universe."[115] Being an amalgam of many and varied elements, we find our lives difficult to order. We can say that every other creature is guided by one principle, but we are pulled in different directions by our differing faculties. The human body partakes in all elements through the quality of the humours that are present in the body. The cold and dry qualities of Earth create melancholy. The cold and moist elements of Water create phlegm. The hot and moist elements of the Air related to the blood, and finally the hot and dry element of Fire found its resonance in the choleric humour of the body. Even our anatomy was seen in correspondence with the universe and its order, but the double nature of humanity partaking in both beast and angel gave rise to the idea of being in a constant battle between Reason or Passion. There was only one solution to this, to seek self-knowledge, as this was considered a path to clear understanding and realizing the truth of God. The knowledge of self was considered "the gateway to all virtue" because the great enemy was seen resting within. Without seeking to understand this aspect of the self, we could never be victorious and realize ourselves as the little world, the mirror of the cosmos, and our place within it.

---

[115] Thomas Taylor, *Iamblichus' Life of Pythagoras* (Inner Traditions, 1986).

Spells of Binding and the Sorcerous Road

The effective mage or sorcerer will ultimately be a good person, free from moral judgment, someone whose understanding of the divine order reflects respect for creation and the connectedness of all things in their life and craft. They have a solid foundation resting on truth achieved through experience and a certain pragmatism in the creative handling of the fundamentals of the tradition.

The art of binding must be founded in the embrace of a theory of creation and nature that are universal, where we see the sympathy between things and forms. The most direct example of binding is what we find in knot magic, a practice found in all the world's corners throughout all ages. Bruno, in his *De vinculum in generis,* presents a clear account of the nature of bonding and what constitutes an effective binding. He starts his discourse by drawing attention to the various bonding agents we have. He lists them as God, demons, souls, animals, nature, chance, luck, and fate. It is through these agents that power is found and thus moves the hand that binds. This means that for a binding to be effective, we need to understand the various things involved in the relationship and to see how they are ordered in terms of influence.

If we take a common romantic relationship between two people, we can dissect matters into several categories: subtle and crude. The bonding is constituted by physical attraction, intellectual attraction, various forms of pledge, emotional bonds, finances, children, possessions, stars, and the natures of the body as well as the psyche. To use the language of modern psychology, an effective bonding in a modern relationship is to find the discriminative stimulus that reinforces your partner to want to stay with you. These can be varied and depend on the partners' preferences. Bonds can then be forged by lust, smell, gifts, enmity, love, compassion—the list is virtually endless, just like the golden chain of being itself. Things move with more ease towards that which they are inclined.

As Bruno comments: "An artisan binds with his art, for art is the excellence of the artisan."[116] This is the premise for the cunning binding as well. It is truly about having a sense of the principles that constitute

[116] Giordano Bruno, *Cause, Principle and Unity* (Cambridge University Press, 1998) p.156.

effective bonding and being aware of the bonding agents used. The one who is cunning in this art needs to have an understanding of the things in creation that they seek to bind. Its habits, inclinations, temperaments, qualities, uses, and so forth need to be understood by the one that is attempting to bind them. A binding must be done along some relationship of sympathy, either a connection that is already there, or the link can be forged by artificially creating a bond by repeatedly performing a series of bonds that, by the grace of Lady Luck, will force the desired result to happen. Eros is the most strong and radical of all bonds, for under the sway of Eros we weep, beat, and fall in and out of obsession. It is hard to come by a greater grief or joy than those given by Eros.

Bonding is further dependant on the appetite in the moment, the available powers in the moment and situation, as well as the "appetites" of the objects or things subject for the binding. There are also agents for binding that bind by their own power, what in Vodou is referred to as *pwen* or "point." Several natural items are considered natural pwens, such as a hagstone or a tree struck by lightning are endowed with a particular natural power that is ready for use. Bruno summarizes this elegantly in the following way:

> *A bonding agent does not unite a soul to himself unless he has captured it; it is not captured unless it has been bound; he does not bind it unless he has joined himself to it; he is not joined to it unless he has approached it; he has not approached it unless he has moved; he does not move unless he is attracted; he is not attracted until after he has been inclined towards or turned away; he is not inclined towards unless he desires or wants; he does not desire unless he knows; he does not know unless the object contained in a species or an image is presented to the eyes or the ears or to the gaze of an internal sense. Bonds are brought to completion by knowledge in general, and they are woven together by feelings in general.*[117]

The senses, nature, and imagination are the faculties utilized in order to effectuate this art, and for the observant one, it should be easy to see that both mundane and celestial relationships are ruled by the

---

[117] Giordano Bruno, *Cause, Principle and Unity* (Cambridge University Press, 1998) p.156.

same mediating factors. To bind the stellar rays extracted at a carefully elected astrological moment, and thus draw the essence of a celestial body down into an image, object, or talisman to invest it with the soul of the celestial body in question, observes the same rules of sympathy and harmony as any other form of bonding. Someone who is hungry will eat whatever kind of food placed in front of them, while another who has eaten their fill will not be bonded as easily to the food. Similarly, someone who considers you ugly and repulsive will naturally be inclined not to be bound to you. Whatever the situation, it must be analysed with scrutiny and mediated by the knowledge that arises from a secure foundation of cosmic harmony.

Simple spells, such as boiling the name of the person you seek to calm in sugar and water, will almost always accomplish their aim because people are inclined to be sweetened by sweet things. Spells that seek to harm people—to bind accidents, misfortune, and death on another person—are far more difficult to accomplish, and the situation needs to be properly understood in terms of all its harmony, sympathy, and antipathy.

It is necessary to understand the four basic factors involved in bonding: mind, soul, nature, and matter. The mind is stable, the soul is moveable, nature is partly stable and partly moveable, and matter is moveable and stable. Basically, these factors are related to the senses and imagination. Imagination as related to *Nous*, the divine mind, is stable and to the point, while the sensual world is subject to a vast number of conditions and preferences, predispositions, likes, dislikes, and so on. A person who comes across as being predominantly eagle-like in their ways will most likely be bound by the same bonding agents and things that will bind an eagle. Someone who manifests qualities we ascribe to Venus will most likely be bound by the very same agents that attract Venus. Likewise, the stars have specific dominion over geographical locations, about the temperament of various people and things. The more we know about the target, the more we can forge Cupid's bond, and the more we can wreck malediction or benediction on the person. This knowledge can be related to general preferences of the thing or person, as well as astrological dispositions and many other elements that can use the mind and senses as a vehicle for the agent.

Necromantic practices, curses, and the manufacturing of a poppet in the image of the person one seeks to heal or harm follow the same basic thinking. In these areas of the Art, it is essential to have nails, bones, hair, fluids, a piece of cloth, or photo of the person in question, as this will infuse the image with the essence of the person. To take the footprint of someone, as well as use their name itself inscribed on metal, virgin paper, or tablets of wax or clay, can also create the vinculum needed to make energies travel from the thing symbolized to the thing itself. These avenues are then solely related to the use of imagination (and faith, according to Bruno), and the efficiency of the spells woven depends on the artist's capacity and mastery of one's understanding of the integrated harmony of creation.

The popular hermetic axiom "as above, so below" is crucial for realizing the foundation of effective bonding and is also why everything possesses a certain quality. Agrippa and Thomas Aquinas realized that everything, from buildings and garments to all kinds of organic life-forms, receive a certain quality from the stars. As Agrippa comments in the second book's chapter 35:

> *...for the beams of the celestial bodies being animated, living, sensual, and bringing along with them admirable gifts, and a most violent power, do, even in a moment, and at the first touch, imprint wonderful powers in the images, though their matter be less capable.*

In plainer words, all forms of action and creation are moved and mediated by the celestial powers ruling the moment. This factor is what can cause good fits to result in bad consequences, strikes of luck, and misfortune related to action and creation.

The most classical form of bonding by images is the use of talismans and objects that naturally carry the desired potency. We find here images, colours, metals, plants, animals, stones, angels, astrological days and hours, constellations, planets, and so forth...all of them various manifestations of the golden chain of being, all of which reflect a particular aspect of the rainbow waters in front of God's throne—or Source, if you will. For instance, Agrippa says of the images of Venus the following:

> *From the operations of Venus they made an image, which was available for favour and benevolence at the very hour it ascended into Pisces, the form of which was the image of a woman with the head of a bird, and feet of an eagle, holding a dart in her hand. They made another image of Venus for to get the love of women, in the lapis lazuli, at hour of Venus, Venus ascending in Taurus, the figure of which a naked maid with her hair spread abroad, having a looking glass in her hand, and a chain tied about her neck, and nigh her a handsome young man holding her with his left hand by the chain, but with his right hand making up her hair, and they both look lovingly on one another, and about them is a little winged boy holding a sword or a dart. They made another image of Venus, the first face of Taurus or Libra or Pisces, ascending with Venus, the figure of which was a little maid with her hair spread abroad, clothed in long and white garments, holding a laurel, apple, or flowers in her right hand, in her left a comb. It's reported to make men pleasant, jocund, strong, cheerful, and to give beauty.*[118]

Agrippa's first book of *De Occulta Philosophia* (Book of Occult Philosophy) deals in detail with the vast field of what we call natural magic. The premise for natural magic is exactly what we have described in the previous passage concerning bonding. It is possible to bind anything to love or hatred, working on sympathy and antipathy, just like the planets have a natural sympathy and antipathy with each other, but these relationships are, in some aspects stronger and weaker in others. The many spells that tell how to manufacture oils and unguents from various animal parts during the peak of Sirius, the Dog Star, in the month of July, work on a natural relationship between Sirius rising high in the heavens alongside the Sun, and thus influences thieves—for good

[118] Henry Cornelius Agrippa, *Three Books of Occult Philosophy* (Llewellyn Worldwide, 1993) p.387.

or for ill. At this astrological window remedies for protection against theft, as well as making the bandits' business more prosperous, were reputed to be done. For instance, the infamous Hand of Glory, which was the severed left hand of a hanged criminal, was said to give powers of domination, especially for the protection of robbers. Likewise, the manufacturing of candles made with the earwax of criminals was said to make one invisible when one went to someone's house to steal.

Hair, nails, skin, and body fluids represent the person, and through the virtue of their significance, they give access to the generation of an avenue of power that affects the totality of that entire person. Likewise, a tree hit by lightning will naturally take on the power of the lightning and can be used for purposes of protection. The witch-bottles made for protection were usually constructed using sharp objects and the owner's urine. Urine is a magnificent anti-witchcraft remedy, a substance similar to blood in vibration but with an amazing repelling effect on hostile influences. Pliny says that a menstruating woman walking naked amidst the corn fields in the hour before sunrise will repel all insects and plagues, but this done at midday will make the crops wither. Pliny also writes about the manufacturing of fumigation made with animal parts that are said to have a tremendous and lasting effect, like burning the lungs of a donkey will repel all flies from the place. The power of herbs, perfumes, and fumigations were so great amongst the predecessors of the witches that, up to the fifteenth century, it was continentally common to refer to witches by words such as *venefica*, or poisoners. The court of King James I was riddled with sorcerous scandals involving poisons and love charms. This image of the witch as a poisoner and herbalist has been projected on rootworkers and conjurers more and more over the last few decades—particularly famous are the various magically prepared poison powders of the mischievous Bokor that can turn one into a mindless zombie.

We have here two examples: the poppet and the mojo bag (also known as a *patuá* or charm bag), both of which frequently make use of a range of plant, mineral, and animal materials in order to gain efficiency. The mojo bag and the poppet have become deeply associated with Vodou over the last seventy decades or so, both due to the attention given to New Orleans witchdoctors Drs. John and Marie Laveau, but in truth, these universal tools have been in the witches' cunning arsenal for centuries.

A Poppet Spell for Healing

For this spell, obtain something from the person in need of healing and fashion a doll in the likeness of that person. You can make the doll from clay, solid paraffin, beeswax, or some other substance. You will then take marigolds, rue, rosemary, thyme, and basil, dry them, and mix them with the doll. Separately, you will make a heart from pure beeswax and place it on a bed of roses on which you have written the name of the afflicted one on at least seven of the petals. You will pray by the heart of Jesus over and over again that the person gets well. Do this by the light of a single white candle and the presence of spring water.

Next, make a cavity in the doll's chest and place the heart inside. Make a brush from fresh coriander, rue, and basil, wet with the water from your prayers, and softly whip the doll with this water. Take an egg and pass it over the doll on all four sides, throwing it out to the south of the house. Then, once again take some water and clean the doll with the brush. Take a white linen and the petals of seven roses and place the doll upon it and the brush on top of the doll.

Place the water and candle at the feet and head respectively of the doll and say:

All sickness good St. Peter whipped away,
All infirmities will now go to Hell.
The third time belongs to good St. Peter.
As the whip withers and dries,
So will your sickness wither and disappear.

A Poppet Spell for Harm

Make a bread figure from flour, salt, hot peppers, and vinegar. While you curse the person, place the items that represent them inside the mixture, making sure to build up a blind anger while making and forming the doll. Put it in the oven and watch it while it turns black. Curse thy enemy constantly, and when the doll is blackened, take it out and make sure that you burn yourself a little. Then throw the doll into a filthy place away from your home with the words:

Like a burned pig, turn back to the filth
from whence you came, (name the person)!

Say this three times, turn your back, spit three times over the left shoulder, and walk home without looking back.

A Mojo Bag for Warding Off Malefica

You will take the following ingredients: coffee beans, sea salt, rue, seven thorns from a red rose, an iron cross, tobacco, roots of fern, and root of spinach. On the day of Mars in its hour and free of affliction, call upon the Lord of Spirit, War, and Protection by using his signs and tokens. Light three red candles and offer him tobacco, Campari, and red wine.

Mix the ingredients together in a red cloth. Tie it up with a black cord three times around it. Then take three sips of the Campari and spray it on the mojo bag with your mouth. Fumigate the bag with tobacco and leave it between the three candles until the next day.

These workings can be accomplished due to one's inherent power or the use of external agents, be they material or spiritual. The Cunning Craft uses a natural power that some people are gifted with while others resort to various means. These powers can also be inherited and even be given through the cunning meeting or congress, as explained in the first chapter of this work.

It is also of great relevance to understand how a planetary virtue is found in the spiritual and material kingdoms, and the concept of sympathy, or what causes resonance between these forms. This means that the performance of sympathetic magic is what Agrippa, Bacon, and others called "natural magic," as it uses the naturally empowered substances found in creation which are then used to create discord or harmony. This idea grew to prominence in the Renaissance and was fundamental to Florentine Neoplatonism which saw the material world as a manifestation of the celestial world by virtue of *sympathia,* a principle used to explain magic and sorcery on the basis of sympathy—the resonant connection between ideas and forms and objects in the world of matter and spirit.

As an example of sympathy we find the mirror, a reflective surface that holds the power of revealing oneself which also serves as a lunar gateway to "the other side." This potential was also present in the eye, especially the witches' gaze and its prudence towards fascination, or *fascinous* from the Latin *fascinum,* a word that has been used to refer to enchantments and charms caused by witchcraft since the seventeenth century. This propensity is well known through the effects of the "evil eye" that stems from the idea that the witch is indeed a wicked one, a *maleficia,* who, consumed by saturnine envy, seeks destruction upon a foe, cattle, or land with their wicked, evil gaze. In *The Magus,* Barrett gives a great explanation of what this faculty is and why it works. This explanation clearly rests on a Neoplatonic foundation, but also it takes the ideas of rays and bonds found in Bruno's teachings into account. He writes:

> *So the eye, being opened and intent upon any one with a strong imagination, doth dart its beams, which are the vehicle of the spirit, into whatever we will affect or bind, which spirit striking the eye of them who are fascinated, being stirred up in the heart and soul of him that sends them forth, and possessing the breast of them who are struck, wounds their hearts, infects their spirits, and overpowers them.*
>
> *Know, likewise, that in witches, those are most bewitched, who, with often looking, direct the edge of their sight to the edge of the sight of those who bewitch or fascinate them; whence arose the saying of "Evil eyes, &c [sic]." For when their eyes are reciprocally bent one upon the other, and are joined beams to beams, and lights to lights, then the spirit of the one is joined to the spirit of the other, and then are strong ligations made.*
>
> *So great power is there in fascination that many uncommon and wonderful things are thereby effected, especially when the vapours of the eyes are subservient to the affection; therefore collyries, ointments, alligations, &,c. are used to affect and corroborate the spirit in this or that manner: to induce love, they use venereal collyriums, as hippomanes,*

> *blood of doves, &c. To induce fear, they use martial collyriums, as the eyes of wolves, bear's fat, and the civet-cat. To procure misery, or sickness, they use saturnine, and so on.*[119]

The belief that the art of fascination was a distinct property of the spirit of the witch was common during the Renaissance. Even today if we turn to Western Africa, the power of fascination, to control people, or to alter events by simple gaze, word, or action is considered to be the effect of a particular spiritual make-up—that of the witch, as we are here speaking of "bewitchment," to fall under the spell of someone. We see the remembrance of this effect in the use of the word "charm," or when someone is called "charming" because of that "something" we really cannot put a finger on and define. Apuleius describes the effect of bewitchment as the eyes of the witch sliding down his own eyes and stirring up his heart and marrow. Agrippa sees this as a variety of rays that the witch can deliberately project from their eyes. These rays are rooted in the heart, and the eyes serve as the projector or magnifying glass. Various forms of collieries are used to maximize the Eros, the desire projected. For instance, they could use the civet of cats, or the eyes of a wolf turned into collieries to induce fear, or vaginal secretion to induce lust and attraction. Naturally, this was used against the witches during the witch trials in the period of Reformation as a part of the cleansing of heresies within the Church. Lust could be provoked in the investigators who, in turn, blamed this on the witch, resulting in acute sexual paranoia. A women could be arrested and charged with *fascinous* or *maleficia* simply because she was too beautiful or because her presence provoked lust in the heart of the Church's emissaries. This innate power was gradually demonized and considered malefic, as one saw only the damage casting the evil eye could do by provoking lust, or it could be used for control and domination of people or nature. The study of optics amongst people like Albertus Magnus and Francis Bacon was probably motivated by the acceptance of this, that some people were naturally capable of allowing what was in their heart to flow out from their eyes and influence their surroundings. This suggests that this natural erotic power is somehow more poignant in some people than in others.

---

[119] Francis Barrett, *The Magus* (Samuel Weiser, 2000) p.49.

Fascination can be described as a highly condensed and well-directed vapor from the realm of Eros, from that place where the heart of the world and the heart of the witch beat as one, with the eyes used to dominate and control or to evoke lust within the target. These rays stem from the world of imagination, and thus the eyes can conduct a great variety of rays, be they Martial or Venusian in their erotic aroma, like in the cord spell described below.

Lylet's Curse Cord

Mark yourself with oil of destruction on the forehead, the palm of the hands, the heart, and the genital area. For each point, say the following:

Lamassu—Izorpo—Lamassu—Ik—Thiltho
Lilithu—Lilithu—Lilithu
Odam—Odam—Odam

Take the cord and make nine knots with the chant below, tied with the name of the offender placed inside each knot. With perfect focus, see your desire in your mind's eye and tie up the enemy.

The first knot I tie to bind your will, *Lil—Odam Ha!*
The second knot I tie to bind your heart, *Lil—Odam Ha!*
The third knot will bind your mind, *Lil—Odam Ha!*
With the fourth you are mine, *Lil—Odam Ha!*
With the fifth I drive you away, *Lil—Odam Ha!*
With the sixth I tie you down, *Lil—Odam Ha!*
With the seventh I take your sight, *Lil—Odam Ha!*
With the eighth I take your voice, *Lil—Odam Ha!*
And may the ninth render you harmless! *Lil—Odam Ha!*
This I pray as She is my witness!

Here, make use of either Thanatos or Eros to make the final charge while reciting the following in a repetitive fashion, holding the cord in your hands in front of your mouth charging it with your breath:

Lilith, Naamah Agrat bat Mahlat.

Put the cord in a jar or in a bottle full of sharp objects, spikes, and vinegar. Spikes can also be tied in the cord together with the name of the enemy.

State your will three times and recite:

Abito—Abyzu—Amizu—Avitu—Lamassu—Zahriel—Zefonith
Partashah—Satrina—Bituah—Lilith—Odam
May my will be done
May the evil be gone!
This I pray
And so it
Will be done
Odam!

Take the cord and place it at a proper place, which should be evident after the spell is done: in front of the image of Lilith, at the crossroad, desolate place, stream, or graveyard.

CHAPTER SIX

THE CRAFT OF THE WISE

The Goal of the Wise

It is crucial to distinguish between eclecticism, both critical and uncritical, and synthesis. Practising discernment while striving to maintain a constant connection to one's daimon or fetch is essential for those seeking recognition as a cunning one or wise individual. Another characteristic of the Cunning Craft is the use of "the Book," which may be a collection of spells, such as a Black Book, a compendium of magical knowledge like the *Ars Notoria*, Agrippa's *Three Books of Occult Philosophy*, Barrett's *The Magus*, and others. Apart from Agrippa's *Three Books of Occult Philosophy*, the grimoire or magical handbook that perhaps most influenced European sorcery and magic was the Arabic manual the *Picatrix*.[120]

Picatrix, The Goal of the Wise, is attributed to the ninth century and encompasses a wide range of influences, serving as a grammar and compendium of magical lore and techniques from various corners of the world. The book is an astrological manual in its entirety, with all procedures, techniques, thoughts, and talismans resting upon a holistic,

[120] Liana Saif, *The Arabic Influences on Early Modern Occult Philosophy* (Palgrave, 2015).

geocentric, and Ptolemaic worldview. This worldview represents the reality of our connectedness to all things as perceived from the Earth. The geocentric worldview has been criticised for being erroneous, as it does not reflect the actual organisation of the universe. However, perspective and placement in time and space are crucial—ultimately, it is about what is effective and useful. Approaching situations from the perspective and placement of an angel residing in the Sixth Heaven would not aid us much in our earthly journey. To navigate the map, we must start from our current location, not from an ideal one. We need to recognise who we are and understand which station the Fates and Dame Fortuna have in store for us, as well as the nature of our surroundings and how they influence us—and then embark on our journey.

For an art to be considered traditional, it needs some level of consistency in being passed down, typically over an extended period. A tradition does not emerge instantaneously; it gradually becomes a vehicle for maintaining connectedness with the sacred centre through its capacity to preserve wisdom and adapt to changes.

In the case of the *Picatrix,* we find a comprehensive nigromantic manual for the talismanic arts, all presented within the embrace of a timeless tradition. However, what often occurs is that this book, like many other handbooks and manuals, is used eclectically. A talisman is made with varying degrees of astrological competence, a spell is performed, and one believes oneself to be practising magic and adhering to traditionalism. More frequently, people use this manual as they would use the *Heptameron* or one of the well-known grimoires, adapting them to a distorted mindset, neglecting that the specific orientations provided are related to particular moments in the Earth's rotation and within the constellations. The manual offers the perfect astrological windows for tapping into any possibility for good or ill. Often, it is the more raw and spicy rituals and procedures that attract attention, while the essential philosophical foundation in Book One is overlooked and the crucial procedure in Book Three concerning the Perfect Nature is not given much attention. Let us pay attention to it now because perfection is so important. A traditional Nigromancer or Magus will strive towards becoming a *Perfecti* in the sense of achieving the soul's perfection. Interestingly, this procedure for perfecting one's nature was said to be given to Hermes Thrice Wise through a dream or from the Empyrean realm. The entirety of the *Picatrix* uses Avicenna as a philosophical foundation, and Avicenna was in the school of Aristotle. However, it should be added that Avicenna was a heretical Aristotelian who brought Aristotle's thinking closer to Plato than anyone before him. The author(s) of the *Picatrix* begins this chapter by quoting from Aristotle's *Astimech*, where we read: "Perfect nature strengthens he who seeks wisdom, firms his intelligence and wisdom, allowing him to succeed more easily in all his works."[121]

The instructions in the *Picatrix* suggest that this ritual was performed once a year, and it is reasonable to assume that this was linked to one's birth, as one's good daimon was particularly close during this time. However, it could not be on the exact birthday, as the astrological observation calls for the Moon to be in the first degree of Aries, in its horns. Quite intriguing is the fact that the stars in the horns of Aries are Sheratan and Mesarthim, which possess the nature of Mars and Saturn. We see here a reference to the great benevolence of Mars as the god of pure spirit and Saturn as the king of the Golden Age, while today in the Age of Corruption they are regarded as malefics. Note that these two planetary forces symbolize the communion with one's Perfect Nature, demonstrating how far we have strayed from realising the benevolence these planets represent. Christopher Warnock, in his book *The Mansions of the Moon*, comments that this first mansion of the Moon is signified by the Divine Mind (nous), primal transmission, and the power of creation and destruction.[122] The enigma is hidden here: the power that creates is also what destroys. This mansion was of great importance for the traveller, particularly at the beginning of the journey. Thus, it would be appropriate to understand the ritual for making contact with one's Perfect Nature as the start of a journey motivated by the Divine Mind.

---

[121] Liana Saif, *The Arabic Influences on Early Modern Occult Philosophy* (Palgrave, 2015).

[122] Christopher Warnock, *The Mansions of the Moon* (2006) p.40.

The composition of the horns of Aries also calls to mind how easy it is to lose one's way and that we need to measure the amount and type of force we use on our journey.

Ritual of Communion with One's Perfect Nature

The ritual begins with a preliminary step conducted over a well with the intent of gazing into the secrets of the world. In this well, place a candle in a glass to prevent the flame from being extinguished by the wind. Collect earth from the four sides of the well and its centre for use in talismanic purposes. The one seeking insight into the world's mysteries will then position themselves so they can look down into the well securing the talismanic substance and a single burning candle.

The ritual itself is relatively simple in format. This streamlined version can be performed once a month. However, on the day closest to your birthday, you will want to present food, sweets, pie, and flowers on the table, inviting friends to partake in the delights. On this occasion, a cake with a single candle would also be appropriate.

Before the ritual, ensure that the temple or room for the operation is clean. Dress the table with a clean cloth and take four bowls, filling one with real butter, another with almond oil, a third with walnut oil, and the fourth with sesame oil. Place them at the centre of the table with a lit beeswax candle in their midst and two censers at the left and the right of the shrine. Then, take four glasses, fill them generously with wine, and place them at each cardinal direction. Finally, present a bowl containing honey, sugar, and flour on the table.

You will then start to chant:

Meegius, Betzahuech, Vacdez, Nufeneguediz
You are the Wardens of Natura Perfecta
Come forth from the quarters of the heavens and
Sustain my ascent Open the secrets of the World to me
And let me see my Self and the Journey onwards!
Meegius, Betzahuech, Vacdez, Nufeneguediz.

You will then take two censers and light the charcoal, saying:

Oh black as Saturn are you and by Saturn
I expel all malefic forces from you!

When the coal starts to get red-hot, say:

Hot as Mars are you, glowing with the Fire of the Divine Mind,
By Mars I expel all malefic forces from you!

Then take frankincense and mastic and place in one of the censers, and aloeswood in the other. As the smoke rises, say:

Oh rise to the heavens, these vapours of fragrant ascent, rise to the Thorne of God and make Sweet the Divine Mind and the journey onwards.
For you my Angel, My Perfect Nature, I give this offering of scent and vapours, the Love of the World in aerial ascent!

You will then face East and call upon Natura Perfecta seven times with the following petition:

> *I invoke you, O spirits mighty, powerful, and lofty, because it is from you that proceed the knowledge of the wise and the intellect of those who understand, and it is by your virtue that the requests of philosophers are manifested, so that you may answer me, that you may be with me, that you may link me to yourself by your powers and virtues, that you may strengthen me in your knowledge, so that I may understand what I do not understand, that I may know that of which I am ignorant, that I may see that which I see not; set far from me blindness, indignity, forgetfulness, and weakness; make me climb to the degree of the wise ones of old—those who had a heart full of knowledge, wisdom, intellect, and savvy—fasten that in my heart in such a manner similar to the heart of the wise ones of old.*

Once this is completed, mix the oils and butter in the larger bowl containing the flour and other ingredients and place it to the North, turning the mixture into a pie. Add wine if necessary, and while the pie is being prepared, sit down in contemplation, enjoying the spirit of the wine and awaiting the descent of your Perfect Nature. It is also advisable to chant the names of the four elementals that guard the congress.

Alternatively, during this phase, you can use the names cited by Ibn Khaldun for calling upon the Perfect Nature, which are consistent with the more common six-fold summoning in the *Picatrix*, equating to the cardinal directions and above and below—or the horns, if you will.

These names can also be substituted in the entirety of the ritual and are as follows:

TAMAGHIS—BA'DAN—YASWADDA—
WAGHDAS—NAWFANA—GHADIS

You will then consume parts of the pie and give parts of it as gifts to friends and neighbours.

The Perfect Nature, the Familiar Daimon, and Orí

It is quite striking how similar the idea of the Perfect Nature is to the Socratic daimon and to the concept of *Orí* amongst the Yoruba-speaking people in West Africa. Let us first examine the idea of the daimon, also known as the familiar. The origin of the word is difficult to ascertain, but we know that Empedocles in his discourse about the psyche or soul, as early as the fifth century BC, described the daimon as the true self. Heraclitus sheds even more light on this, stating that a person's character is their daimon. The culmination of these thoughts is expressed by Plato, who says:

> *...regarding the supreme form of soul in us, we must conceive that the god has conferred it upon each...as a guiding genius (daimon)—that which...lifts us from earth towards our celestial affinity, like a plant whose roots are not in the earth, but in the heavens.*

As we see, the concepts of daimon and genius are considered the same. For the Romans, the genius was understood to be a tutelary deity, just like the familiar daimon. The Latin root, *genere,* "to generate," is used to describe a generative process of the person in question and was understood to be an external and incorporeal extension of a person, the spirit of their destiny, so to speak. Socrates viewed the daimon as a companion and guide, a quite interesting phrasing as we shall see in the next chapter. Naturally, genius gave its name to the genii, and it is the same word, related to one's true character, that today signifies the spectacular mental capacity we refer to as genius.

Psychologist Dr. Sanford asserts that the cooperation of the ego is required if the daimon/genius is to operate successfully.[123] From the perspective of ego psychology, this makes sense. Yet, this divine aspect of personality may be perceived to operate through the ego, whether the ego is aware of it or not. When we speak of one's "calling," in that context, we do not simply refer to one's profession but rather to the fundamental character, orientation, and activity of the ego, in which the daimon/genius is immanent. The concept is useful because it helps us appreciate the complexities of self-expression in terms of both the personal and the transcendent.

Similar ideas to those concerning the nature of one's genius/daimon/character are at the core of the Yoruba Wisdom tradition, Ifá. Therefore, let us delve into some depth on this, as it will clarify the amazing importance of our Perfect Nature or genius. These ideas harmonise with those presented by Porphyry, Iamblicus, and Proclus. I have chosen to illustrate the concept of the daimon and Perfect Nature in reference to Ifá, both because it offers a more global perception of where we can find the Cunning Craft, and the simplicity and elegance of Ifá makes it easy to see how these Yoruba ideas are also found elsewhere in the world.

Among the Yoruba, the idea of "self" is intimately connected to the relationship between the material and celestial world in ways similar to what we find in the monism of Advaita Vedanta. This concept is known as Orí, which means "to receive myself" and is considered to be the spirit of the Inner Self.[124] This spirit of Inner Self is in Ifá understood to be a spirit unique to our human manifestation that follows and guides us in life, similar to the *fylgja* in Nordic traditions and similar to the Socratic daemon Apuleius writes about in *On the God of Socrates*. The twelfth century poet and philosopher Bernard Silvestris, in his *The Cosmographia*, defines this daimon as an intelligence that comes into being together

[123] E. C. Sanford, *Psychology and Physics* (The Psychological Review, 1903).

[124] Awo Falokun, *Ìbà 'se Òrìsà* (Original Publications, 1994) p.85.

with the soul and will watch and guard over the ensouled being. It is a genius that uses dreams, signs, augurs and inspiration to speak with the soul of the being it is guarding.[125] Silvestris in his neo-Platonic treatise envisions the same relationship as for the ensouled man to be similar with all ensouled things from Nous, the Divine Mind that generates the Endelechia or Universal Soul until any ensouled being in any kingdom, spiritual, animal, or the sylvan realms of plants and woods. This means there is no qualitative difference between anything that possess the divine nous, and all things are alive with divine power. This suggests, as in the philosophy of Ifá, that all things ensouled are accompanied by a daimonic force—the spirit of its consciousness. Let's discuss in some more detail this concept as it is explained in Ifá.

Orí is, at the same time, a person's consciousness, their physical head, and also their most important Òrìsá. Orí can be reminiscent of the idea of a person's Holy Guardian Angel or Socratic daimon, as it is one's personal protective deity that oversees each individual's evolution and assists them in their journey on Earth and the return to Órun. Due to this, Orí is considered to be the most arcane and ancient of all the deities created in Órun, and the most decisive of all deities. Without consciousness, there can be no perception. Orí is further composed of the following segments:

1. *Orí ode*, which signifies the physical head.

2. *Orí inú* refers to the inner head, signifying all forms of consciousness, perception, and our experience of identity and selfhood. The Orí inú is further segmented into two parts: *Apárí-inú* and *Orí Àpeere.*

Apárí-inú pertains to the seat of one's inner consciousness. This aspect of consciousness is responsible for cultivating one's character, which is one of the most conspicuous tasks for our personal Orí to perform—namely, to develop good character. Only by developing good character can one attract good fortune to their life. The development of

125 Winthrop Wetherbee, The Cosmographia of Bernardus Silvestris (Columbia University Press, 1973) p.107.

good character is intimately connected to being conscious. Ifá speaks in this regard about the importance of being conscious of all good and bad things that happen in life. The bad things serve to harden one's integrity and character, providing the lesson that life is indeed a challenge, and it is the way we perceive these challenges that makes the difference between developing good character or not.

This idea is again related to another concept known as *Èrí okàn,* which means "the testimony of the heart." One could say that this concept carries with it the key to unlocking the condition of one's consciousness that enables the development of one's character.

The other concept, *Orí ápeere,* speaks about the standards of Odù's creation and refers to the alignment, the particular àsé, inherited within all that is created. For instance, the element of Water remains the same element but takes on various forms depending on whether it is found within clouds, ponds, beneath the earth, or within creatures on the earth. This means that each and every one is more prone to exhibit a specific elemental feature depending on their constitution, creating diversity among all things created, or variations within the "sameness," if you will. This concept is also related to the transmigration of souls and is, as such, the source of divine afflatus, responsible for incarnating and setting limits on the various forms of consciousness.

Incarnation, transmigration, and related terms naturally raise questions about death, the afterlife, and the nature of the soul. In this regard, Ifá teaches that each soul pre-exists in Òrun. This purely esoteric concept speaks about the elevation of selfhood through successive visits to the Earth. Ifá maintains the view that the invisible abode is our true home. This process of constant purification or elevation is called *Ìpònrì.* This term denotes the circle of incarnations, *atunwa,* and is related to the goal of human incarnations ending in *Àpeere,* denoting perfection or rather an ongoing spiritual transformation until perfection. This concept touches the heart of Ifá, as it speaks about one's destiny and character.

A significant aspect of Àpeere is its connection to destiny. There are two significant aspects to destiny, *Ipin.* The first is called *Àyànmó,* the aspects of one's destiny that are fixed and unchangeable. The second is called *Àkúnlèyan,* the changeable factors related to the development of good character and, therefore, to good fortune. Good character is developed by demonstrating honesty, humility, generosity, honour, wisdom, and kindness—traits believed to evoke benevolence from divine beings, which in turn leads one on their path of destiny. Ifá states in numerous verses the importance of good character, *ìwà pèlè,* as the source for all good things in life—especially wealth, prestige, and prosperity. It is common to consider a person who has achieved good character as cool-minded and calm in the face of joy and sorrow alike, marked by moderation and *ìwà rèrè,* a state of joyful contentment.

The Orí, as the seat for character and guidance from beyond, summarised in the development of one's self, is only one of the factors under the domain of Orí. In addition, there are three centres where spiritual congress or possession by the spirit is made possible. These centres are as follows:

Iwájú Orí refers to a powerful centre within the brow, where the "third eye" is located. This point is said to be the source of divine inspiration and the centre responsible for developing one's character.

Àtàrí is the centre found in the crown of the skull. In Ifá, this centre is referred to *as Láyé-láyé* or *laílaí* and signifies a state in which one experiences the source of creation. One's being merges beyond the confines of time and space and enters into communion with the essence of origin. It is in this realm that the wisdom of Odù is retrieved and, in turn, made manifest by the Babalawo. This centre is activated more strongly as the Babalawo practises the tradition and seeks to unveil destiny and secrets resting within the fabric of creation. During divination, the Awó activates this centre and is said to return, to some degree, to the time when Òrúnmìlà, the "Prophet of Ifá," walked the earth, thus releasing àsé. This àsé can also manifest in the form of visions and dreams, as well as deep insight into the complexity of situations. It is a condition or state beyond the intellectual and relativistic reality, as it is of a purely mystical nature, well-aided by prayers, enchantments, and mysteries embedded in poetry.

Ìpàkó signifies the point in the nape of the neck where the older portion of the human brain is found. This point connects us not only to a variety of animal forms but also to the natural powers of nature, which are usually referred to as *Òrìsà*. Mystical vision can also flow from this point, but it carries a different state of being as it operates on more tangible forces than in the state of Àtàrí and is more easily connected to than laílaí. This centre is also activated by prayers, songs, music, and rhythm, facilitating possession by divine beings that enter the body and consciousness of the worshipper, taking control over the person and using them as a medium for interaction with others.

By delving into such depth on this topic and presenting it from an unexpected angle, I hope to shed light on the mechanisms that enable what we call witchcraft to function. As we can see, the metaphysical explanation of consciousness and its powers and needs from a Yoruban perspective presents a remarkable image of humans as a symbol of the cosmos and all its potential. But let us now return to the Western world and examine the simple symbol of the Sun, the point surrounded by a circle. We should note that we need to move beyond the purely direct association with the Sun and instead recognise the symbolic value of a still point and the landscape it generates, much like our Sun does for us as it constitutes the esoteric North in our geocentric perception of the world.

The Point and the Circle

The Wheel of the Year and the Sabbaths are perhaps the greatest hallmarks of modern witchcraft. But what does it actually mean to trace a circle clockwise and widdershins? Many myths and unfounded ideas have been generated based on the Sabbath. Clearly, the observance of the turning tides, marked by the Sun entering the cardinal signs, as the four seasons begin and end here is of note. Ensuring the stability of the seasons and performing rituals for rain and crop fertility were crucial for agricultural societies and, by extension, those who depended on the earth's bounty. However, the meaning of the circle as sacred space needs to be established in relation to the point or pole that marks the sacred centre. The pole star symbolises the sacred centre in the form of the cosmic North, the dwelling of the Hyperborean Apollo and the Hidden Imam.

The circle is defined according to its centre or origin. This formless point of departure is the source of all things and the landscapes—or circles—that arise from it. This formless centre is indivisible and represents Unity in every sense. Thus, the point is the focus, and the circle is the world generated by the point or pole. This means that a false point can generate an equally false landscape. Walking the circle simply means observing the stages of the Sun as it moves widdershins through the zodiacal signs, bringing changes to the earth. We should also remember that any circular form represents celestial spheres, while every square represents the earth. The Masonic expression of squaring the circle refers to bringing Heaven upon the Earth. The relationship between point, circle, and Sun is evident in the alchemical and astrological symbol for the Sun: a centre within a perfect circle. The cross in the circle marks the cardinal stations of the Sun's journey, while the octagon, which has become an increasingly common representation of Craft mysteries, is closer to the circle than the square. Bringing forth the eight quarters generates the model of the Rota Mundi or Rosa Mundi found in Rosicrucian symbolism. This symbolism bears striking similarities to the Horologium, the "timepiece," in Athens. This tower for measuring time was erected around 50 BC by Andronicus of Cyrrhus and is an octagonal structure also known as the Tower of the Winds. Each of its eight sides carries inscriptions dedicated to the eight winds: Boreas for the North, Kaikias for the North-East, Eurus for the East, Apeliotes for the South-East, Notus for the South, Lips for the South-West, Zephyrus for the West, and Skiron for the North-West.

The eight winds, illustrated on page 152, are associated with the eight angels in accordance with Psalm 104, which tells us that light is the centre and from this light, rays of fire and air are sent forth, along with "those who walked upon the wings of the wind" —the angels.[126] The number eight is also significant in reference to the Eighth Sphere, the dwelling of Seth, the perfected one, where we find the fixed stars, the highest sphere. In Agrippa's correspondences, grace and misery, corruption and incorruption, are all related to this number as if it were the edge of unity. Squaring the circle into eight parts generates the intermediary world, the meeting point between the terrestrial and

---

126 Pedro de Medina, *Arte Del Navegar* (Valladolid, 1545).

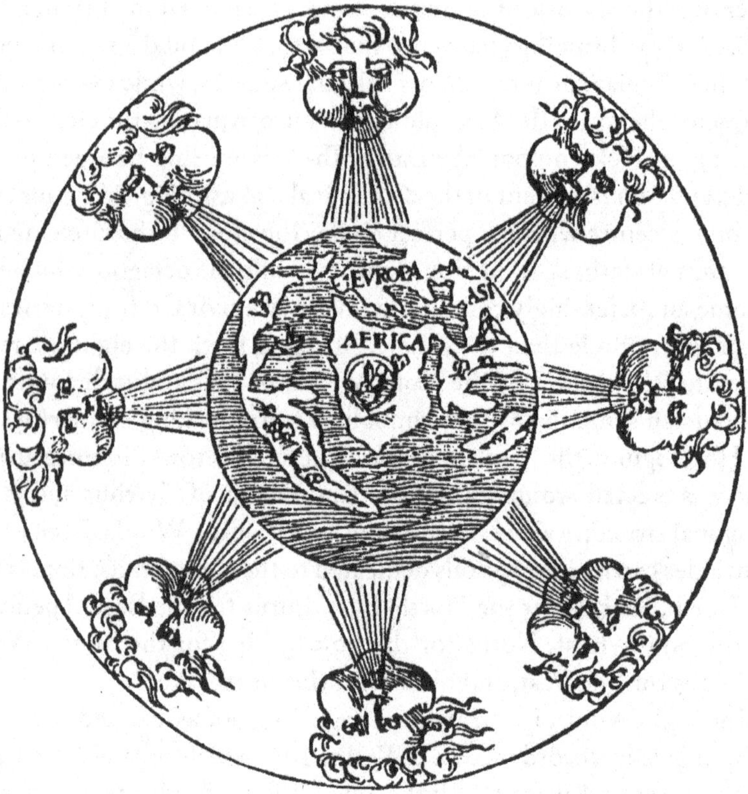
EVROPA
ASIA
AFRICA

celestial worlds. We might say that the eight winds represent the passage from the terrestrial to the celestial world, just like the rose represents the secret hidden within the tower of the eight winds, or the mystery of the rose, protected by eight angelic messengers.

These are, in very brief terms, the ideas contained in the traditional notions of the circle and its meaning. The division of the circle into quarters simply represents the becoming of the point. Observing the physical manifestation of the Sun and its influence on the seasons, we see that squaring the circle into four parts, thereby creating the four cardinal directions, is a completely terrestrial organisation, while squaring into eight carries a different value.

This blending of the celestial and terrestrial is quite evident in contemporary Druidism, where a circle is made, typically with a portal to the circle, and a square stone altar erected. Through its construction, this ritual symbolism connects the axis from heaven to earth, as the ritualist enters the sphere of heaven and then focuses on the earth as a point of entry. The use of stones and their meaning is also significant. It is worth noting the black square Kaaba-stone in Mecca and the Oygigigi of the Yoruba, regarded as the source of the cosmic centre. Nowadays, little thought is given to the meaning of erecting a stone in a burial ground, but the stone is, in truth, the mountain of ascent. Functionally, the stone is akin to the pole or axis, as it connects ancestry to the sacred centre.

The Compass and the Journey of the Soul

The compass is not the circle, the compass is a tool for spiritual direction. Each of the magical squares of the planets are also referred to as "compasses." To strike a compass means to establish sacred space or one's circumstances for generating the way of ascent. The point and the circle establish particular ways of unfolding the sacred centre, while the compass is used to obtain specific intimacy with a particular power. The compass is an instrument of navigation and orientation that points toward the magnetic North, just as the Muslim Qibla compass points toward the spiritual North, Mecca. The Masonic reference to the compass in terms of a building refers to the curved or crooked line that was often the blueprint for the building itself. As such, we should understand the use of the word compass in a craft sense as the laying out of the blueprint that points towards the spiritual centre, the Hyperborean realms. Even today, this instrument of navigation is referred to as the compass rose, and sailors lost at sea always had the option of navigating guided by stars—particularly Polaris. This position also represents the spiritual North, the *Lux mundi,* where the Light descends and calls us back to the original, unfallen state by means of the ladder of light.

The many feast days before and after the winter solstice, the day of Sol Invictus, such as Saturnalia and Larentalia, have the specific function of creating movement and preparing this ladder of light for return. This is also disclosed in the importance of Ursa Major, or the Plough, at this time, being related to Saturn-Sator as the Bull of Heaven and associated with this constellation. These seven stars are also associated with the seven poles of heaven, the guardians of the Hidden Imam. The Plough has the significance of opening the way and indicates the agricultural importance for the fundamentals of hexencraft, or Venus-craft, as we can also call the arts of the countryside. We even see this today in Yule celebrations, where the Christmas tree with its star crowning it is certainly related to the ascent along the axis mundi to the spiritual North, the Polestar. It is not insignificant that Yule has been given the day of Sol Invictus, as here the cosmic law has again reaffirmed the light vault of the Hidden Imam as the point of the world.

We see here the traditional reasons for the eighth and Northern quarter to be a gate of silence and darkness, as here at the gate of the world we access the unmanifested potentiality of all things. Howard and Jackson comment in *The Pillars of Tubal Cain* that:

> *The celestial pole is the secret behind the symbolism of the four-sided spinning castle of the witch goddess. This turns eternally at the heart of heaven and is the gateway to Hyperborea, or the land beyond the north wind. For the initiate of the Mysteries, Polaris is symbolically the sword point, the City of Enoch and Cain, the Iron Star, the Celestial Nail, and the stellar suture in the skull-dome of Heaven, the gateway to the Great Beyond.*[127]

---

[127] Michael Howard and Nigel Jackson, *The Pillars of Tubal-Cain* (Capall Bann, 2000).

This explanation only scratches the surface of the complexity involved in this mystery. The spinning movements of the Queen's castle create a circular motion, revealing the mystery of the rose in the Tower of the Eight Winds to be the gate itself. Lady Venus' motivation for the spinning sets the point and circle in motion, guided by the north star, and from the gate of silence, the formless powers of Light and unity come into being. The tower, its eight airy angels, and the Rose Queen in its centre become a design and compass for the soul's journey back home through the gates of becoming whole again, signifying a return to the Golden Age and the City of Heroes that is the stars in heaven's skull-dome. Similar ideas are found in secret conclaves of the Art in southern France and northern Italy, as well as in the ideas expressed in Haitian Vodou concerning Ville aux Champs, the City of Heroes.

It is also worth noting that north on the wind rose or compass rose used to be marked by the letter T, for *tramontina.* However, "T" is also the Tau cross, Trident, crossroad, or witches' foot. In the fourteenth century, Columbus replaced the T with a fleur-de-lis, which is yet another significant detail, especially considering its use among hidden companies of French pedigree attuned to the mysteries of the undead and French and Spanish monarchs. There is also a timely reference to Mary as the *lilium inter spinas,* "the lily among thorns," as spoken of in the *Song of Songs.* This refers to the importance of the feminine and, by extension, indicates the significance of the relationship between Venus and Luna for the witchcraft mysteries. Choosing the image of a lily instead of the natural flower among thorns, the rose, might indicate the lunar quality of the mystery, as the Moon is the mirror and earth-bringer of celestial influences. The lily is not only a lunar symbol of chastity or virginity in the sense of incorruptibility, but it is also a toxic plant from which the word *delirium* is derived, literally, "from the lily."

The Hebrew *lulav* is a similar design to the fleur-de-lis, made from palm fronds, myrtle, and willow—woods traditionally ascribed to Venus and the Moon. The palm fronds carry multiple meanings, ranging from hiddenness and justice to strength and uprightness, and are often used to decorate the chamber of initiation in many African cults. In art throughout the Middle Ages, the lily was often held by virginal women of strong spiritual aspiration in aristocratic or mystical marriages. We also see the later Latin misspelling of fleur-de-lis as *fleur-de-luce*, "flower of light," which, despite its erroneous etymology, translates the sense of the flower's meaning as being the spiritual light in the hand of the Virgin.

The hidden French convent dedicated to the mysteries of Luna, as she ignites the power of shapeshifting and immortality in the Brotherhood of the Black Lily, also made use of the fleur-de-lis. This was probably because of its multiple references to the state of delirium accompanying the lycanthropic transformation, but also because of its relation to the light of immortality, as found in the star-covered skull-vault of the heavens. This is even replicated in the shield said to belong to one of the families reputed to be part of this convent, a wolf's claw around a pole with the word *on*, meaning "light," written around it. It is also noteworthy that the Black Madonna of Chestochowa is draped in a black cloak covered with golden fleur-de-lis, as is the reference to the custom of branding criminals and witches with this symbol in France, as well as its use among some Franco-Masonic brethren, perhaps most notably Dumas and his Three Musketeers.

The Rite of the Wind Rose

As we have seen, the rose and the compass are indicative of the soul's journey, with the whirling tower of the Queen lying at the heart of the eight winds, the point of return. This rite can be performed either outside on green grass or by using a green altar cloth on a square table. To begin, you will need to fashion a witch's foot from willow, myrtle, and whitethorn, and gather nine roses. Eight of the roses should be pointed in each of the eight directions, with the flower pointing to the compass edge. The ninth rose should have its stem removed and be placed at the centre of the table on top of the witch's foot. You will also need to present a single lily to your left and a chalice of red wine to your right, as well as burn benzoin, rose, and myrrh. Fumigate yourself and the table well, leaving the censer hanging in the north point.

Next, take eight candles—four white for each cardinal direction and four red for the mid-quarters—and anoint them with olive oil. Inscribe the name of each wind on the candle with a wooden quill, preferably made from a nutty tree or whitethorn. Place the candles in their appropriate quarters, leaving the centre either dark or lit by an oil lamp.

Once you have prepared the space, present your petition to the Queen by knocking on the table three times and say:

Fair Queen who holds the great lights in her hands
I stand here in the wilderness of All to seek thy comfort.
Grant me access to thy kingdom
I am here with my heart in my hand
Coming from the ruddy fields to seek thy comfort.

Turn to the North and see there an angel dressed in a heavy black cloth, holding a twisted conch in his hand. Call him by his name: *Boreas.*

Then, turn to the Northeast and see here an angel holding a shield decorated with many symbols of various kinds. Call him by his name: *Kaikias.*

Then, turn to the East and see here an angel holding a clock filled with the abundance of the earth, fruits, and grains, and call him by his name: *Apeliotes.*

Then, turn to the Southeast seeing here a mighty angel using as a shield his heavy cloth to defend against the elements, and call him by his name: *Euros.*

Then, turn towards the South and see here a gentle angel pouring out from his jar a river of fresh water, and call him by his name: *Notos.*

Then, turn towards the Southwest and see here an angel in the form of a boy-child who sustains the mast of a ship and holds the evil winds at bay, and call him by his name: *Lips.*

Then, turn towards the West, see here a youthful angel with flowers in his hair, and call him by his name: *Zephyros.*

Then, turn towards the Northwest and see here an angel with a bearded face holding a pot of bronze filled with hot ashes and burning charcoal. Call him by his name: *Skiron.*

Allow yourself to see the Queen seated in the heart of the rose, resting on the witches' foot, and pray to the winds to guide your journey towards the Tower of the Eight Winds. Let the eight angels lead you on your journey.

CHAPTER SEVEN

THE SILVER KEY AND THE VEIL OF NIGHT

"I am a brother to dragons, and a companion to owls."
—Job 30:29

As we delve into the mysteries of the night, we also enter the realms of fear and prejudice. The night veils all things in its mysterious embrace, making what happens under its cover secret, occult, and hidden. Whilst the Sun was the heavenly luminary ascribed to God, the Truth, and the Church, the Moon was of a more ambiguous, inconstant, and dubious nature. The persecution of the Waldensians and Cathars for heresy in the thirteenth century was not only because they challenged the Church on issues like poverty and possession, but also because these heretical cults sought out the mystery of the free spirit in rituals done behind closed doors, often at night.[128]

The ruler of the night is the Moon, the second luminary of the heavens, a feminine, nocturnal, cold, and moist planet according to the astrologer William Lilly (1602–1681), who happened to be a good friend of Elias Ashmole.[129] The Moon rules over women in general, female aristocrats, sailors, millers, alewives, midwives, nurses, and brewers, among others. In addition, the Moon shares rulership over witch-plants like mandrake

---

128 Jennifer Kolpacoff Deane, *A History of Medieval Heresy and Inquisition.* (Rowman & Littlefield Pub, 2011) pp.6, 69.

129 "William Lilly on the Planets." *Chronos Speaks.* https:// chronosspeaks.com/william-lilly-on-the-planets/

with Saturn, the great cold and distant malefic of melancholy, while the Moon herself rules over the poppy and the mushroom. Another planet of night and women, Venus, is also important to consider here, as she rises as the herald to the Moon and follows the Moon to the western shores of her descent. Venus is a nocturnal and moist planet herself, and as previously discussed, the ruler of all things venereal and the owner of *venefica.* Or, as William Lilly described her: "Common people call her the morning Star, and the learned Lucifer, when she is seen long before the rising of the Sun."[130]

Hence, we see how women, the amatory arts, night and shadows, the nocturnal and moist rays of Venus and the Moon in the realm of Saturn generated a certain discomfort, as in this realm was found the "free soul" that Pope John XXII (1244–1334) saw as the greatest threat to the Roman and Catholic faith in his time.[131] The mysteries of night, of the erotic, and what lies occult under the rule of the Moon and Venus, were the realm of *venefica:* of intoxication, madness, and witches. The figure who proudly absorbed all of these negative epitaphs was Lilith. Isaiah 34:14 describes her as a screech owl that finds her rest among savages and sexual creatures in the wastelands: "The wild beasts of the desert shall also meet with the wild beasts of the island, and the satyr shall cry to his fellow; the screech owl also shall rest there and find for herself a place of rest."

Lilith has been associated with the idea of "witchcraft" as a queen, demoness, vampire, or spirit of lustful vice, with all of these ideas holding a part of her mystery. However, for the cunning one, she represents the witch-mother herself, who, with the fallen host and their offspring, gave the fair daughters of Cain and Seth this special blood that generated the different seed in the world—giving rise to the cunning ones. Lilith, as the first blood spread by many a fallen and wanton angel, ensured that these fallen embers spread in great quantity to lie dormant, awaiting the awakening of their seed in whatever way would move their gestation into self-recognition.

Lilith is the "cosmo-mathematical" antithesis of God, meaning that she is the negative balance to this positive force. When we use words like "negative" and "positive," they are not used in the sense of hierarchical, moral, or qualitative differences, but as a simple way to denote a polar

---

130 William Lilly, *Christian Astrology* (Regulus, 1647/1985) p.73.

131 Alain Boureau, *Satan the Heretic* (University of Chicago Press, 2006).

opposition, much like day and night and the Sun and the Moon are opposite to each other in the same realm. Hence, it follows that apophatic theology, or what is better known as the *via negative,* would be the better approach for closing in on the mysterious Lilith—it is silence, absence, and negation that drive forth the experience of this mystery.

Currently, the idea of "witchcraft" is quite varied and diverse, and to such an extent that we might state that all these forms of "witchcraft" hold merit in one way or the other. Followers of the old persuasion have a tendency to "fly away" from any attempt at definition, and instead, favour the term "the Nameless Art," yet, it is not that simple—the cunning arts never were.

"Witchcraft" is a word largely derived from an understanding of what wicked women were doing in the Middle Ages, a label created by those seeking to reject and expel a category of people. Hence, in relation to Lilith's rejection by Adam, her epitaph as "witch-queen" is quite fitting. At the time the label "witchcraft" was coined, it rapidly became a generic idea for all sorts of *maleficia* and crime, perhaps giving it way too much context. The craft of the witch was predominantly related to liaisons with the diabolic and with the plants and spirits of the wild which gave the witch the ability to effectuate supernatural acts, necromancy, and soothsaying. It still remains to this day that these abilities were made possible by the witch's *famulus,* or familiar, which was largely perceived as a devil. Today, we find that these criteria are often abandoned in favour of sentimentalism and historical nostalgia that focuses on the shunned pagan outsider within the context of the greater accepted social fabric. This nostalgia is radically different from the "witches' nostalgia" that concerns the sacred return to the Golden Age by virtue of the Sabbath, the place where the concept of linear time dissolves in freedom of awareness itself and the resulting sense of connection. Hence, this is encoded in the true meaning of "turning the tides" and going "against the grain," which is the work of restoration and return, *not* the entry into a temporal antinomian rebellion with the social order.

The mage and philosopher Fulvio Rendhell deserves praise for being one of the few to lift the veil of mystery surrounding the domain of the Spirit of Holiness.[132] He revealed how the "Lilithian theme" has been present throughout time from Mesopotamia to modern times, with her

---

132 For an in-depth analysis of his work, see Frisvold, *The Canticles of Lilith* (Troy Books, 2021).

presence appearing in the most unlikely corners of creation. Her form and reputation in the *Alphabet of Ben Shira* in the tenth century, as well as in the mystical and profound interpretations by the Kohen brothers in the thirteenth century, further deepen our understanding of Lilith. She who was and still is the power that holds the heavens together has, unfortunately, been debased as a satanic harlot and the mother of demons, born by stolen sperm. Recently, she has also been portrayed as an archetype of the "dark feminine," used to explain psychological processes that result from abuse, which is actually quite alien to her divine function. As a result, the discovery of the mathematical lunar position called the Black Moon or Lilith has been associated with similarly malefic interpretations.

In fact, the mysteries revealing the identity of Lilith can be found in the commentaries on the Book of Prophecies attributed to Isaiah, where she is referred to as a "tortuous serpent" along with Samael as the "crooked serpent." The book also describes Lilith inhabiting deserted places and ruins and being equated with the screech owl. Familiarity with Islamic lore reveals that she inhabits the same domain as the Djinn, and by extension, we can assume that she is of a similar nature, being of fire, the fire of the Holy Spirit itself. Fire is purgative, as in the infernal halls of Hell, but it is also the nature of the Divine Mind. The fire can strike upwards or downwards, like the serpent-fire in the body, which rests coiled around the root, and can strike upwards to unleash enlightenment or downward to ignite passion, relating to its original meaning of "suffering."

Contemporary analysts of Lilith's nature have essentially fallen into two types of error. The first suggests that the root of her name, *lil,* refers to the hostile spirits of the air, the *lilins,* who are solely understood based on their maleficence and not on their function in the divine design. The other error is to associate her with the psychological "shadow," understood as a deified form of all the depravity we hide from ourselves and refuse to accept, dislocating her from the greater design by reduction to a function of the human psyche. In the words of the Kohen brothers, "happy is he who understands these things as they are."[133]

The whole enigma is contained within the letter Aleph, which represents the polar axis and the point above and below it, as well as its

[133] The Kohen Brothers, *The Early Kabbalah* (Paulist Press, 1986). Edited by Joseph Dan.

turning, spiralling motion, like the axis mundi of the Earth. Aleph is the world, and by its very nature, it does not denigrate the left in favour of the right but recognizes that both the left and the right are entrusted to the central pole they are generated from and sustain. Since Lilith is the space between the stars, the power that creates or destroys creation, the antimatter, or the power that generates black holes, then we understand her as poorly as we understand the function and reasons behind these phenomena. We can rightly speak about a Lilithian theme that stretches from Mesopotamia and Ishtar, and spreads through the world in fine veins, giving its blood to Niritti and Bhairavi, Hel and Freya, the mother of the Djinns, and even to the Holy Spirit itself, where she manifests at the longest and shortest nights during the telluric turn. She is also Algol and Pleiades, Virgo and Venus. She is the power of cataclysmic possibility and the secret of immortality.

We see a similar transition with Hecate, and we shall focus on the format in which she emerged from the time of Plutarch, the Orphic and Homeric Hymns(around 500 BC). In the Homeric Hymn to Demeter, Hecate is mentioned as the *propolos* and *opaōn* of Persephone, her companion and guide. All deities with the ability to lead a *katabasis*, a descent to the underworld, would naturally have mastery of the necromantic and funerary arts of *psychagōgia* or *goetia*—meaning Dionysius, Apollo, Orpheus, and Hermes would be of importance to the likes of Proserpina, Demeter, Core, and Hecate.

By the fifth century BC, Hecate was *megisté*, greatest, and in the company of Zeus and Cybele in the neighbouring Phrygian districts. We find here a multiplicity of aspects related to Hecate. Pausanias honoured her as "bringer of light," an epitaph more commonly used to honour Phosphorus. In the city of Lagina, she was honoured as *kleidos agōge*, "the processor of the key," and honoured most of all as a protector of cities and gates, hence the importance of the blade in her triformis representation. In the city of Thasos, she was placed at each of the city's three gates, and in Rhodes, she was worshipped alongside Apollo and Hermes.

The transition of Hecate from an honoured bringer of light and protector of the mistress of ghosts and a nocturnal patron of the outcast was related to the growing interest in metempsychosis, or reincarnation, and accordingly, speculations about how life and circumstances affected the transmigration of the soul into a new corporeal vessel. Hecate, as the patron of midwives and maidens, had a particular importance in the safe delivery of infants. Hence, an anomaly, like the death of a child, resulted in consequences both for the mother and the child, but the same suspicion was also aimed at women who died before they became mothers. It was conceived to be a form of malediction. In the same way, Hecate's reputation started to wane and change until she was seen as a patron for the outcast and the vile ghosts of the night. She was found at the crossroads of night, and was found at boneyards in association with *skia,* vile souls who turned into angry ghosts, and *aōrai,* literally "someone who dies too young."

There was also a vengeful class of ghosts called *alastōr* that was intimately linked with early death and the failure to fulfil one's destiny, or "human mission." From this, a strong belief in the existence of malevolent female ghosts grew, threatening unborn children and young maidens, which led to the proliferation of amulets against *gelloudes* (hostile female ghosts), as well as *strix, lamiae,* and *mormō.* Hecate, as a gatekeeper, especially to the Underworld, naturally took on many of these vengeful and cold nocturnal aspects. However, her grace and majesty lives on in her tripartite representation of three faces, with Key, Blade, and Torch. She is at the same time the holder of the key, the protectress, and the light-bringer. This transition is similar to what happened to Lilith, who today is seen either as a vile bloodthirsty demoness or a depraved feminist symbol of dominance over male abuse.

It is interesting to note that the three animals sacred to Hecate: the black sow, the mare, and the dog. These animals are associated with second sight (dogs), travel between worlds (horses), nightmares (pigs), with all of them related to fertility and lust. As the companion and guide of Persephone, Hecate is a worthy icon for anyone who seeks to travel the Hel-way. Interestingly, these same animals are also in a particular relationship with Oðin, another traveller of the in-between.

Skin-leaping and the Art of the Undead

The Sabbath of the Witches, night-flight, and their diabolic orgies are elements that have been associated with the idea of witchcraft since the fifteenth century. Perhaps it is here that the similarities between the witch and the vampire-traveller can be found. Since the time of Roman writers Apuleius and Ovid, night-flight has been linked to witches, conveyed through the terms *strix* and *striga,* which are still found in Romanian as *Strigoii,* akin to *Varcolac* or "wolf-coats." This concept also lives on in Latin lands under the term *stregoni.* In Romanian mythology, the term *strigele* denotes the floating lights found in forests and mountains that circle around trees of power on specific powerful nights. These lights were believed to be the fetch bodies of witches, either exorcised or convening in the Sabbath. It is also worth mentioning the remnants of myths that tell how nine spindles are placed on the grave where the strigoi is believed to rest, as the power of the Fates and their spinning of the silver thread of night travel was believed to stop it from rising at night.

The relationship between vampires, wolves, and witches found in myths all over the continent is striking, especially in Slavic regions. The motive indicates that stregonis were intimately linked to earth and air. In life, they set out in the coat of Saturn's beast, the wolf, rising from Saturn's bed of moist, cold earth and from the death-like slumber in the shades of Night. Upon death of the physical body, they went out as bats and birds of night, especially owls.

This mystery is better explained by looking closely at Oðin, as here we find a very complete format for understanding the complexity of the vampire-witch. Fylgja (or fetch), Hugr, and Hamingja are the elements in the esoteric anatomy of the vampyri night. It is also worth mentioning the special band of warriors, alternatively called berserker or *Einherjer,* that was considered to be under the special protection of Oðin. These warriors often wore coats of wolf fur and were well-versed in the arts of Freya (*seidr*). They dedicated their spiritual attention to Oðin as a patron of wisdom and wizardry. These warriors were those who died in combat, and it is said that they continued their battles in Valhalla. Every day they rose to battle, while at night they sat at Oðin's table in Valhalla to eat the flesh of the pig Saerimne and drink mjöd from the goat Heidrun, who lives on Valhalla's roof. These warriors were particularly favoured by Oðin, as they were the bravest who died in battle, picked up by the valkyries and brought to Oðin. Oðin prepares these warriors for the battle of the gods at the hill of Vigrid. Some of these warriors are also taken to Folkvang, Freya's farm. We might say that this special warrior band was "dressing their fetch" in the sense of the *fylgja,* the animal familiar. Warriors were always considered to have a fylgja that was of an aggressive or fear-inspiring nature, such as a wolf or bear.

We might suggest that these special groups were brought together by their familiars, like the berserkers who shared the bear form and the Einherjer who shared the wolf.

We should also mention *ham*, or *hamingja*, which directly relates to the skin, veil, or dress. The ability to change *ham* was considered a particular gift related to magical abilities and, in particular, to provide fertility, and as such, related to *hug* or *hugr*, which is the power that manifests itself in Eros or love. *Hugr* is commonly understood to be a particular power possessed by sages and witches, the word itself denotes warm and passionate feelings, ultimately related to feelings of love and attraction. For instance, King Erik Aarsael, who was the king of the Swedes for only one year from 1087 to 1088, was said to possess this particular power. He was the last of the heathen kings and became a symbol of luck, given his stunning magical powers and ability to fertilize what was considered barren. The last blot in Uppsala was led by this king, and this crucial year places him in a particularly strong relationship with the whole retinue of the Vanir and Aesir, particularly Oðin and Freya, who had an affinity with *hugr*.

Legends of skin-leaping, shapeshifting, and lycanthropy are found everywhere in the world, from the jaguar-allied *canaima* in South America, to the were-boars in Turkey, to the more well-known wolf forms in Europe. In all instances, these myths contain elements of going against the natural order, often against the exoteric religious organization, or a theme of some unavoidable cosmic consequence—such as the special mark on the seventh child of a seventh child who was born accursed. The minister Robert Kirk, who wrote *The Secret Commonwealth*, was said to be the seventh son of a seventh son, curiously noting that he reported intimate dealings with the Sidhe of the local marshlands and hollow hills. The legends of King Lycaon, founder of the kingdom of Arcadia in the mountainous parts of Greece also demonstrates similar qualities. Lycaon was the father of the muse Callisto, and he was raising the son Nyctimus (night) who had been fathered by Zeus. Lycaon slaughtered Nyctimus and served this meat to Zeus. Zeus, appalled by this bizarre offering cursed Lycaon by turning him into a wolf. Pausanias presents a slightly different version of the myth; here, we are told that Lycaon sacrificed a child on the altar of Zeus and the child turned into a wolf. There are several various explanations for this phenomenon, ranging from lycanthropy becoming a reality due to intentional or accidental offense of Zeus to Zeus simply usurping Lycaon's sanctuary. What we do find tied to lycanthropy and other forms of shapeshifting is that certain conditions need to be in place, like seasons and moon phases. The full moon is well known to be the force that causes a transformation from human to beast, as the Moon is also watching over the related phenomena of vampirism and, by virtue of transformation and flight, tied to the mysteries of the Sabbath.

The Power of the Moon

Let us now return to the significance of the Moon and her profound association with the mystery of night. Not only is she the heavenly light by night, but her waxing and waning play a crucial role in the ebb and flow of all fluids on earth, be they water or blood. All stellar rays enter through the Moon, particularly at night, and are imbued with a particular nuance as dictated by the Mother of Night. While all planets have a host of qualities associated with them, why is the Moon, the Mother of Pearls, linked to vampires and the undead? In Book I of *De Occulta Philosophia,* Chapter XXIV, Agrippa states that things under the power of the Moon include:

> *...monstrous blood, of which are made wonderful strange things by magicians; the civet cat also changing her sex, being obnoxious to diverse sorceries, and all animals that live in water as well as on land, as otters, and such prey upon fish. Also all monstrous beasts, such as without any manifest seed are equivocally generated, as mice; which sometimes are generated by coition, sometimes of the putrefaction of the earth.*

As we can see, the Moon is associated with the powers of traversing between realms, and any abnormalities related to water and blood fall under her power. References to the wonderworking properties of menstrual blood and generation by the putrefaction of the earth are significant, as are the Slavic tales that tell of vampires flying to the full moon and colouring it red with their hunger. Skin leapers are said to change into their familiar forms at the full moon, and insanity is said to rage high during its fullness, influencing all living beings with ecstasy and lust. It is interesting to keep in mind that each of the twenty-eight nights of the lunar cycle, during which the Moon moves through her gardens, possess different qualities, thus changeability is one of her essential characteristics.

In Book 3 of the *Picatrix,* there is a formula for enticing the Moon and requesting her favours. The text describes how one should dress like a young boy and perfume the working area with pleasant aromas while wearing a silver ring on the finger. The petition should be presented eloquently and ornately on the fourteenth day of the Moon's journey, while she is free from malefic influences and in a positive aspect with other significant planets. The reference to the fourteenth day likely refers to the fourteenth Mansion, *Al Simakh,* found in the last six degrees of Libra and the first four degrees of Scorpio, a mansion related to the fixed star Spica, which has the nature of Venus. Spica is considered to be highly beneficial, and here we see how a benign aspect between the Moon and Venus can generate wonderful possibilities for gaining gifts from Luna. The *Picatrix* also details how one should wash in scented water, and then turn one's face toward the Moon, saying:

> *May God save you, Luna, O Mistress who is happy, fortunate, cool and moist, even and beautiful. You are the head and the key of all the other planets, light in your movements, you who have a scintillating light, mistress of happiness and pleasure, of goodly speech, of excellent reputation, of fortunate kingdom. You are she who loves religion, who meditates upon the things of the world, full of subtlety in your thoughts. You love and cherish pleasures, songs, and pleasantries, mistress of ambassadors and envoys, skilled at revealing the mysteries. You are free and priceless; you are for us nearer than the other planets, you retransmit their light; by your bounty you improve them, whatever be their state. Everything in the world is beautiful when you are beautiful, and turns to evil when you are turned to evil. You are the beginning of things and their end. You have more nobility and honor than all the planets. This is why I make to you this request.*
>
> *And I conjure you by Celan, the angel that God has placed with you to manifest all your effects, to have mercy upon me, to accept my request, and by the humility that you have towards our Lord of greatness and towards his reign, to make a good reception to me in what I ask of you and for that which I petition you.*

> *I invoke you by all your names: Camar (al Qamar) in Arabic, Luna in Latin, Mehe in Phoenician, Zamahyl (Semele) in Greek, Cerim in Hindu, Celez in Roman, in order that you grant in this place my requests.*

The supplicant then prostrates on the ground and offers incense made from mastic, cardamom, juniper, storax, cinnamon, myrrh, and twenty-two other ingredients including apples, wine, and pine nuts to the Moon. It also follows how to make a Lunar remedy under this aspect which, in the right measurement, can serve as a *vinum sabbati.*

The recipe is as follows:

Gather laudanum, St. John's Wort, apple, roses, grape seeds, pumpkin seeds, lily root, dandelion root, spikenard and saffron, juniper, and cinnamon.

Steep this in wine, put aside for two weeks, strain, and let rest for the next time the Moon moves into the fourteenth Mansion.

Sol Niger & Luna Nigrans

To comprehend the darkness, one must become the Night, the Mercury of the philosophers must be brightened by the radiant Sulphur until what remains are the white bones of matter. At this point, a new Sun can dawn and the oceans of silver can flow freely again, ensouling the bones covered in eagle feathers. The mystery of the Lion's blackening is radical, and the dryness of the Silver is moist, yet many go astray, mistaking putrefaction for rottenness. The vessel breaks, and the foul mixture stains the matter, corrupting the path. The child does not see the crown and the lakes of Night are forgotten in the Dragon's flight. Lost is the valley of the lilies…the fountain is nowhere to be found. This is the pool of self-delusion and misconception that many seekers in search of the Sun and the Moon and the mystery of the Night that surrounds the Black Sun and Black Moon get lost in. The mystery is simple for those who see with the soul, for with the blackening of the Sun, the waters will flow freely back into the garden. It is a release and a return, becoming through ordeal, the mystery of the path becoming the double-headed serpent and the Lady of Milk.

The belief that the Black Goddess is our hidden and suppressed emotional life or unrestrained eroticism is a bewilderment in the land of the blind. Rather, one should turn their soul to the north and draw the flame of silver from the land of Power. Through the Green and the Red, one can be enthroned in the Castle of Silence, where flowers shall blossom from thy hand. The answer rests in the red caverns of one's closed soul, and this is a matter a million times true. To understand darkness, one must realize that it is the fabric of creation, the absence of light, the inhalation, and the annihilation. The fire of Need and the glowing coals of Mystery are veiled. This is the first realization of the moist path of Silver, where darkness is the nocturnal silver, moist and cold.

The Mystery of the Silver Night is often referred to as something pertaining to the subconscious, but this idea is erroneous. It is supra conscious, and the integration of this mystery on the basis of the subconscious is an illusion. One must look outside to the connectedness of all things, not within their own fragmented and veiled psyche. Humanity's modern psyche is a product of their belief in their own greatness and loss of spiritual connection. By these spiritual beings the essence of the natural world is seen as something that dwells in the psychic constitution of humankind. In many ways, this is right, but the modern perception is feeble and wrong. By Eros, one's Psyche is released, and it is not a microcosm in itself. It is the golden chain of being, its connectedness, that allows it to relate to all things through the sensorial apparatus. Only a person of Love and Soul can attract the natural and celestial sympathies. A person encapsulated in their own psyche and fabricated world will attract the sympathies of this construction that they live within. The Dark Goddess and the Black Sun turn into perversity and suicide while the Seeker believes they are unravelling inner secrets. Only from the temple of Venus, forged in the bond of Psyche and Eros, can the Seeker realize the radical paths that go against the grain. This is the eternal return, the dream made flesh.

In 1964, Robert Graves stated:

> *The Black Goddess is so far hardly more than a word of hope whispered amongst the few who have served their apprenticeship to the White Goddess. She promises a new pacific bond between man and woman, corresponding to a final reality of love.... She will lead man back to that sure instinct of love which he long ago forfeited by intellectual pride.*

The Black Goddess is the earth, and the Black Earth is Wisdom herself. She is the river of silver flowing over the blackness of the earth. She is Ishtar, who after seven steps stands naked in the halls of death to meet her fate by the hooks and crooks of the path. She is the Holy Spirit, Giver of Wisdom. She is the power released in sacred communion, the spirit of *maithuna.* She is the Star of all sacraments, and in her glorious manifestation, mankind is prone to place the right foot in the left path and condemn themselves.

To understand the Black Goddess, you need to blacken the Sun for the coming of the Queen. The king must fall at the foot of Her, his grave the wings of Crows, and her Mercy, the touch of Splendour. By this, the Sun is reborn, and the blackness is not only understood but integrated for the sake of Love. The Sun is you, your "I," and Psyche needs to blacken it. St. John of the Cross called this the dark night of the soul, where the putrefaction of all falsehood and misdirected selfishness is brought into the vessel of the Dragons. This is the secret of the North, where true power resides, and if you dare to approach power in its pure form, be well warned, journeyman, that the Path itself has fangs and swords where you expect there should be bricks and wells.

The Black Goddess is not your shameful sexual urges, your denials, and the dark ally of your psyche. She walks there and can rest there, but this awakening is not the Black Goddess, but her ordeal. She is the path's frustration and not the Path itself. She is the Black Light beyond the Emerald Castle, and as such, you cannot reach her unless you are beyond your Self. The only way is the blackening of the Sun, the annihilation of that identity you cling unto as if it was something real and precious. With the *nigredo* of the Sun comes the darkness seeping in, like silent sharks and birds of prey. And in this land, the Black Goddess is Queen, and it is here your release must be. When the Soul takes precedence, the feeling is one of death and despair, a sense of losing yourself—and indeed, losing yourself is what commences. By losing yourself to the Mercy of the Soul, you can be lost or found again. By the blackening of the Sun, Love enters, and in a land where Love is a stranger, the return is painful. By the bitterness of cold night, Love is the three burning coals that burn the way.

It has been said that the Black Goddess is a vampire, a sexual predator, a killer of children, and a thief of semen. Similarly, it has been said of the Black God that he brings suicide into the hearts of men. However, is not suicide the poison of Saturn? Is not the loss of the will to live the drowning of the Sun? Is not melancholia the curse of the philosophers? The path toward enlightenment and integration is not for everyone. Failure will set time in motion and one will fall prey to its consequences. For those who mistake the Black Goddess for a vampire and predator, I say that these are the words of the tongueless. The failure to sacrifice the dross of the Sun brings on the thief. The Black Goddess is Mercy and Love, but those who mistake Mercy for vileness and folly and Love for something crude and immature will reap from their beliefs. And it will be a harvest of seduction and rape, of lust and degradation, all in the name of failure and chaos. This is not the way back; this is the way forward, where the return turns into a time where the perfection of nature is but a dim memory of arcane possibility.

The Black Goddess is the frustrating point of the mortification of the shell, the putrefaction needed to rejuvenate the soul into its rightful state. Again, I say, are you ready to see your Sun go black and abandon all hope for its restitution? The Black Goddess brings Night over your soul, like the drape of corpses she covers you softly with claws and fangs, like a mother prepared to do whatever Need tells her to do. And for the last time I ask, are you ready to confront the Northern Night in all her awe? For the Night is cold and moist, and only with abandonment will you find the coals that will heat the long-gone returning Love.

A Rite for Calling the Silver Guide in the Night of the Dragon

To successfully carry out this ritual, you must first observe the position of the dragon's head in relation to the Moon in the sky. It should apply well to a dignified Moon, and the Sun should not be afflicted in any way. Additionally, make sure the tail of the dragon does not swipe the house of death and sorcery. The optimal conditions are when the Moon is in the sign of the Bull (Taurus). Observing this, you must go to a lonely place during the blackness of the Moon, for it is in her blackness that she bestows her particular pneuma and Mercy. At this point, you will use bone powder mixed with grains of silver to draw the triskelion and in the centre, facing north, you will sit down. At your left side, light a black candle, and at your right side, a white candle. See yourself in the following way:

Your hue is golden like a Sun, but internally you see only darkness and nothingness. Once this visualization is stable, see your golden hue turning black and slowly disintegrating. You will be of the nature of Night itself. At this point, take a cup of red wine collected in a silver vessel and pour it out upon the ground in the north while saying the following:

Oh great Dragon of the North,
May thy head look upon me in this night of rejuvenation.
Dragon who gives hope,
And opens the road to the Mountain of Venus,
I praise thee with your black hue and crown of silver light.
I praise thee, old one who can secure the return,
And I call thee by my silence.

You will now see the Dragon appear from out of the Darkness. Allow your mind to passively appraise the form; be receptive and do not create any expectations of the imaginary. If a scrying ball or mirror will aid you in this, be well advised to use them.

When manifestation occurs, continue in the following way:

The Door has been opened by the Old Dragon's kiss
The Night is upon me and from within the night, I call thee:
Holy Spirit of the North, Black One of the North!
Claw-handed and goat-footed One!
By your wings and talons, I call thee!
Nameless One, by Bereshit, I call thee!
By the Forgotten Names, I call thee!
By the Spirits of the Air, I call thee!
By the Dragon's Head and the Moon's embrace, I call thee!

You will now take another black candle and anoint it with ylang-ylang oil. Remove your clothes and sit naked in the triskelion. Place your clothes and the candle in the northern gate. Focus on the candle flame and recite the following prayer:

I am what I am, a homeless Soul,
I am what I am, Matter and Spirit,
I am what I am, and I shall become my Fullness!
This skin I offer to the night,
This flame I offer to the Spirits of the Night.
And I say, hear me, ye spirits of the night,
For I need ye to intervene for me so I can reach the throne of your Queen.
The Queen of the Night, I beseech thee!
I pray to thee, I call upon thee,
I am a lost Soul calling upon Love!
I pray that you in your Mercy, release Love upon me.
I seek the union of All, teach me,
What was born from the old skin, I give to thee.
Your blessings I ask, my gift is my own essence.
This token I give for this oath to be taken.

You will at this point give a sacrifice from yourself: saliva, tears, blood, semen, vaginal fluid—or your ecstasy. Then lie down in receptive meditation and wait for the Queen's arrival. In the moment of sacrifice, visualize the starry and moonless sky of night turn into the form of a beautiful woman with a crown, wings, feet of a bird, and claws, taking her form in the night. If your ecstasy is the offering, you must call forth and focus this form during stimulation, and at the peak of ecstasy, lie down and embrace her form in your mind's eye.

It is crucial that you approach this ritual with a sense of complete abandonment and willingness, as it may seem simple, but its soft commencement can lead to dramatic consequences.

Close the ritual in the following manner:

Recite Psalm 22:1–15 and offer wine to the left and right, extinguish the candles, and, in the darkness of the night, say:

I have approached thee,
Lead me on the Path towards the union of Soul with Love.
I am yours for the sake of my wholeness.

Teach me and temper me,
Let me be on the ground to do my work,
Because underground I can do nothing.
I must be on the ground.
Bless me so that I shall succeed to conquer myself.
This is my prayer to the night,
This is my cry to the Queen of Witchblood,
This is my will to return,
Bring me from the womb,
Like a phoenix from the fires,
May the coal of Love set my Soul aflame!
Amen! Amen! Amen!

This rite must be repeated at each darkening of the Moon for nine months, and the practitioner must monitor their life carefully considering the rite's purpose and the mystery it holds. This rite contains the key to immortality, as well as the potential for doom and redemption, Love and Mercy, and all shades of death.

CHAPTER EIGHT

AGAINST THE GRAIN

"To the sinful and vicious I am evil;
But to the good—beneficent am I."
—Mirza Khan, Ansari

St. Anthony, upon deciding to live as a hermit, was visited by Satan who tried to tempt him to renounce his faith through visions and hallucinations of a maddening character. Satan's tactics differed when he tempted St. Benedict, using lust to try to make him give in to his desires. Satan also attempted to seduce St. Augustine and St. Catherine of Siena. Hubris and hunger were the temptations Satan used when he walked with Jesus in the desert for forty days. Satan was typically associated with the seven deadly sins, a mirror of the seven celestial virtues. Therefore, Satan preyed on human doubts and tendencies towards anger, lust, despair, vengeance, cruelty, and other antisocial and anti-Christian impulses. Satan was the Lord of the Forbidden, the Tzar of Deception, the prince of the material realm, and the owner of the Earth. When Satan, in the guise of devils, demons, and familiar spirits, came to tempt people, they often gave in and made a pact with him through breath, blood, or coitus. They chose to go against what was good and to side with the enemy of humanity. This led to scatological accounts of the infamous "pact with the Devil," as described by Claude Tholosan in his *Ut magorum et maleficiorum errores.*[134]

[134] Kors and Peters, 2001. p.164–166.

Tholosan's account describes how witches use the Devil's urine as a sacrament and how they sacrifice infants to prepare unguents for entering the diabolic sabbath. They fly out and strangle children and afflict others with illness. Some engage in lustful play with shadows that paralyze and weaken their targets. They render people insane and barren, while the witches are inflamed with insatiable sexual lust that overrides every taboo. Charles Zika demonstrates how the lustful aspect of witches was predominant in the fourteenth and fifteenth centuries. However, witches were *also* considered to be children of the Great Melancholy, the children of Saturn. This transition from Venus to Saturn meant that the witch was found in the company of the Dead, magicians, and all things that lurk in dark, lonely, and desolate Saturnine places. Thus, in the sixteenth century, Saturn, as the ruler of diabolism, became conflated with Satan to such an extent that they both became largely synonymous. However, Zika also adds that: "Allusions to Saturn in witchcraft iconography are found from the first decade of the Century."[135]

It is also worth mentioning the mysterious connection between Saturn and the Sun in alchemy, where lead is the hidden gold and the metal for auric transformation. The solar quality is well expressed in historically famous witches like Circe and Medea, while the Saturnine element is present in the memory of Robert Cochrane. Cochrane, representing the Saturnine cunning one, was not afraid to go against the grain and call a spade a spade.

The bane that Cochrane chose for himself and the ally he went away with can speak to us about the influence of Venus, Sun, Moon, and Saturn in Cochranes' life. After falling into the embrace of Venus, his Sun shining too brightly for him to manage to stay true to his own simplicity, he chose to go away through the path of Saturn and Moon, through the paralyzing embrace of the Lady Belladonna. These planetary influences, with an emphasis on Saturn, were balanced in ways that played heavily on fate, fortune, and wisdom in his pellar craft.[136]

The premises for Cochrane's vision of the Craft were quite simple. He says in one of his few essays: "All mystical thought is based upon one major premise: the realization of truth as opposed to illusion." And

---

135 Charles Zika, *The Appearance of Witchcraft* (Routledge, 2007) p.205.

136 The Cornish term for a cunning one, maybe originally derived from "expeller," someone who exorcises and throws out negative spirits and knows how to bless and consecrate.

this truth is "in essence, means by which man may perceive his own inherent divinity." He uses the dispute over the nature of witchcraft in the 1950s and 60s as a mirror of this fact when he comments that there was as much superstition and illusion in witchcraft, or rather the ideas people held about witchcraft in his time, as in the outside world. "The Faith is finally concerned with Truth...bringing as it does man into contact with Gods, and man into contact with Self."[137]

Cochrane objected to the dogmatic ways and superstitions he saw growing up in relation to Wicca, which he conceived of as very different from his own craft, the true persuasion. As he wrote: "The inherent philosophy of the Craft was always fluid, and fluid it must become again before it gasps its last under a heap of musty nonsense, half-baked theology, and philosophy."[138] This he demonstrates greatly in the essay *The Faith of the Wise* from 1965 where he emphasizes the importance of "Experience, Devotion, and Vision" as the tools toward embracing the truth. This is because the faith has no secrets in the sense that there are certain formulas that can be readily understood and taught. On the contrary, he says that the truth can only be grasped by "hard devotional work," which leads to the great vision in which one has a direct experience of truth.

It is evident to see here the emphasis on the lunar qualities in Cochrane's vision of the Craft. Both the techniques and goals along with the dangers warned against are all under the influence of the Moon. Cochrane was very much aware of the peril involved in the Craft, and his ritual suicide might indicate that we who are left with his legacy in writing and feel drawn to his spirit should take note of it. He says: "First and foremost, the Roebuck in the Thicket represents the spirit of sacrifice and leadership. It can also represent the idea of fate or destiny in the form of the old Anglo-Saxon 'Shapers' who create the future we have to live out."[139] He understood very well the peril and dangers of taking up the heritage of the Craft, and as his fascination for Graves' book *The White Goddess* and his insight into this mystery demonstrated that he knew the mystery of how Mother Moon can both feed her offspring and eat them. In a way, we can see in Cochrane the difficulties of

---

137 Robert Cochrane and Evan John Jones, *The Roebuck in the Thicket* (Cappall Bann, 2001) p.49, 51, 56.

138 *Ibid,* p.51.

139 *Ibid,* p.85.

balancing Lady Fortuna and Lady Wisdom in one's life. Understanding through the path of vision and inspiration is different than having our ferocity tempered through the challenge of Tubal Cain, the challenge given in the context of what Cochrane refers to as "overcoming Fate." This challenge can also be seen in Cochrane's idea of initiation: "When the initiate takes the full coven oath, they are submitting themselves to the will of Hecate. In a sense, by doing this, they then become the Roebuck in the Thicket because they have chosen to follow the path she has selected for them."[140]

To embrace one's destiny and overcome it can be allegorically seen as embracing the Moon while armed with Saturn. It is all related to the concept of time, to Cronos, and through subduing Father Time by understanding the connectedness of all things outside of the concept of time. Through this, we can establish an unshakable foundation for understanding creation and a deep overcoming of all challenges, even Fate herself. Cochrane understood the importance of Death, another domain profoundly related to the Saturnian sphere. Without understanding its nature, Saturn can easily turn into depression and harbouring malefic elements, leading to a negative outlook on life and fatalism. As Luna can give a visionary experience of profound truth, she can also give the painful stroke that leads to a fall into delusion—into a pit where Saturn and Moon engage in an uncanny union. Cochrane knew this, but apparently, he was unable to raise himself from the heavy influence of this union of powerful malefic forces in his life. Lady Wisdom gave him a clear mind, but he chose to enter into the Castle of the Never-Dying Rose with Mother Moon's aid. As far as death is concerned, his ideas and considerations were beautiful and to the point. He said:

> *Nothing is gained by doing nothing, and whatever we do now creates the world in which we exist tomorrow. The same applies to death, what we have created in thought we create in that other reality. We should also remember that Desire was the first of all created things.*[141]

And yet, he escaped from the path Fate laid before him by passing on to the Castle in the way he did rather than overcoming her. It is almost

---

140 Robert Cochrane and Evan John Jones, *The Roebuck in the Thicket* (Cappall Bann, 2001) p.92.

141 *Ibid*, p.70.

as if Cochrane went against his better insight by inviting Belladonna to take him away, as he said: "The Three Sisters were also considered to be the keepers of the Cauldron of Creation, which is one place where past, present, and future are as one yet still in a state of flux, movement, and promised potential"[142] which again leads to the final challenge: "So, in a sense, when we start to seek out the Goddess and her magic, we are, in effect, becoming the hunter. Yet when we have found her, we then become the hunted because the Goddess pins us down and makes us hers forever."[143] It is in this challenge, when the tables turn, that we need to stand strong and focus on overcoming through understanding our experiences and actually using it through practical application—this is growth.

Without Saturn, there would be little progress, and without the Moon, there would be little vision. The joining of these forces in a higher unity of acceptance, as everyone's destiny is unique and grandiose, no matter how significant or insignificant in the great scheme it might be seen. Destiny is still the greatest force in the life of each and every one of us. Fate is not related to misfortune; actually, we should perhaps rethink the term misfortune in light of the power Fate presents us with in terms of the challenges from which we can extract lessons of growth. Armed in the likeness of Tubal Cain, we can participate in forging our destiny; we embark with courage on the ordeal of overcoming, and it is in this light that the element of sacrifice, related to Roebuck, is better understood, for it is by way of sacrifice that makes the person whole. In other words, when Fate presents challenges and we see them as misfortune, then we focus solely on the blindness of Lady Fortuna, and by cursing her wheel of fortune, we reject Lady Wisdom and miss the whole opportunity. With the curse, we fall to the lower strands of Father Saturn's being and engage in a process of disintegration and self-pity, blinding us to the solutions and useful tools willingly offered by Master Tubal Cain during our battle in the silent castle where we meet not only Her, but in this tower of ordeal, we also witness all the atrocity and all the beauty contained in what we conceive of as "Self."

One significant point to make here is related to fate or fatalism in a more philosophical context. There seems to be a gap between fate and

---

142 Robert Cochrane and Evan John Jones, *The Roebuck in the Thicket* (Cappall Bann, 2001) p.88.

143 *Ibid,* p.90.

fatalism, where fate can inspire the embrace of destiny in ways understood as "good" or "bad." In the past, when fatalism was a philosophical doctrine, there was nothing significant that differentiated fate and fatalism, as fatalism referred to submission to fate akin to Cochrane's ideas. It carried nothing intrinsically evil or bad, as in terms of misfortune. In cases of fatalistic thought centred around some catastrophic misfortune, something glorious always came in its wake. However, today, fatalism usually refers to some unavoidable misfortune that is about to strike one's life, referring to a negative state and outlook on life.

We can also mention the Stoic ideal where suicide could be turned into an act of dignity in front of fate, as one could be given the option of ingesting the poisoned chalice like in the cases of Socrates and Seneca. An important point to note here is that the suicide of these philosophers was demanded by the emperor. It was not a *choice* by fate, but an *acceptance* of fate, an honourable way out of a situation that could not be turned to one's favour. Maybe Cochrane saw his ritual suicide in this way, as a reflection of Mother Moon, of Hecate's will, the unavoidable way out of a situation that could not be turned for the better.

There is an interesting passage in one of the letters to Joe Wilson that might indicate such an attitude. Cochrane says in regard to "witch laws" the following: "Do not do what you desire—do what is necessary. Take all you are given—give all of yourself. What I have...I hold! When all else is lost, and not until then, prepare to die with dignity."[144] Maybe he saw his ritual suicide, by willingly ingesting the poison fate gave him, as a dignified way of leaving the terrestrial body behind in favour of the Hidden Company. Another quote of his can be understood in such a way:

> *Seeing the Lady is just not enough...because in fate, and the overcoming of fate, is the key to inspiration and death itself is gained stayed. There is no fate so terrible that cannot be outfaced and overcome, whether by a concrete victory gained by action or the deeper victory of the spirit engaged in the solitary battle of self. Fate, destiny, and doom is the trial, the Castle Perilous, in which we all must meet to win or die.*[145]

---

144 Robert Cochrane and Evan John Jones, *The Robert Cochrane Letters* (Cappall Bann, 2002) p.50.

145 Robert Cochrane and Evan John Jones, *The Roebuck in the Thicket* (Cappall Bann, 2001) p.161.

This can be read as Cochrane seeing himself defeated by fate. His meeting in the Castle and his battle granted him death.

Cochrane defined the Craft as being about truth, experience, and devotion. All these elements he placed under the mercy of Hecate, Mother Moon, Lady Fortuna, and Lady Fate. It seems that he might have forgotten something in his identification with the Roebuck as the symbol of sacrifice and leadership, namely ferocity and courage. Still, his legacy lives on, and his spark of spirit continues to inspire. What to make of his early death and its untimeliness or timeliness is still subject to a multitude of opinions, and in the end, it probably does not matter, since the visions and teachings he shared with those who continued his legacy are still there to learn, digest, and take spiritual nutrition from. By seeing the growing interest in his legacy alone, we can see that he gained, after all, eternal life. Both the lessons he learned and mastered and those lessons that defeated him are there serving as a compass on the path of the pilgrim, helping the seeker understand the depths of Saturn's well of wisdom and how it can affect our life and craft. Let us now turn to the solar manifestations of the witch.

Circe: Regina Nymphae

Circe represents a most typical image of a witch, represented as a regal goddess who married the king of the Sarmatians, whom she later poisoned. She was the daughter of the Sun, Helios, and Perse, an Oceanid or saltwater nymph, and, by extension, the granddaughter of Poseidon. Her natural affinity with Sirens, the dreadful beings of utmost beauty and danger, was due to this connection. She was born of divine seed and carried fairy blood from her nymph mother. The name Circe means "falcon," a reference to the predatory flight of her fetch. Her association with royalty in Greece, such as the king of Colchis, highlights her special pedigree.

Earlier in this book, it has been suggested that the divine origin of witchblood is from Shemesh, the Sun, the centre of Luciferian awakening in its phosphorous radiance. Circe is associated with shapeshifting, the ability to transform people into animals, and, more than anything, the imprint of the witch as *venifica* or poisoner. Her knowledge of drugs, plants, cures, and poisons was her most poignant feature.

Circe lived secluded on an island, Aeaea, which was said to be the abode of Helios himself. Lions and wolves, animals associated with Lilith, prowled around her home as guardians. She captured Odysseus' men and kept them drugged, but Odysseus was helped by Hermes, who gave him the herb "moly" (an herb known as "snowdrop" or Lily of the Valley) as a ward against Circe's magic. This herb, which is outside the domain of the witch, recurs in several myths. The subtle references to Circe as a sexual predator or dominator of Odysseus' men are further suggested by Odysseus becoming her intoxicated lover for one year, despite Hermes' protection. The three children she begot with the hero became kings, notably Latinus and Telegonus, who became king of the Etruscans. There are many variations of the number of sons and their names, but the latter remain more or less constant. Her daughter, Aega, was said to be born from the ocean and that she was like ice or lived within a shield of ice.

Circe, when she realized that she could not seduce Glaucus into loving her, is reputed to have transformed Scylla, Glaucus' beloved, into a six-headed monster. Interestingly, one myth says that Scylla was the daughter of Lamia, the Queen of Libya. Although her association with water has made her largely a lunar goddess, there is also reason to see her as a manifestation of Venus, largely formed in the image of Ishtar, and along with Ishtar, we are now firmly in the heart of the witch-identity.

Medea: Granddaughter of the Sun

The accounts of Medea date back to at least the sixth century BC. In the stories of Medea, we once again see the impact of love and the multiple ways in which these rays of Venus can manifest. The fates of Ariadne and Apuleius were two other incidents brought on by Aphrodite. In Medea's case, her father, King Aietes, had offended Juno, who then brought Aphrodite into the scene. With Eros' aid, Medea fell hopelessly in love with Jason, and she used her witch powers inherited from her aunt, Circe, to aid and protect Jason in his travels to obtain the Golden Fleece from the Garden of Ares. It is with Medea that Hecate enters the world of witches as their protector, as it was with Hecate's assistance that Medea protected and ensured Jason's success. With Hecate's help, she enchanted the dragon that guarded the fleece, and when Jason and his Argonauts finally entered the island of Crete, the spirits of death were called upon to overpower Talos.

When the mission was accomplished, Medea's father sent his half-brother, Apsyrtos, to bring her back. To avoid being brought back, the two lovers ambushed Apsyrtos and killed him. This senseless act of cruelty brought on the fury of Zeus, and even Medea's aunt, Circe, turned her back on her. Further attempts to bring her back also failed, and cruelty walked in the footsteps of the love-intoxicated Medea. Especially memorable is her encounter with the daughters of the recently deceased King Pelias, Jason's uncle, whom she promised to rejuvenate if the daughters feasted upon the flesh of their father. The murder of Pelias was, of course, part of a greater plot by Jason and Medea. The daughters did as they were told, and Medea left with the business unsolved. It might be from this incident that cannibalistic accusations were affixed to the witch.

Thereafter, the lovers went to Corinth and experienced ten years of happiness, after which Jason fell in love with the daughter of King Creon, Glauce, and left Medea. Medea took a horrible revenge: she sent a beautiful robe to the bride that consumed her with fire when she put it on, thereafter killing all the children she had with Jason. She went to Athens, where she married Aegus, but after an attempt to poison Aegus' son, the hero Theseus, she had to leave Athens and finally went home. As for Jason, some stories say that misfortune followed him until his death, and other accounts say that, when he received the news of Medea killing off his future legacy, he took his own life.

Herodotus says that the failure to bring back Medea was the indirect cause of the Trojan War, as this gave a reason to justify the kidnapping of Helen. Legend tells us that Medea finally emigrated to Persia and that the Aryans living in the area where she found rest changed their names to Medes in honour of her.

Saturn: the Hidden Sun

The fusion of Sun and Saturn can also be seen in the conflation of Satan and Lucifer, as noted in 2 Corinthians 11:14 (King James) which states: "For Satan himself is transformed into an angel of light." Therefore, it is worth exploring the main themes of this mystery.

The fusion of Lucifer and Satan was completed through the letters of St. Paul. The interpretation of the spirit in Job 1 and 2 and the identification with the spirit mentioned in Zechariah 3 created a total fusion between Lucifer (from *lux* + *ferre*, meaning "bringer of light") and Satan. They were understood to refer to the same being, and by the fourteenth century, they were both also referred to as *diavolo.* This symbiosis occurred partly due to a lack of distinction in translation, theological dogma, and historic necessity.

In Job 1:6, we read: "Now there was a day when the sons of God came to present themselves before the Lord, and Satan came also among them." In Zechariah 3:1, we read: "And he showed me Joshua, the high priest standing before the angel of the Lord, and Satan standing at his right hand to resist him." The scene in Zechariah 3 is a judgment regarding Joshua's right to be anointed to priesthood or not. One can make a parallel to the anointing of Jesus Christ, where the Devil constantly challenged his right to be "Christened," which means anointed after "chrism." In Job, the issue is of a theological nature that expounds on the dilemma of the need for a moral order in creation, especially the conditions for worship. The question these two verses pose is whether Satan is a spirit being, or if it is simply an office acting from some sort of necessary duty. In both instances, Satan is presented as someone who questions the validity of either Job's reasons for worship or Joshua's right to the priesthood—someone who challenges, quite similar to the prosecutor in a trial.

Looking at the root of the word "Satan," it is revealed that the word itself is most likely a noun derived from the Hebrew *sâtãn.* This word is subject to some variation through interpretation, as it can be constructed from the Hebrew root *sth,* meaning "to stray," or *swt,* referring to "fall away" and "the act of revolt or rebellion." It can also be derived from the root *sth,* meaning "to seduce." If one assumes that the additional "an" is a suffix, the word itself, *satan,* is an abstract noun. However, the etymological roots are unclear. It might be that the limited reading of the etymological root of *satan* resulted in the figure of Satan being subject to the qualities of these root words. However, if we add the additional "n" or "nun," the matter changes, and we have a name with fuzzy etymological roots. P. L. Day suggests that the meaning of this name is better discerned from its occurrences and context in the Scripture, given that the common meaning of the noun is "adversary," both in terms of the Hebrew *sâtãn* and the Aramaic *satana.*[146] This Hebrew word was substituted with *Diabolus,* meaning "slanderer," and *Ho Satanas,* referring to God's opponent, as the Holy Scriptures were translated into Greek and Latin. Accordingly, Satanas and Diabolus became used as a reference to the same supernatural power.

It is interesting to note that, outside the Hebrew scriptures, there are no other references to the use of the word "satan." This suggests that the word was created to serve some kind of meaningful purpose. The question is: what kind of meaning would this word serve? It is possible that the word was derived from the Acadian legal system, which had three types of office, all translated into "accusers." These offices were referred to as *bêl dabâbi, bêl dini,* and *akil karsi.*[147] They were used to designate legal opponents, either celestial or terrestrial, and can be seen as a representation of the same contextual meaning as what is found in the use of the noun "satan." This indicates that, despite the lack of an etymological relationship, there is a meaningful relationship based on historicity.

One example given by Day is a reference to the use of the deities Nanay and Mâr-Biti in the legal system. Oaths were sworn to these deities, and if the accused turned out to be a liar, he had to answer to the wrath of them. Note that in the Acadian legal system, the celestial council was an integrated and supreme part of the legal system, serving vital functions in the prosecution itself. One can speculate if the present custom of swearing on the Bible is actually a remnant from this practice of swearing on the names of wrathful deities. If so, it means that one's oath made upon the Bible is an act that can bring about a curse from the celestial court, if oaths are broken or one is found to be untruthful. Thus, one invites in the confrontation with the accuser, with Satan.

Returning to the challenge in the case against Job, we see that the word used for the accuser, according to Day, *hassatan,* is a common noun meaning "accuser," which is a word used in legal references. Given the definite article of the word, it seems highly unlikely to be a name and thus a position. A similar role is found in Numbers 22, where we find the story of Balaam and the donkey whose mission is hindered by a *hassatan,* in a reference either to Jahveh himself or one of his divine

---

146 P. L. Day, *An Adversary in Heaven: sâtãn in the Hebrew Bible* (Brill Leiden, 1988).

147 "Asharu Tradition." https://covenantofbabylon.wordpress.com/tag/asharu-tradition/

messengers. This means that this "satanic office" is administered by God himself. The role described is similar to what happens to Joshua, who is also challenged by his *hassatan*. This indicates that choice and aspiration on the path will, at all times, be challenged by a spiritual entity that aims to make us strong by presenting the poison of insecurity and corruption. Thomas Aquinas comments on this in *Summa Theologica:*

> *Further, scandal denotes an obstacle that is put in a person's spiritual way. Now even perfect men can be hindered in their progress along the spiritual way, according to 1 Thess. 2:18: "We would have come to you, I Paul indeed, once and again; but Satan hath hindered us." Therefore, even perfect men can suffer scandal.*[148]

As such, the role of hassatan often leads to an understanding of this office as "against humanity." In truth, it is more a lack of understanding of this office and its relationship to our spiritual and moral growth than some sort of inherited evil curse.

To turn to modern-day legal references, the prosecutor or accuser in a trial, at times, suffers the same interpretation—degenerated, perverse, or evil—in spite of them performing the function of their office, the task assigned by the government. One can say that we have the right to a defence, in a similar way we also have the right to be accused.

The Greek word *diabolus* means "a slanderer" or "attacker" in an abusive and vulgar sense, unrelated to a legal office. After the Vulgate, translations of the Bible fused *diavolus* and *daemon,* which were originally separate terms in the Vulgate, into a single term seen as synonymous with Satan. The office of *hassatan* was reinterpreted from a legal function to an expression related to violence from a meaningless mob. The meaning reappeared in the term *advocatus diaboli* in the mid-seventeenth century in the Vatican, referring to the one assigned to the task of speaking against the canonization of a candidate for sainthood.

The association between Lucifer and Satan arose from the equating of the Fall of Lucifer and his angels in Isaiah 14:12 to Satan or *diavolos,* now being identical with the enemy of humankind—the Devil. However, there is a lack of meaning both etymologically and in contextual use. Perhaps the difference was breached by equating Phosphorus, which in Hebrew is *Helel ben Shahar,* the same as Lucifer. Thus, the rebellious

---

148 Thomas Aquinas, *Summa Theologica* (1274).

spirit who stole the light from the gods was equated with Lucifer, now considered as God's antithesis instead of divine accusers in a celestial court.

Due to his symbiosis with Phosphorus, Lucifer, the Angel of Light, was imposed with the nature—or, shall we say, the office—of *Ho Diavolo* rather than *hassatan,* and with the battle against the heretics of the Church, they became assimilated with the adversary of God. Within a short time, Aquinas' increasingly diabolic interpretations of theology led to Lucifer-Satan transformation into the fallen angelic genii that would manifest later as the antichrist. The term "angel" is from the Greek *angelos* meaning "messenger," which in turn is translated from the Hebrew *malakh,* also meaning "messenger." In both cases, "messenger" in both Greek and Hebrew and refers to a spiritual being in the court of God with specific tasks in the celestial government. Lucifer is accordingly the messenger of divine light but given the association with the angelic rebellion and Fall, his light was considered corrupt and diabolic.

The same fate befell the Philistine god worshipped at Ekron according to 2 Kings 1:2, Beelzebub. The name is probably a contraction of the name *Baal Zebub,* meaning the "winged lord," but the deity became demonized by the Hebrew tribes into a gigantic evil-minded fly. This misrepresentation was, perhaps, because a foreign celestial being with wings could be taken for an angel, a messenger of God, which would be highly improper. Since the word *zhebub* could refer to a fly as much as a winged being, the transition from angel to supernatural fly was done with ease. In the same way, the Pauline letters bring back the meaning found in the etymological Hebrew and Acadian roots of what became the name of God's opponent, Satan, as an accuser, and combined with imagery amongst the Hebrew prophets, one would understand Satan as the fallen and evil angel, jealous, corrupted, and hateful, God's adversary, and the enemy of humanity.

There is much theological speculation to be derived from this quotation, but for the purpose of this essay, the transformative aspect is of particular interest. Aquinas argues that it is not a dangerous error to mistake a wicked angel presenting itself as good for being good. This remark is likely made because of the transformative process itself. An angel transformed into light is light. This transformation can be seen in the context of a seeker who has successfully navigated challenges on the path of light. He has been found victorious in the "trial" and has thus by wisdom and insight, rejected the *Kakodaimon* (bad angel) in favour of the *Agathodaimon* (good angel). The celestial image of the Kakodaimon, as well as Agathodaimon, is a serpent, the true angelic form. As such, one can imagine a situation where a seeker stands before a good angel and a bad angel, with both constituting a divine balance that presents choices for the seeker, giving opportunity to follow the guidance of their good angel and walk their destiny. The accuser will challenge the seeker's choices, making the seeker conscious and aware of their choice instead of automatic behaviour, for the accuser's aim is to make the seeker's light luminous or the seeker will perish by the path itself.

The Amoral Witch and the Path of Ordeal

The witch is a child of Venus and Saturn, yet beyond them in terms of moral qualities. The witch is amoral rather than immoral. Divine descent by Sun, Venus, Saturn, and fairy blood come together in the imagery of the witch where "the other side" opens up through life ordeals and spiritual gifts.

Amongst the Babylonians, Ishtar was the divine incarnation of the planet Venus. Venus was seen as the deity of both love and war, a courtesan deeply associated with sexuality, aphrodisiacs, and sensualism. Her sacred city, Erech, was famous for the courtesans of the goddess and temple prostitution. Ishtar was said to be the courtesan of the gods, and this was reflected in her as a goddess who drank the ecstasy of pleasure and the sensual, and as the protector of divine and arduous passion, indulging in eroticism to the fullest. The lion was depicted on the pillars leading to her city, the same fetch and lover presided over by Lilith. Here, the lion represents the Sun, and by this, Regulus, the Royal star at the heart of Leo. Ishtar was the daughter of the Moon god Sin, and indirectly influenced the Sabaean cult that grew up in Harran, portraying the powers spoken of in the Dance of the Seven Veils, related to the mysteries of the seven planets. This is enacted when she enters the Underworld, challenges its Queen, and loses seven pieces of cloth on the journey towards the mystery, which are then regained on the return.

As in the case of Circe and Medea, Ishtar's love was a fatal drug which revealed the ecstasy and pleasure, as well as the insanity and cruelty, of love. References are seen to Aphrodite, Astarte, and Freya, where the same theme concerning love and cruelty is depicted in the spirit of Venus' holiness, influencing her avatars and vessels. From this early representation, the image of the witch ventured through time as an unruly seductress, a poisoner and a hedonist, a social recluse veiled in mystery and rumour, until the end of Jules Michelet's romantic presentation of the witch in *Le Sorceress* in the final years of the nineteenth century.

There are a few essential factors that define the nature of the witch. We speak of a special pedigree, of someone with a solar seed, whose blood is partly from the "other side." This gives access to secrets only revealed to those who possess the second sight, natural for this particular pedigree, often referred to as "the mark." A genuine connection with the formless truth of the Source is another way of describing this. This is further seen in the witch's ability to converse with spirits through various forms of divination as well as possession of a vast knowledge of herbs for blessing or bane.

The witch is a liminal being that must be connected to nature to feel content and complete. Consequently, the constant degeneration of the natural world into an illusory civilized, and orderly moral universe induces resistance in the witch. This resistance provokes actors in society, as the witch appears as someone who insists on standing still in the face of progress. The truth is that the appearance of standing still is a rejection of the crooked way of profane progress and an insistence of remaining in the sacred centre, enabling the return to the Golden Age.

As mentioned earlier in this work, the Golden Age was a time of freedom before the introduction of law and civilization to the world. Therefore, the path against the current and back to the Source often takes the form of the witch being lewd, amoral, and shameless, but with purpose and wisdom.

We can understand the witch as a being of nature deeply associated with the craft of peasants and dwellers in untamed regions of the world. The witch stood apart from the general populace in terms of perception, attitude, knowledge, and social actuation. The constant communion with the fairy realm and the "other side" fuses with occult knowledge and natural wisdom, giving rise to the Cunning Craft. To remain in uncultivated nature and maintain the legacy of the fair-folk will naturally provoke those who consider the chains of civilization as freedom and who see ambition as the journey to the summit of meaning.

Even today, country dwellers, the *paganus,* continue to provoke modern humanity as they enter a mutual symbiosis with nature and the wildness found in the freedom of the woods and springs—inspiring them to reject religious morality and profane modern law in favour of the freedom granted by Venus and her nymphs. In this way, the true secrets of witchcraft lie in the natural freedom of the witch and the realization of oneself as a fair being living in harmony with the various kingdoms. The witch continues to be a mirror and a living critique of progress and law through their lewd, lawless insistence on freedom.

There is a notion that going against the current or the grain represents some sort of "anti" mentality, rooted in a mentalist and profane view of the sacred science. If the current is unhealthy, going against it is an act of restoration, healing, and restitution. To go against the current, in the real sense of the word, we need to first locate the dimension we find ourselves in. Today, the idea of going against the current conveys the notion of rebellion, the work of fire and transgression, and a satanic impulse, but in a world that is slowly grinding towards its own collapse, to go against the grain might very well be an act of cosmic restoration.

And yet, going against the current is the very hallmark of the witch. We might say it denotes a sort of nostalgia within the witch where they act upon the remembrance of the Golden Age, where there was no need for control and law because humanity knew how to conduct themselves in natural harmony with one another and the world around. This does not give rise to rebellion for the sake of rebellion, but rather resistance against *civilis* and a preference towards *naturis.* Seen through modern eyes, this might generate the idea of the witch as anti-social, lewd, and somewhat morally shocking. This gives birth to more labels, as the witch is opposed to modernity, a lack of will to be confined, "sorted out," or labelled. It is the blood of ancestry stretching back in straight lines to the source of all things, to the tomb of beginnings, that motivates this seemingly resistant iconographic witch

In concluding this chapter, an inspired rendering of the Gospel of Judas as it applies to the journey of the soul "against the current" is presented here. It is common to see Cain as the ancestral witch-father, but it is important to view Cain's role in a greater design as "the man who does what needs to be done," or even the Man of Desire—St. Martin's vision of the man of ordeal, representing the Greek and Gnostic stage of *psychikos.* If we look at Master Cain from the perspective of necessity, sacrifice, and restoration, we find him to be functionally similar to Judas Iscariot. Cain, as witch-father and son of Lilith, testifies to the importance of standing strong as Azazel, the scapegoat of the world. The witch is the Devil in deed, the Devil we need, and few are those who accept that this is the consequence of "that other blood" that Shemyaza and Lilith gave to their children, to stand strong as Azazel on the tortuous path of ordeal, to shed the skin every year and a day, to work with both hands with Sun and Saturn as guides, even when they take the shape of Lucifer and Satan...to be cursed for the sake of restoring the world.

The recently rediscovered Gospel of Judas is a useful compass, as it points the pilgrim towards the polar axis in its initiatic aspiration. Let Orpheus and Calliope guide this presentation's words in this final sequence, attempting to give some form to the formlessness of truth, which is the beginning, becoming, and marks what going against the current entails.

The Ordeal of Powers' Concealment

"For I am the voice that speaks through your fear.
I am the power that enters when you have no more."
—Liber Combusta[149]

The path itself presents four ordeals, each aimed towards self-overcoming. These four ordeals are represented by the winds of the elements and the spirits within them. The first ordeal is by air, the second by water, the third by fire, and the fourth by earth. Resting within these ordeals are the timeless virtues of the Sphinx.

The Ordeal of Air

The ordeal by the winds that bring the beings of Air challenges our sense of separation, mind, thoughts, thinking, goals, and identity. Air can be like a mighty wind, giving food for the waters to raise themselves in rage, for the fire to die, and for the earth to vanish. The nature of the first wind ordeal is to stand strong in the challenges of the Devil and not let the waters rise, the fire die, nor the earth erase our memory.

149 Privately circulated text in the cunning sodality of Via Vera Cruz.

What makes the path challenging is spoken of in the Gospel of Judas where we read in the introit that, in this time, "some walked in the way of righteousness while others walked in their transgression." The Master speaks not of a division between people, in bad and good of sorts, but rather about the estate of his followers, seekers in general whose hunger for the gardens of honeydew and milk outside the temple of the everlasting one can only be quenched by transgression.

Oh, woe upon the pilgrim of the lonely road, woe upon the one who willingly took the mark of the first sorcerer. Woe upon the accursed blood, for in the curse is the holy work of salvation. The holy work of transgression will be accomplished by the deeds of Jezebel and Judas Iscariot, Delilah and Herodias, so we can be righteous and forever standing. Without transgression, there can be no salvation. The Devil is the first one of the Air, and he will split the winds in four ways—this will open for confusion or focus, choice of the right kind, or the unright kind. Air is the breath, which separates us from the corpse and the somnambulists of the decaying world. Air is divine, so the ordeal is in the realization of this and the further divinization of the god-giving life-sustaining air.

The Ordeal of Water

Regarding the second ordeal, we read in the Gospel of Judas: "When Jesus observed their lack of understanding, he said to them, 'Why has this agitation led you to anger? Your god who is within you has provoked you to anger within your souls. Let any one of you who is strong enough among human beings bring out the perfect human and stand before my face.'" A lack of understanding sets the waters in motion when confronted with the ordeal. This ordeal is from the she-devils, from the obscure caverns of dark lustful secrecy. From the sores of your soul and the scars on your heart, inflicted by failing to understand the Water, the Water itself will return to test you.

One could argue that we are speaking about control. Controlled powers are not wasted, and powers not wasted are powers at hand. It is this power that the Devil will challenge you to relinquish. But I say, do not give him what is rightfully yours! This is where the curse and the kingdom lie. True transgression lies in not succumbing to the demands that lurk in the moist darkness. This is the matter of the heart, whether it will be of darkness or light. Without a heart, there can be no love, and without love, there is no passion. And without passion, the path will never materialize. As the mark is taken and the curse bestowed, a fire is kindled. And by igniting the lantern of the lonely pilgrim, they will go forth into the world as an outcast.

The Ordeal of Fire

The third ordeal is where the curse and its burden can feed the lantern, your guiding light—or you can return to the wind and water that will extinguish it. Our ancestors referred to this stage as *rubeata,* "the reddening of the profane," to infuse the profane with holy fire. In this ordeal, we find belief. It is belief that will challenge our right to the holy fire. At each forked road, the Devil will take on his masquerade and force you to demonstrate that you truly, by mind and heart, broke the veils of ignorance, that you truly woke up, that you willingly and knowingly took on the curse. In belief, we find loneliness. We need to understand this particular solitude or loneliness as the essence of "oneliness," as being of *One.* We encounter here the silence of our belief, the flickering flame kindled in our hearts to bring balance to the waters. And this is the silence that we fill with our own doubts, insecurities, and distractions, which take us one step astray from the path—backwards. In the silences of fire, spirit speaks; it is in silence that we measure our worth. The fire will challenge you in terms of your worth, your endurance. In the silence of fire, there is no self-pity, no going back, no remorse, no forgiveness. You must become One or perish!

The Ordeal of Earth

With thy lantern, you will walk the earth, and the last ordeal is always what lies under our feet, the earth itself, the mystical north. Her name is Foundation. And know this, oh journeyman of the accursed road, that if you have no foundation, the earth will swallow you as it did with Koran and his profane rebels when they challenged Moses and demonstrated the great failure of the test of fire. Because the failure of fire will bring the waters to vanquish the fire, the air to gather the dust of the earth—and by this, your memory will be lost forever. In the fourth ordeal, the Devil will challenge you for the powers gained, and you shall wrestle with your demons and the djinns of the world in a battle where you will either ascend or perish. By the holy transgression, you will be named righteous, and thus the Devil will be a companion and a beacon of undying light. Only by Foundation will the gifts of air, water, and fire be sustained within the arms of the True Cross, and only by this can we station ourselves in the centre and take the horned skull of ancestry in our hand and say: this is in my likeness, this black skull of our bloody beginning is rightly mine to hold and take. I am the One from beginning to end. And so it shall be!

Know, pilgrim, that the path to power is one of ordeal. There is no other way to achieve true power, and it is only through true power that true mastery can be attained. One cannot exist without the other. This mastery is over oneself, and transgression is the holy work that leads to our salvation, allowing us to stand in the gardens of secrets within the divine courtyard, feeling the divine breath, the mighty passion, and the fire of inspiration upon a solid foundation. This is the legacy of holiness achieved through ordeal, the exaltation of wise blood, and the straightening of the crooked road into a ladder of light for the ascent of righteous ones who emerged from the tribulation of transgression with the light of holiness blazing like a torch of victory in their hands.

Let us conclude the path of ordeal with the gospel of the holy Judas Iscariot, for with each victory, even greater forces will rise from the servants of Saklas, not to challenge our victory, but to destroy it.

You will become the thirteenth,
and you will be cursed by the other generations
And you will come to rule over them.
In the last days they will curse your ascent to the holy.

BIBLIOGRAPHY

Anon. *Ghayat Al Hakim. Pictarix*. Ouroboros Press, 2008.

Anderson, Jeffrey, E. ed. *The Voodoo Encyclopedia*. ABC-CLIO, 2015.

Ankarloo, Bengt and Stuart Clark, ed. *Witchcraft and Magic in Europe*. Six volumes. University of Pennsylvania Press, 2002.

Agrippa, Henry Cornelius. *Three Books of Occult Philosophy*. Llewellyn Worldwide, 1993.

Baroja, Julio Caro. *The World of the Witches*. The University of Chicago Press, 1965.

Barrett, Francis. *The Magus*. Samuel Weiser, 2000.

Best, Michael R. and Frank H. Brightman, ed. *The Book of Secrets of Albertus Magnus*. Oxford University Press, 1973.

Bonatti, Guido. *The Book of Astronomy*. The Cazimi Press, 2007.

Boureau, Alain. *Satan the Heretic*. The University of Chicago Press, 2006.

Briggs, Katharine. *The Vanishing People: A Study of Traditional Fairy Belief*. Batsford Ltd., 1978.

Bruno, Giordano. *Cause, Principle and Unity*. Cambridge University Press, 1998.

Burkert, Walter. *Ancient Mystery Cults*. Harvard University Press, 1987.

—. *Greek Religions*. Harvard University Press, 1995.

Cascudo Luís da Câmara. *Dicionário do Folclore Brasileiro*. Grupo Editora Global, 1952.

Cassirer, Ernst, Paul Oskar Kristeller, and John Herman Randall Jr. *The Renaissance Philosophy of Man*. The University of Chicago Press, 1948.

Cavendish, Richard. *The Black Arts*. Perigee Books, 1967.

Christian, Paul. *The History and Practice of Magic*. Citadel Press, 1963.

Churton, Tobias. *The Magus of Freemasonry*. Inner Traditions, 2007.

Clark, Stuart. *Thinking with Demons*. Oxford University Press, 1997.

Cochrane, Robert and Evan John Jones. *The Roebuck in the Thicket*. Edited by Mike Howard. Cappall Bann, 2001.

—. *The Robert Cochrane Letters*. Cappall Bann, 2002.

Corbin, Henry. *The Man of Light in Iranian Sufism*. Omega Publications, 1971.

Cristiani, Mgr. Leon. *Satan in the Modern World*. Barrie & Rockliff, 1961.

Crowley, Aleister. *Goetia, The Lesser Key of King Solomon*. Sut Anubis, 1904.
Dhalla, Maneckji Nusservanji. *History of Zoroastrianism*. Oxford University Press, 1938.
Davies, Owen. *Cunning Folk. Popular Magic in English History*. Hambledon & London, 2003.
Day, P. L. *An Adversary in Heaven; sátán in the Hebrew Bible*. Brill Leiden, 1988.
Deane, Jennifer Kolpacoff. *A History of Medieval Heresy and Inquisition*. Rowman & Littlefield, 2011.
Dreyer, J. L. E. *A History of Astronomy from Thales to Kepler*. Dover Publications, 1953.
Duffy, Eamon. *The Stripping of the Altars: Traditional Religion in England 1400-1580*. Yale University Press, 1992.
Falokun, Awo. *Ìbà'se Òrìsà*. Original Publications, 1994.
Frisvold, Nicholaj de Mattos. *Arts of the Night*. Chadezoad Publication, 2009.
—. *Serpent Songs*. Scarlet Imprint, 2013.
—. *Trollrún*. Hadean Press, 2021.
Ginzburg, Carlo. *Ecstasies: Deciphering the Witches' Sabbath*. Penguin, 1992.
Goodare, Julian. *The European Witch-Hunt*. Routledge, 2016.
Goodare, Julian, Rita Volmer, and Liv Helene Willumsen, eds. *Demonology and Witch-Hunting in Early Modern Europe*. Routledge, 2020.
Grant, Kenneth. *Images & Oracles of Austin Osman Spare*. Fredrick Müller, 1975.
Green, Arthur. *EHYEH: A Kabbalah for Tomorrow*. Jewish Lights, 2004.
Guénon, René. *Symbols of Sacred Science*. Sophia Perennis, 1995.
Heselton, Philip. *Gerald Gardner and the Cauldron of Inspiration*. Capall Bann, 2003.
Hodne, Ørnulf. *Trolldom i Norge*. Cappelen Damm, 2008.
Howard, Michael and Nigel Jackson. *The Pillars of Tubal-Cain*. Capall Bann, 2000.
Howard, Michael. *The Book of Fallen Angels*. Capall Bann, 2004.
Huson, Paul. *Mastering Witchcraft*. Penguin Putnam Inc, 1970.
—. *Mystical Origins of the Tarot*. Destiny Books, 2004.
Hutton, Ronald. *The Triumph of the Moon*. Oxford University Press, 1999.
—. *The Witch*. Yale University Press, 2017.
Jackson, Nigel. *Call of the Horned Piper*. Capall Bann, 1994.
—. *Compleat Vampyre*. Capall Bann, 1995.
—. *Masks of Misrule*. Capall Bann, 1996.

Kaplan, Aryeh. *Jewish Meditation*. Schocken Books, 1995.
Kieckhefer, Richard. *Forbidden Rites*. Penn State Press, 1997.
Kirk, Robert. *The Secret Commonwealth of Elves, Fauns & Fairies*. New York Review Books, 2007.
Kittredge, George Lyman. *Witchcraft in Old and New England*. Oxford University Press, 1929.
Lebling, Robert. *Legends of the Fire Spirits*. I.B. Tauris, 2010.
Lecouteux, Claude. *The Pagan Book of the Dead*. Inner Traditions, 2020.
Levack, Brian, P., ed. *The Witchcraft Sourcebook*. Routledge, 2015.
Lilly, William. *Christian Astrology*. Regulus, 1985.
MacGaffey, Wyatt. *Religion and Society in Central Africa*. University of Chicago Press, 1986.
Maguire, Henry, ed. *Byzantine Magic*. Dumbarton Oaks, 2008.
Martin, Luther, H. *Hellenistic Religions. An Introduction*. Oxford University Press, 1987.
Ma'shar, Abu. *The Great Introduction to the Science of the Judgments of the Stars*. The Cazimi Press, 2020.
McGrath, Aliester E. *Christian Theology. An Introduction*. 2nd edition. Blackwell, 1997.
Michelet, Jules. *Satanism and Witchcraft*. Citadel Press, 1992.
Murray, Margaret. *The Witch-Cult in Western Europe*. Oxford University Press, 1921.
Naudon, Paul. *The Secret History of Freemasonry*. Inner Traditions, 2005.
Patai, Raphael. *The Hebrew Goddess*. Wayne State University Press, 1990.
Pearson, Nigel, G. *Blackthorn—Whitethorn, Ways of Witchery*. Troy Books, 2023.
Pennick, Nigel. *Secrets of East Anglian Magic*. Robert Hale, 1995.
—. *Witchcraft & Secret Societies of Rural England*. Destiny Books, 2019.
Ristic, Radomir. *Balkan Traditional Witchcraft*. Pendraig Publishing, 2009.
—. *Witchcraft and Sorcery of the Balkans*. Three Hands Press, 2015.
Russel, Jeffrey B. and Brooks Alexander. *A New History of Witchcraft*. Thames & Hudson, 1980.
Russel, J. S. *Satan: The Early Christian Tradition*. Cornell University Press, 1981.
Saif, Liana. *The Arabic Influences on Early Modern Occult Philosophy*. Palgrave, 2015.
Schnieders, Paul C. and Robert H. Charles. *The Books of Enoch*. International Alliance Pro-Publishing, 2012.
Scot, Reginald. *Discoverie of Witchcraft*, 1584.

Sommer, Benjamin D. *The Bodies of God and the World of Ancient Israel.* Cambridge University Press, 2011.

Shah, Idries. *Oriental Magic.* Arkana Books, 1956.

Smith, Meyer W. and Richard Smith. *Ancient Christian Magic.* Princeton, 1999.

Stephens, Walter. *Demon Lovers.* The University of Chicago Press, 2002.

Summers, Montague. *Witchcraft and Black Magic.* Rider & Co, 1945.

Sussol, Max. *O Livro dos Benzimentos Brasileiros.* DCL. SP., 1995.

Swartz, Michael, D. *Scholastic Magic.* Princeton University Press, 1996.

Taylor, Thomas. *Iamblichus' Life of Pythagoras.* Inner Traditions, 1986.

Taylor, Charles. *A Secular Age.* Belknap Harvard Press, 2007.

Thomas, Keith. *Religion and the Decline of Magic.* Penguin, 1971.

Thorndike, Lynn. *A History of Magic and Experimental Science.* Volume I and II. The Macmillan Company, 1929.

Tillyard, E.M.W. *The Elizabethean World Picture.* Vintage Books, 1942.

Trachtenberg, Joshua. *Jewish Magic and Superstition.* Atheneum, 1987.

Turner, Alice, K. *The History of Hell.* Robert Hale, 1993.

Vere, Nicholas de. *The Dragon Legacy.* The Book Tree, 2004.

Walter, Philippe. *Christianity; The Origins of a Pagan Religion.* Inner Traditions, 2007.

Walker, D.P. *Spiritual and Demonic Magic.* Penn State University Press, 2000.

Wetherbee, Winthrop. *The Cosmographia of Bernardus Silvestris.* Columbia University Press, 1973.

Weyer, Johann. *Witches, Devils and Doctors in the Renaissance.* Center for Medieval and Early Renaissance Studies. University of New York, 1991.

Wilby, Emma. *Cunning Folk and Familiar Spirits.* Sussex Academic Press, 2005.

INDEX

J

L

M

N

O

P

Q

S

T

V

W

Z